THE
MAN
IN THE
SHADOWS

My father was very sure about certain matters pertaining to the universe. To him all good things . . . come by grace, and grace comes by art and art does not come easy.

—Norman McLean, A River Runs Through it

You always know you have Coe's support. He fights for you. . . . He's the man in the shadows who makes it all possible.

—Tad Mosel

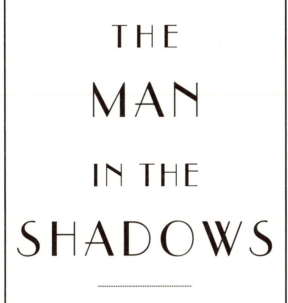

THE
MAN
IN THE
SHADOWS

Fred Coe and the Golden Age
of Television

Jon Krampner

Rutgers University Press • New Brunswick, New Jersey

Manufactured in the United States of America

Library of Congress Cataloging-in-Publication Data
Krampner, Jon, 1952–
The man in the shadows : Fred Coe and the golden age
of television / Jon Krampner.
p.   cm.
Filmography: p.
Includes bibliographical references and index.
ISBN 0-8135-2359-1 (alk. paper)
1. Coe, Fred, 1914–1979.   2. Television producers and directors—
United States—Biography.   I. Title.
PN1992.4.C64K73   1997
791.45′0232′092—dc20
[B]   96-8339
CIP

British Cataloging-in-Publication information available

To my mother,
Dr. Bernice B. Elkin

And to my father,
Robert Krampner

CONTENTS

PREFACE

I asked many questions while working on this book, and in return was asked one more than all others: Why are you writing a book about Fred Coe?

The most obvious answer is that he was the sparkplug that ignited the period of live New York television drama remembered as the Golden Age of Television. Telling his story also provides the opportunity to tell a larger story: how the Golden Age came into being, what made it important, and why it started to decline almost as soon as it began. Coe's career on Broadway was also important, and he made several good films.

Fred Coe, born in Alligator, Mississippi, was an important, colorful, and ultimately tragic figure. Yet he is the best-kept secret in postwar American cultural history. There are several reasons why this is so: he championed so many top dramatic artists in so many genres and media that his works have no identifiable stylistic imprint save that of enduring quality. And while Coe raised live television drama to the level of an art form, he unfortunately did the same with modesty. As such, he lacks the notoriety that flashier but less substantial figures have achieved. Also, the field which he defined no longer exists: Fred Coe is the forgotten master of a lost art.

He is an elusive figure as well. One evening when I had dinner in Atlanta with John and Laurence Anne ("Laurie") Coe, his son and daughter by his first marriage, they asked two pivotal questions about their father. John noted that by the time Coe arrived in New York as a young man on the verge of greatness, he had acquired a script doctor's ability to see through a story, take it apart, recognize why it isn't working, and do something about it. How did he acquire that ability? And why, Laurie added, couldn't he apply it in his personal life?

After five years of extensive research, interviewing, and thinking about the subject, I've arrived at the same answer to both questions: I don't know. Fred Coe was neither introspective nor confessional. He left no journals we're aware of, nor did he court personal publicity. Although he had a distinctive and memorable personality, his ultimate opaqueness resembles that of another pioneer to whom many, including Lillian Gish, have compared him: D. W. Griffith.

Because the world of live television drama has been all but forgotten, it's easy to caricature the 1950s as a period of fluff and escapism, the decade of lightweight whitebread All-American sitcoms that ignore life's grittier and darker side. Kinescopes of shows have disappeared, key figures have died, and documents have been lost. While recent in historical terms, much of television's Golden Age has vanished.

Fortunately, Fred Coe patronized and befriended a generation of dramatic artists, notably writers, whose varied voices recall him in a rainbow spectrum of eloquence. Larry Ceplair's 1982 *Emmy* magazine article about him was titled "Fred Coe—Forgotten Genius." Since then, there have been another fifteen years for his reputation to fall further into eclipse. It is the purpose of this book to remove him from the shadows, and to place him in the spotlight that has long been his due.

ACKNOWLEDGMENTS

My thanks go first and foremost to Delbert Mann and Alice Coe, who kept the faith. Without their help, this book would have been impossible.

Although I've spent countless hours alone in front of the computer, I was nonetheless surprised at the extent to which writing a book is really a corporate endeavor. As such, I wish to thank the members of my board of directors: Lou Goth, Penelope Niven, David Drum, Gail Polevoi, Norman Corwin, Dennis Johnson, and Dave Farrell of the *Detroit News*.

For librarianship above and beyond the call of duty, thanks to Darell Brown and Helene Mochedlover of the Los Angeles Public Library. Thanks also to Hank Rieger, publisher of *Emmy* magazine, who commissioned the article this book grew out of.

My cousin John Krampner did yeoman research and thoughtfully warned me I was becoming "Coe-dependent."

Harry Miller of the State Historical Society of Wisconsin was immensely helpful, as were Marcia Winter of the Yale School of Drama, Sandra Willis and Ann Fogle of the Town Theatre in Columbia, S.C., Patricia LaPointe of the Memphis Shelby County Public Library and Information Center, and Ann Wilkens of the Wisconsin Center for Film and Theater Research. At the UCLA Film and Television Archive, thanks to Dan Einstein; thanks and a box of cookies to Lou Kramer.

I'm also grateful to my attorney Jonathan Kirsch, members of the Bio-Group (Bernice Kert in particular), the Independent Writers of Southern California (IWOSC), Iris Berl, Nancy McKey, Elizabeth Seton Stone, Mary Anne Knefel, Jan Jessel, Richard E. ("Dick") Davis, my brother Michael J. Krampner, Sharon L. Green, Elsie Premacio, Bob Costello, Harry Muheim, and the 1972–1974 English department at Occidental College, notably my adviser, Dr. Jean Wyatt.

Some of my most helpful interviews were with Jeanne Bodfish, Arthur Cantor, John Coe, Joyce Coe, Laurie Coe, Sam Coe, Sue Coe, Eleanor Cogbill, Mike Dann, Vera Coe Dawes, Dominick Dunne, Horton Foote, Herb Gardner, William Gibson, Bo Goldman, Everett Greenbaum, Roger O. Hirson, George and Phyllis (Adams) Jenkins, JP Miller, Priscilla Morgan, Tad Mosel, Bill Nichols, Arthur Penn, David Shaw, Ira Skutch, David Swift, Porter Van Zandt, Pat Weaver, and Kate Wells.

And last, but not least, thanks to Leslie Mitchner, my editor at Rutgers University Press, to Marilyn Campbell, managing editor at Rutgers, to my agent Mike Hamilburg, to S. W. Cohen and Associates, Inc., to Joanie Socola, and, especially, to Sungmi.

A NOTE ON NOMENCLATURE

Fred Coe's signature show during the Golden Age of Television was known as *Philco Television Playhouse* between 1948 and 1951, and as *Philco-Goodyear Television Playhouse* between 1951 and 1955. It was also known, and is also referred to in the text, as *Philco*, *Philco-Goodyear*, and the *Television Playhouse*.

THE
MAN
IN THE
SHADOWS

ACT I

Amateur Night
in Dixie

The Class Poet is little Fred Coe,
He'll probably be a Burns or a Poe.

—Seventh Grade Class Notes,
The Volunteer
(Peabody Demonstration
School Yearbook)
Nashville, 1928

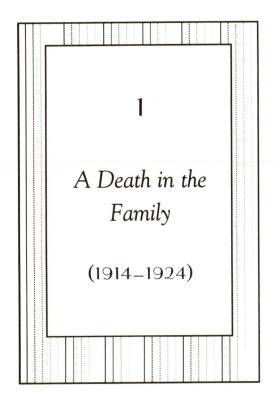

1

A Death in the Family

(1914–1924)

For nearly two centuries after they arrived in America, the Coes were a family of stalwart Connecticut Yankees. Robert Coe was born in rural Thorpe–Morieux in Suffolk County, England, in 1596, the year Shakespeare wrote *Romeo and Juliet*. Coe sailed for the New World in the spring of 1634, next year helping to found a plantation at Wethersfield, today a suburb of Hartford. His grandson, Captain John Coe, spent much of his youth in New Haven two generations before the founding of Yale in 1718, and Phineas Coe of Durham and Hartland, Captain Coe's great-grandson, fought at Lexington in the Revolutionary War, one of the militiamen who fired Ralph Waldo Emerson's "shot heard 'round the world."

But starting in 1818, the males of the line became restless. That year, Phineas Coe's son Anson moved to Ohio. His son, Dr. Hayden Coe, studied medicine at the City University of New York in 1846, then settled in Atlanta, founded only nine years earlier. A year after the Civil War began in 1861, the fifty-year-old Dr. Coe died at home, leaving a widow and three children, including one-year-old Hayden Lumpkin Coe, Fred Coe's grandfather, who eventually went into railroading.

By 1880, the young man from Atlanta had an entry-level job in South

Carolina. The village of Richland was in the Oconee County foothills of the Blue Ridge Mountains, an area South Carolinians call the Upcountry. A few hundred feet higher and several inches a year rainier than the rest of the state, it is geographically and psychologically at the opposite end of the state from coastal, sophisticated Charleston. Its residents are direct and unpretentious, and speak in Southern accents that shade into an Appalachian twang.

In Richland, Hayden Lumpkin Coe fell in love with and married Sara Hughs. They remained in Richland for fifteen years, having eight children; the third, a son born in 1884, was Frederick Hayden Hughs Coe, Fred Coe's father. Ben Robertson, who grew up in this region at the time Coe's father did, describes it lovingly in *Red Hills and Cotton: An Upcountry Memory*:

> It was a land of smokehouses and sweet potato patches, of fried pies and dried fruit and of lazy big bumblebees buzzing in the sun—a country of deep dark pools, of the soaring spirit, of little rooms stored with apples and of old Confederates and tenant farmers and colored people and swarms of politicians and preachers. . . . Sometimes the valleys are filled with showers, melting into yellow light, and in the evening in the depths the woodthrushes sing. It was a disturbing country that rested us and somehow never let us rest. There seemed to be a divine discontent, a searching for its soul.

Frederick Coe's brothers were serious, but he was light-hearted and full of fun. His hair and complexion were dark, as opposed to those of his brothers, who were lighter in appearance if not in temperament. Frederick Coe's disposition also differed from that of his father.

Hayden Lumpkin Coe was fair but strict; and when he was away at work on the railroad during the week, his wife kept the children in line by threatening to report their misdeeds when he came home. For when moved to anger, Hayden Lumpkin Coe displayed the wrath of an Old Testament prophet. Although he never met either man and knew little of them, Fred Coe usually had his father's genial disposition, but, when angered, his grandfather's explosive temper.

About 1895, the Southern Railroad promoted Hayden Lumpkin Coe to roadmaster, and the Coes moved to Blacksburg in Cherokee County, 100 miles northeast of Richland. Though Coe's family grew there—three more children arrived, making eleven in all—disaster, in the form of epidemics, struck them in Blacksburg: nine-year-old Edwin or "Little Berkeley" dying of typhoid fever in September 1901, and his older sister Nell Louise dying six weeks later of tuberculosis, which claimed another sister, Sara Hughs Coe, in January 1904. The hand of death stayed close to this family, and on March 11, 1904, it claimed the patriarch, Hayden Lumpkin Coe, who died of kidney failure at forty-three.

After her husband's death, widow Sara Hughs Coe took the younger children back to Richland. There was nothing to hold Frederick Coe in Blacksburg, and the profession of railroading his father had taught him would get him out. The Blue Ridge Mountains loomed on the western horizon of Cherokee County, beckoning him to adventures beyond. By 1908, the year Henry Ford introduced the Model T, Frederick Coe was a chief clerk for the Southern Railroad in Memphis.

• • •

Memphis was a vibrant commercial center, having recovered from the devastation of the Civil War and the yellow fever epidemics that followed. By 1909, it had 200,000 people and was the largest inland cotton port in the world. Steamboats lined the waterfront of the Mississippi River and Ed "Boss" Crump was mayor.

One day early that year, twenty-four- or twenty-five-year-old Frederick Coe was running alongside a moving engine in the Southern Railroad's Memphis train yard, talking with the engineer. His pants leg got caught, and he was dragged under. The horrified engineer stopped as quickly as he could, but Coe's leg was hopelessly mangled and had to be amputated. Coe was in the hospital a long time, waiting for what was left of his leg to heal so he could be fitted with an artificial limb.

The student nurse who looked after him was Thursa Annette Harrell, who had a disposition as serious as her patient's was light-hearted. She had come to Memphis in 1907 from Houston, a town on the Natchez Trace in the hill country of northeast Mississippi. Her father, James W. Harrell, Jr., was a farmer there, as was his father before him.

When Frederick Coe was well enough to leave the hospital, he returned to Richland, where he convalesced at his mother's home. Even the loss of a leg didn't dampen his spirits: when his seven-year-old sister Vera came upstairs one morning to wake him, she was startled by his artificial leg, which he left standing by the door, dressed like a scarecrow to frighten her.

By July of 1909, Coe had recuperated enough to resume working for the Southern Railroad. During his travels, he wrote to his former nurse. In the few remaining letters which preserve his voice, he sounds cheerful, good-natured, and utterly besotted by love. Writing from Chicago on July 14, 1909, he says, "I have it bad and am proud of it. You are the dearest girl in the world and I am a mighty lucky boy to have your love and no one realizes it more than myself." In a postscript, he adds, "My pulse indicates I must be in Memphis next Saturday."

Frederick Hayden Hughs Coe and Thursa Annette Harrell were secretly married in his Memphis apartment on December 29, 1909. It was apparently kept quiet because married women were not allowed in Annette Harrell's nursing program. Frederick Coe then went to Cumberland Law

School near Nashville. Although his wife remained behind in Memphis, her salary probably helped finance his studies.

Back in Memphis, they lived in the impressive new Colonial Apartments, whose comparative luxury reflected Frederick Coe's success as a lawyer. In a letter to his wife five days after they were married, Frederick Coe wrote, "If we do grow old as the years pass we are always going to have our growing love to make us happy." She would grow old, however; he would not. He had chronic appendicitis, and Annette Coe pressed him to see a doctor, but he kept putting it off. His condition worsened, and on April 29, 1914, he entered St. Joseph's Hospital in Memphis. On July 23, his swollen appendix burst, and he died of septicemia. He was only twenty-nine.

Frederick Coe was buried in Elmwood Cemetery, but left behind a legacy: four weeks before he entered the hospital, his wife became pregnant. Although she maintained an abiding love for Frederick Coe and never remarried, Annette Coe almost never spoke of him or his classically American family history again. Nor did she speak much of her own. "It was as if she came from nowhere," says Laurie Coe, Fred Coe's daughter by his first marriage.

. . .

Following the burial of her husband, Annette Coe wrote to Sue Smith, a friend from nurses' training. Smith had married Dr. Samuel Wells and moved with him to the Mississippi Delta hamlet of Alligator. In Bolivar County, it was surrounded by cotton fields and a lake, formed by Mississippi River flooding, that was indeed infested with alligators. The Wellses invited their pregnant and widowed friend to come live with them.

Local lore says the Mississippi Delta begins in the lobby of the Peabody Hotel in Memphis and ends on Catfish Row in Vicksburg. Millenia's worth of flooding has created some of the richest farmland in the world, and its cotton plantations are large and productive, although workers' lives are oppressive: black field hands working on Delta plantations in the late nineteenth and early twentieth centuries created the blues. Despite its agricultural bounty, the Delta was the last part of the state to be developed. A journalist covering President Theodore Roosevelt's big-game hunting expedition near Bolivar County in 1902, described the area as almost "unbroken wilderness."

Because its sprawling plantations embodied the Southern myth cherished by viewers of *Showboat* and *Gone With the Wind*, the region has been called "the most Southern place on earth." Plantation owners, or planters, had casual and indulgent attitudes toward drinking, and lived life like riverboat gamblers, fearlessly going into debt on a regular basis, confident that future increases in the price of cotton would erase those debts.

From the train windows as she rode into the Delta, Annette Coe could see cotton fields and red clay roads, plantation manors and sharecroppers' shacks, cypress swamps and piney woods. The Delta was a land of expansive vistas, with the darkened silhouettes of trees stretching the length of the western horizon at sunset. In Alligator, the Wellses lived in a one-story house on the banks of Alligator Lake.

Fred Coe was born in the back bedroom of the Wells home on December 23, 1914. Conceived during springtime by a happy young couple with bright prospects in the big city, the only child of Frederick and Annette Coe was born in winter to a grieving widow in a rural outpost. Perhaps it was moist and chilly, what Tennessee Williams called "one of those milky white winter mornings peculiar to that part of the country."

The young boy's world featured startling contrasts between affluent white planters and the poor black field hands who worked for them. Although he had the social status of neither, Fred Coe later displayed characteristics of both: he would have the boundless faith in his dramatic artists that planters had in the rising price of cotton. His increasingly generous use of alcohol, however, would not only reflect patterns of the white aristocracy, but the poor blacks who poured into juke joints on Saturday nights. Fred Coe had the soul of a Delta planter, but like those who labored for them, he would always be dogged by the blues.

His full name was Frederick Hayden Hughs Coe, the same as his father, although he never used it in its entirety. Coe had only a vague idea of where his father was from, later indicating his birthplace was "South Carolina, U.S.A." The hazy, unreachable form of his father would overshadow his life. Even to those close to him, Coe was enigmatic, a trait typical of posthumous children (a category including another Southerner, President Bill Clinton). Leslie Stevens, who wrote the screenplay of Coe's debut feature film *The Left-Handed Gun*, notes that his own father, an admiral, was also posthumous. "It makes them extremely capable, but moody and distant," he says. "He had a mysterious quality, a mystical overtone which came from looking for a non-existent authority figure in his life."

The young Fred Coe had an abiding curiosity about his father, but learned nothing of him from his mother. Kate Wells, daughter of Dr. and Mrs. Wells, guesses this was because Coe's father was her only love, the only thing she ever had that was truly hers. Young Fred Coe would know as little of his family history as it's possible to know short of being an orphan, and sometimes wondered if he were illegitimate. This would strain relations between mother and son: she supported him and worked hard to make his future possible, but stole his past from him.

"He probably never had a chance to learn who he was," Kate Wells says. "That's why he was so good at drama—the playacting." His mother's silence created an identity for him to fill with a character and a history—an identity he would assume in an idealized form, inspiring a generation of dramatic artists (if not all of his own children) to gratefully regard him as a father figure. But he had few scraps of information to base this identity on. In time, young Fred Coe's desire to learn about his own father was ground down to indifference by his mother's silence and his somewhat imperfect creation of himself as his own father.

He was not a healthy baby: as a result of childhood rheumatic fever, Coe developed a heart murmur, and also suffered from colitis. As an infant, he didn't talk until he was two years old. One day, the Wellses had duck for supper, and he blurted out, "Duck—Mo! Mo! Mo!" ("More duck!") It was a modest first step for the man who would preside at the birth of a new literary genre, the original dramatic teleplay.

An attractive blonde who carried about her the scent of talcum and rose water, Fred Coe's mother was devout, with a wry sense of humor. She was also intelligent and well-read, with a bookshelf including *What's Vital About Religion* and *Your God Is Too Small*, works suggesting she approached her religion with a questing spirit. Annette Coe was abidingly fond of her only child, but did not spare the rod when she felt it was warranted.

In 1919, Sue Wells gave birth to her daughter Kate. The Wells house was more crowded, but Annette Coe apparently remained until 1922, when her son was seven years old. Fred Coe's enduring gratitude to the Wellses in providing an anchor for him and his mother during this period is reflected in the names he gave his children from his second marriage: Sue and Sam.

When she left Alligator, Annette Coe took her son to Jackson, Mississippi, to visit relatives. Probably through church authorities there, she got a job as a nurse at a Presbyterian mission in rural Kentucky. It would provide the rudest of cultural shocks for her son.

• • •

Buckhorn is an isolated village in the Appalachian highlands of Eastern Kentucky. A 1902 report by the Society of Soul Winners, the group that established the Presbyterian mission there, described it as an area "beyond schools, beyond roads and rivers, beyond the light of the gospel."

Eight-year-old Fred Coe was alone in Buckhorn. He had lost both his father figure and second mother, and Annette Coe was often away at work. Instead of warm weather and the expansive vistas of the Mississippi Delta, there were long, cold winters and the endless ridges and hollows of Eastern Kentucky, a claustrophobic, primitive, and isolating landscape. Running along creek beds, roads across the mountains were impassable during storms, and it was a two-and-a-half-hour ride by horseback to the nearest train station.

Brainard Memorial Hospital, where Annette Coe worked, was a one-doctor, one-nurse facility. She helped to care for victims of malaria, pneumonia, typhoid, injuries, and gunshot wounds, the latter often resulting from the region's notorious feuds. Annette Coe and a Dr. Turner usually worked at the hospital, but also rode on horseback into the mountains if a patient couldn't get to them. When she was gone, her son waited by the window for hours on end, never knowing if his mother would return—and many nights, she never did, leaving Coe with a lifelong fear of being alone.

In Buckhorn, he had no usable past, a bleak and isolated present, and no sense of the future. While all of his later problems can't be ascribed to the lack of male influence in his early years, or the oppressive sense of loneliness he felt in Buckhorn, it does seem that to escape that loneliness, he later poured all of his energy and creativity into the theater. But he never developed the skills to cope with the drama of his own life. He was like a seal that swims gracefully, but flops around awkwardly on land. In the theater—especially the electronic theater of 1950s television—his instincts and training lent a decisive quality to his actions. In his personal relations, though, he lacked the navigational equipment that was second nature in his professional life.

In 1924, after two years there, Annette Coe decided Buckhorn was no place for her son to get an education, and returned to Tennessee.

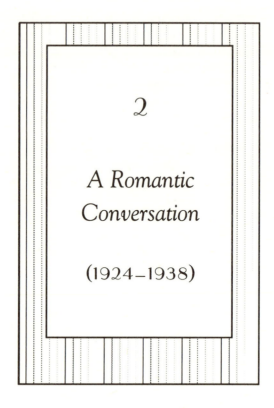

2

A Romantic
Conversation

(1924–1938)

Culturally, Nashville was the most exciting place in the American South during the 1920s. Memphis, Birmingham, and Atlanta had more commerce and industry, but Nashville's many colleges gave it a richer intellectual base. Literature, music, theater, and painting flourished in the self-designated Athens of the South. The symbol of the Nashville Renaissance was the Parthenon, a full-size replica of the original. Its concrete exterior was completed in Centennial Park in 1925, a year after Annette Coe brought her son to Nashville.

Another reflection of Nashville's cultural efflorescence was the Ryman Auditorium, later the home of the Grand Ole Opry. During the 1924 season, the Ryman showcased John Philip Sousa and his band, Metropolitan Opera star Giuseppe de Luca, violinist Jascha Heifetz, Shakespearean actor Fritz Lieter, and two marionette shows. Although it could not have been easy on her public health nurse's salary, Annette Coe frequently took her son to the Ryman, where he started to develop a love of the arts.

Summer evenings in Nashville were humid, languorous, and fragrant with the scent of magnolia, but days were not as pleasant. Until Nashville received electric power from the Tennessee Valley Authority in 1939, coal smoke from factories often hung over the city. Still, the city's air didn't harm the cultural effervescence of its citizens. In 1927, writer Donald Davidson, a member of the "Fugitives" literary group, noted, "Everywhere and every day, I meet people who are projecting or writing novels, poems, plays, biographies, histories, articles, and essays. Ideas are in the air."

Although Nashville regarded itself as the Athens of the South, there was nothing Athenian about its public school system. As a result, Annette Coe enrolled her son in the fourth grade of Peabody Demonstration School in 1924. It was an expensive private school, and for Coe's mother, sending him there was not easy. To some of Coe's Nashville friends, Annette Coe was a strong-willed, positive woman who spoke her mind, to others, a woman with a Cheshire Cat smile, polite but elusive. Despite their ongoing tensions, mother and son loved each other, and her active interest in culture would be an eventual key to his success.

During the 1920s, they lived in a red brick duplex on 18th Avenue South. Along with Spiller Campbell, the landlady's son, thirteen- or fourteen-year-old Fred Coe put on puppet shows, perhaps inspired by the marionettes at the Ryman. He and Spiller had a box with a proscenium arch and lights, for which Coe's mother sewed the curtains. The boys also engaged in a crude form of filmmaking, inking cartoon figures onto film strips, then running them through a 16-mm projector and charging neighborhood kids a few cents for shows.

As a student at Peabody Demonstration School, Fred Coe was more noted for acting up in class than for academic excellence, although he wasn't a bad student. And he began to attract attention for his writing skills: in 1928, the yearbook called him the seventh grade's class poet for writing a play that was performed in the school auditorium.

When her son was in the ninth grade, Annette Coe moved with him to an apartment on Pierce Avenue, closer to the street car line that took her to the city health department. Soon afterwards, the Depression came to Nashville with the November 1930 failure of Caldwell and Company, Nashville's largest banking firm.

The Depression put an end to the Nashville Renaissance, and led to scenes like those across the country: large numbers of poor and homeless camped out in settlements along the Cumberland River; others wandered through downtown looking for work or panhandling. There were reports of infant malnutrition and food shortages. For Annette and Fred Coe, the Depression appears to have made little difference in their standard of living: they lived simply, as they had before.

• • •

One of many high-school boys in the congregation of the Hillsboro Presbyterian Church, Fred Coe quickly became the nucleus of a group known as "the gang." Although popular and usually good-natured, Coe had a hair-trigger temper. His best friend, Donald Phillips, was as calm and steadfast as Coe was mercurial. Morrell Fisher liked to clown around, was bright, and shared Coe's lack of athletic ability. The three led a group whose pranks made them irritatingly familiar in the neighborhood of the church.

Despite Coe's affability, his temper, when it surfaced, could be frightening. Once he got into a fight with another member of the gang and started pounding his head against the church steps. Donald Phillips felt it was only his intervention that prevented Coe from killing the other boy. JP Miller, who later wrote *Days of Wine and Roses* for Coe, says this blinding rage stemmed from Coe's insecurities. "His ferocity came from a deep, deep, deep-seated lack of confidence in his own powers and his own masculinity," Miller says. "Anything perceived as a challenge evoked a neurotically attacking response. He was gentle as a lamb most of the time and that was his true nature. But when he felt threatened, he over-responded."

To find an outlet for the gang's energy, W. F. Christopher, the church's genial director of religious education, suggested to Coe that he and his friends start an amateur theatrical group. The idea took root, and sometime in 1930 or 1931, a simple theater began to appear in the Sunday School room in the basement of Hillsboro Presbyterian Church. It was the birth of the Hillsboro Players.

The stage was only a foot or so above floor level, no more than fifteen to twenty feet wide. The curtain hung from wires, with spotlights in tin cans. One side of the stage was a wall with a door leading to the hallway, but the other side was completely within the Sunday School room. An actor entering from that side had to be there before the curtain rose. There was room for an audience of sixty or seventy, usually parents of cast members.

In addition to Coe and Morrell Fisher, one of the troupe's most talented actors was Rebecca Rice. She was tall and self-conscious, but when Coe directed her, he put her at ease, joking, "Stand up, Becky! I was tall once myself!" Behind the scenes, mischievous Red Evans was in charge of lighting. His technical assistant was Max Souby, who put in an occasional on-stage performance as a dead body. Most of the Players' Friday and Saturday night shows were one-act plays featuring religious themes, often dramatized versions of Old Testament stories. Eventually, though, the group would perform secular works such as *The Late Christopher Bean* and *Waiting for Lefty*.

Coe directed many shows, often took a leading role, wrote several plays, and was actively involved in production design. The group started out haltingly. But driven by Coe, it was eventually in rehearsal for up to three plays at a time and members didn't even think about making weekend social engagements without checking their rehearsal calendar. Coe would later repeat this three-at-once act as producer of the *Philco–Goodyear Tele-*

vision Playhouse. The skills Coe developed leading the Hillsboro Players would prepare him for the pressurized world of live television.

For the young director, live performances in the basement of Hillsboro Presbyterian were full of risks. In *The Clockmaker*, one actor accidentally jumped from his second speech to his final speech, and the play was over as soon as it started. In another show, a maid who meant to say her employer was prostrate said, "She's upstairs, lying prostitute on the bed." There was a collective gasp from the audience, then a few giggles, and the play lurched forward. As the producer of *Philco–Goodyear*, Coe would not forget these moments: when outraged by what he felt was slipshod work, he would yell, "This is amateur night in Dixie!"

Since their intensive rehearsal schedules left little time to seek out new acquaintances, the members of the Hillsboro Players socialized with each other. On Sunday evenings, Fred Coe and half a dozen or so boys from the Hillsboro Players would pay court to Jeanne Stephenson or one of the other girls from the group, who would invite several girlfriends to her home.

These would seem to have been the best of times for Fred Coe. But when asked about this period in a 1967 interview, he only said, "I can't remember very much about high school, because those years weren't very happy for me. I hurt my knee the fourth day of football practice, which knocked me out of football, and I didn't do much else." It's remarkable for him to gloss over the activities of the Hillsboro Players, which he began around his sophomore year of high school, only to complain about not playing football. It ties in, though, to his not having had a father and later, not serving in the military during World War II—another ritual by which a young man could define his masculinity was denied him.

• • •

In the fall of 1933, Coe enrolled as a freshman at Peabody College for Teachers. After five years, the director of the Hillsboro Players would still not have enough credits to graduate, to the probable irritation of his mother, whose salary paid his tuition. We don't know much about his college career: what his major was, or if he even had one. He didn't take classwork very seriously, though: on a political science test, he was asked to name the current U.S. ambassador to Italy and given the choice of three statesmen and Joe DiMaggio. He picked DiMaggio, later explaining that the least obvious choice is often the correct one.

On the first day of his sophomore year, Coe was in American history class when he was spotted by an attractive blue-eyed brunette. "See that boy in the blue sweater?" freshman Alice Marie Griggs asked her friend Dorothy Duncan. "I'm going to marry him."

"Do you know him?" Dorothy asked. No, Alice admitted, she didn't. But

Dorothy did and introduced the two several days later at the soda fountain of a nearby drugstore.

Unlike Fred Coe, Alice Griggs grew up in a family that was happy and intact. The first of three daughters of Cardwell William Griggs, a retired World War I army officer who ran a franchise custom-tailoring shop, and the former Mattie Nelson, she was born in Yeager, Oklahoma, on July 20, 1916. It was not an easy birth: Alice was a seven-month baby weighing 2 1/4 pounds. Her birth set the pattern of her life: she was a fighter, Alice would later reflect. She was meant to live. When she was seven, they moved to Nashville, where she was a Girl Scout and a good student. Despite the onset of the Depression, it was, in many ways, an idyllic childhood. Alice's good looks, popularity, and calm strength made an impression on Fred Coe.

But Alice, who soon joined the Hillsboro Players, presented him with a dilemma. Coe was dating Jeanne Stephenson, and now he had to break up with her. One Sunday night in the fall of 1934, the gang gathered at member Cornelia Gamble's house. Separately, Coe instructed Jeanne and Donald Phillips to go outside, sit in a jalopy in the driveway, and have a romantic conversation. At the end, they were supposed to embrace and fall in love.

Awkwardly, the two got in the front seat of the 1923 Dodge touring car and acted out their roles. But instead of embracing, they burst out laughing. The "romantic conversation" was a flop. Directing his friends was not as easy in Cornelia Gamble's driveway as in the basement of Hillsboro Presbyterian Church. This episode crystallizes the central paradox of Coe's life: his aptness in the theater and lack of adroitness in personal matters. "His work life was his life, which he could manage," Alice Coe later mused. "His personal life he couldn't manage."

But that realization was a long way off on Christmas Eve of 1934. At the Griggs home Alice was in bed when someone scratched on her window. It was Coe. "I've decided to go with no one but you," he told her. For Alice, who was now the leading lady of the Hillsboro Players, it was the best possible Christmas present.

In 1935, Coe's love of theater took him out of the South for the first time, to a summer workshop in Lowell, Massachusetts. Among his fellow students was Vincent Donehue, later one of the "Murderer's Row" of directors Coe assembled on *Philco-Goodyear Television Playhouse* including Delbert Mann, Arthur Penn, Coe himself, and Gordon Duff.

Coe's thoughts often drifted home, though, and he resumed his courtship of Alice when he returned to Nashville in the fall. A year later, on September 20, 1936, Coe and Alice drove up to Franklin, Kentucky, where they were secretly married by a justice of the peace. It was an era when good girls "didn't" without benefit of clergy, and Coe, still a student in his last year at Peabody, could not support a household. Both continued to live separately at their respective homes, keeping their marriage a secret for years.

Outwardly, little had changed for Coe and Alice. They were often in the basement of Hillsboro Presbyterian Church, working on his next play. When they wanted to go out, they went to Hettie Rae's, west of town on Nine-Mile Hill. There, they danced to "Stardust," or went to the Wagon Wheel for the live music of Jimmy Dorsey and his orchestra. Even then, the gang still moved as a group. For Alice, the lack of free time alone with her husband was the one thing missing from their lives. But they were committed now; he was hers.

• • •

By the late 1930s, the New Deal had begun to alter the landscape of Nashville, bringing a new Tennessee Supreme Court and the majestic Davidson County Public Building and Courthouse, among other impressive public buildings. President Roosevelt developed programs such as the NYA (National Youth Administration), which many members of Fred Coe's gang worked for at fifteen cents an hour. Meanwhile, Coe's passion for drama found a new outlet in the Nashville Community Playhouse. While the Hillsboro Players performed in a cramped Sunday School room in a church basement, Playhouse performances were staged in a full-sized theater on Belcourt Avenue.

Coe and Alice, along with other members of the Hillsboro Players, participated actively in the Playhouse. Director Fritz Kleibacker, a graduate of the Yale School of Drama, took note of the theater-struck leader of the Hillsboro Players, casting him in several major roles. In the Playhouse production of Maxwell Anderson's *Winterset*, Coe and Alice (listed in the credits under her maiden name), appeared together. Also in the cast was a tall, shy student from Nashville's Hume-Fogg High School whose role consisted of the line "Hello. Did you see a couple of girls go this way?"

Director-to-be Delbert Mann had met Coe a year earlier when, as the head of the Hume-Fogg High School Dramatic Club, Mann coordinated a visit of the Hillsboro Players to Hume-Fogg, where they performed Coe's play, *The Dawn Salutes*. For Mann, theater helped him to break out of his shell and overcome his shyness. It was a way of finding himself, just as for Coe it was the place where he could lose himself.

The two became such good friends that when Coe left for Yale in 1938, Mann escorted Alice to Playhouse parties and served as her date on a stand-in basis. Coe could not afford to support a household; Alice understood this and was willing to wait the three years it would take him to get his master's degree. One day in the fall of 1938, she accompanied him to Nashville's Union Station, and saw him off to New Haven, where, unknowingly, he would spend the next few years in the shadow of his ancestors. New Haven was where Captain John Coe had passed much of his youth 250 years earlier.

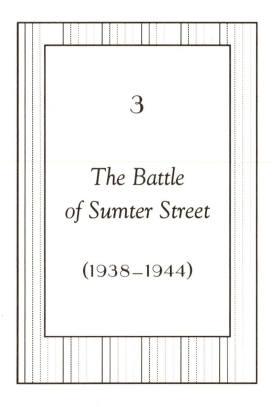

3

*The Battle
of Sumter Street*

(1938–1944)

As Fred Coe arrived at Yale in the fall of 1938, the nation was growing edgy at the prospect of war in Europe. In September, British Prime Minister Neville Chamberlain capitulated to Adolf Hitler at Munich. A month later, on the evening before Halloween, Orson Welles and the Mercury Theater broadcast *The War of the Worlds*. People believing an invasion from Mars was under way swamped police stations with calls, dug World War I gas masks out of closets, and called priests wanting to make confession.

Things were quieter at the Yale School of Drama, where Coe was known as capable and hardworking, a pleasant Southern gentleman. He wrote occasionally to Alice and rarely to his mother (who was still paying his bills), so rarely that Alice asked him to forgo his letters to her and write to his mother instead.

But as a graduate student in the directing program, he focused his energy and thoughts exclusively on the theater. Classmate Melville Bernstein was the head of a property crew for one show, and assigned Coe the task of building and maintaining a huge tom-tom. "There was not a day that passed that he didn't go back into the prop room, take the drum out, wet it down and make sure it was taut," Bernstein recalls. "He tended it like an infant."

Coe had his first brush with television in 1939 when Alice joined him at Yale for spring break and they went to New York, where they saw TV demonstrated at the World's Fair. RCA's broadcasts from the Fair represented the first regularly scheduled public broadcasting available to the 100 to 200 people around New York with television sets. Coe and Alice were fascinated by the exhibit and thought television might amount to something one day.

The young Tennessean's directorial debut at Yale came in February 1940, with *It's Morning*, a one-act play written by one of Coe's classmates and staged at Yale University Theatre under the guidance of Otto Preminger. The play was a Civil War–era drama of slaves on the eve of the Emancipation Proclamation. Although it was a celebration of their freedom, it featured such unpromising dialogue in blackface as "Barbacue! Um-um—Ah can smell hit!", to which a second soon-to-be-ex-slave responds, "Mah mouf am waterin' down!"

Nonetheless, Sarah Click Ferry, who acted in it, says Coe directed with skill and sensitivity. And at least one of Coe's instructors also thought highly of his work. "Fred seemed to make a deep impression on Otto Preminger," Ferry says. "Mr. Preminger was a very hard taskmaster. And he seemed to be going a lot easier on Fred, to like him a lot more, than the other young directors." Coe is one of only two of his Yale students Preminger mentions by name in his autobiography.

Because of its prominence and closeness to New York, Yale Drama became a kind of Triple-A farm team for live television drama. In addition to Coe, major producers of that era who trained at Yale were Coe's classmate Herbert Brodkin (*Studio One* and *Playhouse 90*) and George Schaefer (*Hallmark Hall of Fame*).

Yale alumni from *Philco-Goodyear Television Playhouse*, Coe's signature show, would include directors Delbert Mann and William Corrigan, writers Tad Mosel and JP Miller, and scene designers Otis Riggs and James Russell. Bob Costello, the unit production manager of *Mr. Peepers*, another Coe show, was also a Yalie. The *Philco-Goodyear* theme song was a pleasant, innocuous fanfare, but with this lineup, it might well have been "Boola Boola" or "The Whiffenpoof Song."

• • •

During his two summers at Yale, Fred Coe returned to Nashville, where he directed Shakespeare with an experimental twist at the Nashville Community Playhouse. Before leaving for graduate school, he had been an actor and stagehand in the theater on Belcourt Avenue; directing large-scale productions there was a kind of triumphal homecoming.

In the summer of 1939, with Delbert Mann as his assistant, he directed a modern-dress version of *Julius Caesar*. Such versions were popular at the time, drawing parallels between dictatorship in ancient Rome and the rise of modern fascism as exemplified by Hitler and Mussolini. The subject couldn't have been more timely: on August 1, two weeks before the show was staged, Germany invaded Poland, starting World War II. The Nashville *Tennessean* questioned how well *Julius Caesar* worked as a cautionary parable about modern fascism, but called it one of the most artistic and provocative shows ever at the Nashville Community Playhouse, giving much of the credit to Coe.

Coe chose farce, almost burlesque, as the experimental angle for a 1940s *Twelfth Night*. Costumes were gaily colored and Coe hired an electric organ for slapstick sound effects as well as background music. Delbert Mann again served as Coe's assistant, and helped set the play's comic tone as Feste the Clown. The Nashville *Banner* said the show was "a credit to its young director" while the *Tennessean* said *Twelfth Night* was less daringly experimental than *Julius Caesar*, but more successful. At age twenty-five, Fred Coe was a confident young director working successfully in both comedy and tragedy.

●　●　●

Instead of returning to Yale for his third year of graduate study in the fall of 1940, Coe took a job as director of the Town Theatre in Columbia, South Carolina. The post, which he learned about from a fellow grad student, paid $1,500 for a seven-play season. On December 28 in Nashville, he and Alice reaffirmed their marriage with a public ceremony at Hillsboro Presbyterian Church; their "honeymoon" was a three-day drive to Columbia, where they lived as man and wife for the first time in their four-year marriage.

In 1940, despite its population of 50,000 and status as a state capital, Columbia was a sleepy, small Southern city. Living in the Cradle of the Confederacy, many white South Carolinians regarded the Civil War with an almost proprietary fondness. Allen Whitehead, a young North Carolinian, worked at the Town Theatre with Fred Coe. In a history class at the University of South Carolina, Whitehead had made the mistake of referring to "the Civil War." A deathly silence followed, then he was frostily corrected, "You mean 'the War Between the States.'" Fred Coe would later affectionately parody this spirit of Old South boosterism in his teleplay *This Time Next Year*.

In 1940, though, the war foremost in Columbians' minds was World War II. On the east side of the city, in what had been a desolate area of piney woods and sand hills, Fort Jackson, built during World War I, was reactivated. Building it up to accommodate nearly 50,000 soldiers generated so much economic activity that it helped to end the Depression in Columbia.

The Town Theatre was in downtown Columbia on Sumter Street, a short walk from the University of South Carolina, whose elegant and gracious "horseshoe" quadrangle, with antebellum classroom buildings and dormitories, recalled a Southern plantation. A few steps another way was the State Capitol, whose western facade displayed several stars to highlight where it was struck by General Sherman's cannons before he entered the city and burned much of it to the ground in February 1865. It was—and still is—a landscape evocative of Faulkner's observation that in the South the past is not dead, it's not even past.

As he began his job, the twenty-five-year-old director was slim and sandy-haired, with an affable smile and an uncommonly youthful appearance. One day, a man from the Rockefeller Foundation came to the theater looking for Coe. When he found him atop a ladder in a pair of grimy coveralls working on the scenery, he thought Coe was a student working part-time after school.

If it was easy to mistake his age, though, there was no mistaking his enthusiasm: a local reporter sent to interview him noted that he began talking excitedly without waiting for the first question, and at one point had to pause in mid-sentence to catch his breath. There was also no question about the steely determination behind Coe's smile: he told another reporter that plays for his first season at the Town Theatre had been selected without regard to production difficulties. "If we have hard production problems," he said, "we are going to solve them."

Coe felt it would be difficult finding good plays to stage. He told a reporter from a Columbia newspaper that he hoped to keep up with Broadway, but doubted he could, since so many top plays were held back for professional production before release to amateur groups such as the Town Theatre.

When Coe took over, the Town Theatre's finances were a mess. "They were in debt, and I do mean in debt," Alice later recalled. "We couldn't charge nails [at the local hardware store] or anything else." As the theater's business manager, Alice set about restoring its solvency. To attract larger crowds, ticket prices were lowered. Life memberships were sold, and sales of season tickets increased. Different sources indicate theater membership either doubled or tripled during Fred and Alice Coe's four years in Columbia.

Alice also served as the business manager of their marriage after Coe bounced a check their first week in Columbia. She was the stabilizer who took care of everything, a friend notes. So much so, Alice later mused, it sometimes seemed she was more Coe's mother than his mother was.

Although some Columbians felt Alice lacked Coe's glamor and dynamism, most felt her quiet, low-key efficiency masked an inner strength that was a welcome counterpoint to his artistic temperament. Coe was quick to party, usually at get-togethers Alice organized for cast and crew when a show finished its run. The serious drinking problems he later developed in New York were nowhere in evidence here. "We never drank in Columbia. We drank coffee," Alice says. "It all seemed to sort of start with *Philco*."

• • •

Fred Coe provided the Theatre with a boost unlike any it had ever known, according to Town Theatre historian C. Robert Jones. Jo Brown, who as Jo Zula was a frequent leading lady in his productions, agrees: "We've had some good directors since then, but never a person with the drive, the brilliance, the sparkle that man had. We were all amateurs, but Fred could take somebody who was just adequate and bring out the very best in him. I think that's where Fred's real talent lay."

As a director, Coe was quick to improvise. On *Twelfth Night*, hapless knight Sir Andrew Aguecheek was played by Charles Wickenberg, a freshman at the Citadel about to go into the military. His costume included a hat with a tassel and ball at the end of it, an old-style sleeping cap.

In dress rehearsal, the tassel kept falling in Wickenberg's face. Instead of pushing it away, he blew on it in an idle, distracted manner. "Fred just thought that was great," Wickenberg recalls. "He came running up on the stage and said, 'Leave it in, do it, do it, keep it in!'"

The young director was adept at the theater's technical and performance sides as well. His lighting for *Liliom* drew praise from the theater critic of *The State*, a Columbia newspaper, and he designed the stage set for *H.M.S. Pinafore*. He also acted capably in about a quarter of the twenty-nine plays he directed during his four-year stay in Columbia.

Coe had another distinctive characteristic which foreshadowed his ability to pluck writers such as Paddy Chayefsky, Tad Mosel, and JP Miller from obscurity: supreme confidence in his literary taste. In an unsigned director's note in the program of *Liliom*, Coe said many outstanding plays had been written since Ibsen, but fewer than ten in the modern period could be called great, and that *Liliom* (which was later turned into the musical *Carousel*) was one of them. It is a remarkable display of self-assurance from the twenty-six-year-old director of a small community theater. (In that same note, Coe showed his geographical skills were no better than his knowledge of contemporary diplomacy. Saying *Liliom* was first staged in Budapest, he added that it only ran for about thirty performances "when first produced in the Rumanian capital.")

On December 7, 1941, Coe and Alice were listening to the radio on Sunday afternoon when the broadcast was interrupted by news that Pearl

Harbor had been attacked by Japan. The country was at war. Columbia, whose military population would soon equal its civilian population of 50,000, responded with wartime salvage drives such as the "Share Your Clothes With Russia" campaign. Rationed items included tires, gas, sugar, meat, coffee, and canned goods. There was a highly-charged, live-for-today atmosphere; women with husbands whose units at Fort Jackson were on alert had to worry they would be shipped overseas the next day.

Classified 4F because of a heart murmur left by childhood rheumatic fever, Coe would not fight in World War II. But the build-up of Fort Jackson had a major impact on him and the Town Theatre. He had a file of 175 enlisted men interested in acting. For the convenience of servicemen, the theater's upstairs lounge was redecorated and equipped with a radiophonograph. "The room will be open every afternoon and night," *The State* noted, "and the Fort boys . . . are invited to drop by."

Servicemen volunteering for roles in Town Theatre productions could have been excused for wondering which was more rigorous: basic training or their rehearsal schedule under Fred Coe. For a one-month period, rehearsals began every night at seven, frequently lasting until eleven, sometimes later. "It was for anyone who didn't mind rehearsing until eleven o'clock, one more run-through, okay," Jo Brown recalls. "Fred would say, 'It's lousy. We're going to take it from the top. Act one, scene one.' And we'd do it.'"

This effort paid off in some memorable shows. In Coe's March 1943 staging of Clare Booth's *The Women*, Brown says Coe found women who perfectly fit all of the play's forty-one roles, a coup in a town the size of Columbia; when he directed Daphne DuMaurier's *Rebecca* that June, he did so a year and a half before it reached Broadway, winning a Hollywood contract for Gloria Saunders, who played the title role; *Green Grow the Lilacs*, later the basis of the musical *Oklahoma*, was, according to Allen Whitehead, "so simple, so plain, but so deep." While not a work of enduring significance, *Show Me First*, a musical comedy about the Wacs written by Coe and several members of his staff at the Town Theatre, appears to have been popular with local audiences.

During his four years in Columbia, Coe's idea of community theater evolved from one of an organization that staged Broadway shows as soon as available to one that could serve as an experimental outpost. The ideal community theater, he told a Columbia newspaper in February 1944, does not attempt to be a carbon copy of Broadway. It should also be a workshop where new plays, not necessarily by local authors, are tried out.

Coe never actually used the Town Theatre in this way, sticking with the tried-and-true fare Columbia audiences preferred. But he would later repeat this growth curve at *Philco-Goodyear Television Playhouse*, where he started out airing reworked versions of Broadway plays, then became the first producer of live television drama to broadcast original works by unknown writers on a regular basis. In doing so, he would turn *Philco* into the most remarkable writers' workshop in the history of American TV.

Community theater prepared Coe well for live television. The stories that worked best in live TV were intimate, character-driven stories delivered with a minimum of special effects to a small audience (a TV audience can number in the tens of millions, but consists of individual families and viewers). Even today, many of the best teleplays from the 1950s—such as JP Miller's *Days of Wine and Roses*, Horton Foote's *The Midnight Caller*, and Reginald Rose's *Twelve Angry Men*—appear not on Broadway, but in community theaters around the country.

In her February 1944 profile of Coe, Columbia journalist Miriam Glovier Rabb noted the Mississippi native still had a Southern drawl. "I was beginning to lose it at Yale," he said, "but in Columbia it's gotten thicker than ever." Columbia made an impact on Coe, but he had a greater impact on Columbia. Recalling his work and that of his protégé Delbert Mann (the Town Theatre's director from 1947 through 1949), Jo Brown says, "Not to be maudlin about it, but those years of Fred and Del were kind of the golden years for the Town Theatre."

• • •

Of all the shows Coe directed at the Town Theatre, *Pygmalion*, in May of 1943, would prove the most important to him. "A couple of nights after we opened, Fred ran backstage and was higher than a kite," Jo Brown recalls. "'My God, you'll never believe what I'm going to tell you,' he said. 'Lester Shurr is in the audience.'" A leading New York theatrical agent, Shurr was stationed at Fort Jackson. He told Coe he belonged on Broadway, not in a little theater.

Also among the "Fort boys" who dropped by the Town Theatre was a stage-struck young infantryman from Philadelphia named Arthur Penn. Coe told him to come by the theater anytime he was free, and when Coe and Alice had cast parties, he was invited. "The theater was a little oasis of culture," Penn recalls. "A number of us would hang around the theater and then we'd go over to the Coes' and hang out there. If you had a three-day pass and no place to sleep, he'd say 'Stay here,' so we'd sleep on the floor. Fred was always very generous."

Shurr and Penn brought more than enthusiasm to the oasis of culture on Sumter Street; they also brought food, such as bacon and eggs, in short supply because of wartime rationing. Alice would then prepare and serve it at cast parties.

But Shurr brought something even more important: the confidence of a Broadway insider that Fred Coe could make it. He got a secretarial job for Alice in the New York office of Jack Davies, another theatrical agent. She went to New York in March 1944, three months ahead of Coe, whose work as director kept him in Columbia. When word of the Coes' leaving Columbia got out, it was felt as a loss to the community. "His resignation, and that of his gifted young wife, who has contributed so greatly to his success here, are to be regretted by all," Margaret Vale wrote in *The State*. "But good wishes go with them, and all prophesy for them both a future of distinguished achievement."

Coe joined Alice in June of 1944, just as Allied troops stormed the beaches of Normandy on D-Day. In later years, he usually said he arrived in New York after the war, which suggests he felt awkward about being stateside during his generation's defining conflict. This was particularly the case since many of his friends and those he worked with had seen active duty. Paddy Chayefsky was wounded by a land mine in Germany. David Shaw, another *Philco-Goodyear* writer, fought against Field Marshal Rommel's Afrika Korps. Donald Phillips, Coe's boyhood friend from Nashville, survived a direct hit on his destroyer by a Japanese kamikaze in the Pacific.

Fred Coe only fought the Battle of Sumter Street, the struggle to put on a good show every month. Combat experience—or at least affiliation with the military—was the union card of masculinity for men of Coe's generation. While he was legitimately 4F and had nothing to be ashamed of, he rarely acknowledged the actual date of his arrival in New York.

Fred Coe's final show at the Town Theatre, staged in June of 1944, was *The Pursuit of Happiness*. Once the sets were struck and some loose ends tied up, he followed Alice to New York to pursue his own happiness. He was brimming with confidence and ability, but it made things easier knowing Alice had secured a beachhead for the now-unemployed director's assault upon Broadway. "She helped him get started. She supported him. She was working when he was scratching," says Ira Skutch, who worked with Coe at NBC. "Fred owes his career to her, really."

ACT II

The Golden Age

It is difficult to describe—or even to keep alive in our memories—worlds that cease to exist.

—Howell Raines, *Grady's Gift*

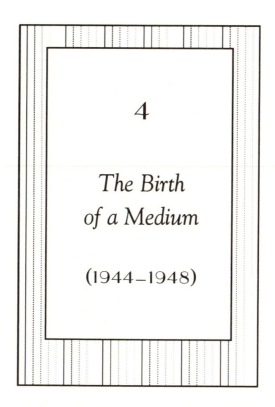

4

The Birth
of a Medium

(1944–1948)

When Fred Coe arrived in New York that June, Alice was camped out in their small apartment four floors above the Stage Delicatessen several blocks north of Times Square. She was sleeping on a cot, and cooking in pots and pans borrowed from her boss, theatrical agent Jack Davies, and his wife. The Davieses had done what was nearly impossible, finding an apartment in space-starved wartime New York for Coe and Alice.

After depositing the few pieces of furniture he brought up from Columbia, Coe set about looking for work on Broadway, but found nothing. He and Alice lived on her secretarial salary of forty-five dollars a week. Fortunately, their rent was only seventy-five dollars a month.

During the war, Manhattan still glowed with what John Cheever called the city's "river light": the reflection of the sun from the East and Hudson rivers, a glow lost now that the city is more densely packed with skyscrapers. In an era soon to witness the terrifying modernity of the atomic bomb, the city's East 35th Street police station was still lit by gas and Nicholas Murray Butler had been president of Columbia University since 1905. The city was firmly planted in the past, although one of its greatest chapters lay just ahead.

New York was gearing up for a period of unrivaled prosperity, but the Coes were not sharing in it. Alice only had one blouse and one pair of stockings, which she washed every night. During their first Christmas in New York, she bought a small, scraggly Christmas tree in an open-air lot and dragged it home several blocks although they had no money for ornaments.

Several months earlier, Jack Davies had found Coe his first job: as stage manager of a show called *The Day Will Come*, with a small acting role as well. The play, which opened on September 7, 1944, in Broadway's National Theater, was a historical fantasy in which the Wandering Jew meets Hitler. Its title comes from a line in the Jewish prayerbook: "The day will come when all shall turn with trust to God, hearkening to his voice, bearing witness to his truth." But when critics turned to the show, they largely did so with disdain. The *New York Times* called it "confused" and "a mixture of would-be realism and fantasy, neither successful," and it closed after a brief run.

Jack Davies soon found another job for Coe, as stage manager of *Bonanza*, a comedy about a Nevada mining town that springs to life again, Brigadoon-style. However, there were several ill omens before the play's out-of-town opening in Pittsburgh on New Year's Day, 1945. A lead actor quit the show because an astrologer said the stars weren't right for him in Pittsburgh. A lead actress died suddenly. And, the *Pittsburgh Press* added puckishly, "a few minor roles have found other miners."

Bonanza had two more strikes against it: the weather and its script. When it opened, Pittsburgh was in the grip of near-blizzard conditions, and local critics took equal offense to the blizzard and the play. *Bonanza* never made it to Broadway, Coe was on the street again, and in March, Alice learned she was pregnant. To bring in some money, Coe took a part-time job as a delivery man with hat-maker John Fredericks. The firm had few thirty-year-old delivery boys, but the youthful-looking Coe got the job by saying he was a college student.

As spring wore on and the birth of their first child approached, Coe was no closer to finding work on Broadway. He went up to Yale, where the drama school had a job lead for him: serving as director of another small community theater. Alice told Jack Davies they were preparing to leave New York. Before they did, though, Davies made one more effort on behalf of his secretary's husband.

• • •

John Royal was the vice president in charge of television at NBC, still primarily a radio network. When Royal was put in charge of TV, it was done in the spirit of sending him to Siberia: he was not a popular man at NBC.

The large, balding Royal could be gruff, but he was also a lone voice of showmanship among NBC's time salesmen and deal-makers, a flashy man of effusive warmth who wore a flower in his buttonhole. Nonetheless, he had strict and conventional values. Before coming to NBC, he served as a booker in vaudeville. After watching Mae West perform, he disapprovingly cabled his superiors, "Mae West could read the Lord's Prayer and make it sound dirty."

Jack Davies sent Fred Coe to meet Royal in April 1945. Coe made a good impression (his 4F status also made him available when many men were away at war), and Royal hired him as a floor manager for $270 a month. Coe would retain an enduring fondness for the man who gave him his career break.

"I always felt John Royal was *his* father, the father he always wanted," says Academy-Award-winning screenwriter Bo Goldman, later Coe's assistant on *Playhouse 90*. "Fred never said 'Mr. Royal' and he never said 'John.' It was always 'John Royal.' I have the feeling he was a very courtly man."

The post of floor manager was like that of stage manager in the theater. Coe worked with Ernest Colling and Edward Sobol, the two directors at WNBT, NBC's New York television station. He served as a production assistant, ordering props and costumes, preparing the studio for broadcast, and holding the script to prompt actors during rehearsals, among other tasks.

When Coe was hired, WNBT was broadcasting over Channel 3 to 3,000 pre-war television sets in New York. In April 1945, it began to air Sunday night dramas on a semi-regular basis under the title *NBC Television Theater*. Coe did his job as stage manager well, and John Royal promoted him to director in September. And on November 29, 1945, the day Alice gave birth to their son John, Coe was promoted again, to producer-director.

All of WNBT's live TV shows came out of Studio 3H, a twenty-five-by-fifty-foot pint-sized space crammed with three large and bulky iconoscope cameras. They were not only big, but difficult to operate: a cameraman looking through the optical viewfinder saw an image that was upside down and reversed left to right.

The iconoscope also needed a great deal of lighting to generate a broadcast-quality image. As a result, studios were intolerably hot. Temperatures rose to 100 degrees, causing Coe's floor manager Ira Skutch to lose eight to ten pounds a day. (After-hours beer-drinking sessions in nearby Hurley's Bar helped to replenish those fluids.) Don Pike, one of the cameramen, never forgot the stifling heat. "We used to call the lighting director the heating engineer," he says, adding in a petulant tone, "It got warm!"

• • •

Although New Yorkers are accustomed to thinking of their city as the center of the world, at the end of World War II they may have been right.

Berlin and Tokyo had been destroyed. London had been savaged by buzz bombs, Paris was recovering from Nazi occupation. New York, alone untouched, stood poised on the brink of a remarkable period of cultural and economic vitality. "It was the town of all towns, and this was the culminating moment in its history," author Jan Morris writes, calling Manhattan in 1945 "the unexampled island at [an] unrepeatable moment of its history."

Soon after he and Alice joined the half-million New Yorkers who packed Times Square to celebrate victory over Japan on August 14, 1945, Coe began to direct dramatic shows on a regular basis for NBC. One of his first shows, *Bedelia*, aired on October 21, 1945. Coe adapted Vera Caspary's story of a sinister young widow with a mysterious past who attempts to kill her new husband. The show displayed his increasing confidence and artistry as a television director.

Until this time, television plays had mostly been staged on a "point-and-shoot" basis: directors would set up one end of the studio like a stage and point their three cameras at it. This would give them a choice of a wide shot from the center camera or closeups from the two side cameras. On *Bedelia*, Coe wasn't content with this.

For the home of Bedelia and her husband, he had stagehands construct sets that, shot in closeup, looked like the upstairs and downstairs of a Connecticut country home. In cramped and sweltering Studio 3H, these partial sets looked like three-dimensional examples of cubist art. But on the home screen, they looked realistic.

Don Pike, one of the cameramen on *Bedelia*, recalls Fred Coe as "a bright taskmaster." A transition Coe asked Pike to make from a mid-range shot to a closeup on *Bedelia* using the iconoscope camera illustrates why. "One of the difficult elements for me was to get a medium shot of the lady (Leonora Corbett, who played Bedelia), then tilt the camera down and do a fast focus on the keyhole," Pike says.

The problem was that the camera's focus mechanism was in one of the handlebars Pike had to hold in order to maneuver the camera from the mid-range shot to the closeup. If he kept his hands squarely on the handlebars, he could not adjust the image of the keyhole, and it would appear on home screens out of focus. To solve this, he simultaneously pushed his arm down on one of the handlebars to get the closeup of the keyhole and rolled his arm forward across the handlebar as far as his elbow to bring the shot into focus. All the time, he was looking at an upside-down image that was reversed left to right.

Coe, then thirty-one, was a generation younger than his directing colleagues, Edward Sobol and Ernest Colling. They had more experience in theater, but had a harder time adjusting to live television. Unlike stage directors, television directors could not make set changes between curtains, and unlike movie directors, they didn't have time to stop and build a new set between shots. Then there was the technical crew. "Altogether, there are nineteen persons directly involved in studio operation of a television play—not counting the cast," Edward Sobol wrote in the *New York Times*. "A miscue on the part of any one . . . can mean ruination."

Sobol and Colling were initially viewed by the trade press as the standard-bearers of quality at NBC. But with his instinctive grasp of the medium, Coe was poised to surpass them. "Fred was aware of the restrictions of those cameras as they existed, and didn't ask us to do impossible things, which the other directors did," Don Pike says.

• • •

In 1945, television was still the stepchild of radio. When Adna Karns, a Yale Drama classmate of Coe's, visited him at the RCA Building, the lobby guard had never heard of television and directed him to the wrong floor. The Waldorf-Astoria had already wired its rooms and installed televisions, but much of the time the screens sat blank and empty, with no programming to fill them.

Few saw television as a serious competitor to radio. "This new form of entertainment will be supplementary to existing forms, and will not disturb them in the least," John Royal wrote, proving that he may have been a great showman, but a poor seer. For television would grow with dizzying and exponential swiftness in the next few years.

In 1946, there were seven commercial television stations in the country. In 1949, there would be 51; in 1950, nearly 100. In the fall of 1944 and 1945, network schedules were virtual blanks, with a few sporadic evening programs. The first daytime show, *Swift Home Service Club*, didn't air until 1947, and only in 1948 did the networks begin the wall-to-wall prime-time schedules American viewers now take for granted.

The NBC television network consisted of a coaxial cable between WNBT in New York and WPTZ in Philadelphia, along with a short-wave link to WRGB in Schenectady. Two years later, in 1947, the cable was extended to Washington, D.C., while Boston and Richmond were added to NBC's short-wave relay system. By July 1948, NBC had eight more stations on the air. Not connected with WNBT in New York by either cable or short-wave, they showed kinescopes, poor-quality 16-mm filmed copies of TV shows made by pointing a film camera at a television monitor broadcasting a live show. But by year's end, the coaxial cable would reach many of these stations, most of them in the upper Midwest.

One of the first events to stir public interest in television was the June 1946 Joe Louis–Billy Conn heavyweight title fight. It had the then-impressive audience of 150,000, most of it in bars, as TVs were not yet a standard household appliance. The next sporting event to grab the public's attention, the 1947 World Series between the New York Yankees and the

Brooklyn Dodgers, had an audience of 3.9 million (3.5 million of them in bars).

And when the Texaco Star Theater starring Milton Berle premiered on June 8, 1948, it was, according to Harry Castleman and Walter J. Podrazik's *Watching TV*, "as if television had been re-invented." In the years between 1948 and 1957 Fred Coe would perform the pioneering role in television drama that Berle did in comedy and variety, and under his guidance, the same authors observed, "the performers, scripts and direction were top notch and, almost single-handedly, Coe made NBC the leader in serious TV drama for a decade." This is the period when he honed the skills that made that dominance possible.

• • •

After *Bedelia*, Coe's next show on Sunday night's *NBC Television Theater* was *Petticoat Fever*. Airing on November 25, 1945, it's the story of what happens when several women suddenly drop in on a radio operator in the remote Canadian wilds who has gone too long without female company. "These full-length plays WNBT is producing each Sunday night might well put a crimp in theatre grosses someday when there are more video receiving sets in circulation," *Variety* noted. "Producer Fred Coe kept the laughs coming fast."

During March and April of 1946, there was a television blackout in New York City. RCA's transmitter on the Empire State Building, also used by CBS and the DuMont Network, was shut down to readjust station frequencies in keeping with FCC rulings. NBC got a competitive boost from the transition: although WNBT was moved from Channel 3 to Channel 4, TV sets needed no alteration to receive WNBT on Channel 4. But viewers had to take their sets into the shop to continue receiving CBS and DuMont.

Two years later, NBC proposed the construction of Television City, a huge facility in the Flushing Meadows area of Queens, which all the networks, pressed for space, could use jointly. But the other networks, perhaps recalling the transmitter episode, didn't trust NBC and declined to go along. Ultimately, the failure of the Television City plan was an early warning of the death of live New York television, and of the move of most television production to Los Angeles in the late 50s.

One of Coe's first shows once NBC got back on the air was the television premiere of *Lights Out*, broadcast on June 30, 1946. He produced and directed the show, which had originally been a staple on NBC radio. On *First Person Singular*, the series premiere, Coe and writer Wyllis Cooper made the camera itself the leading character—a man who kills his shrewish wife. He is never seen: the camera sees what he would see, and his thoughts are voiced by an actor off-screen. It was an innovative use of TV technology to heighten the medium's story-telling powers. Although *Watching TV* authors Castleman and Podrazik say the series failed to make a successful transition from radio to television, *Variety* critic Bob Stahl praised it enthusiastically.

> It's usually considered in bad taste for a reviewer to use superlatives in describing a show. Sometimes, however, such a course cannot be helped. . . . Coe achieved some admirable effects with the camera, drawing the viewer both into the killer's mind and into the action. . . . Use of a spiral montage effect bridged the gap between scenes very well and the integration of film to point up the killer's dream of a cool, placid existence and to heighten the shock effect as the hangman ended his life was excellent.

"First Person Singular," a landmark in the young medium of television, was innovative even by the standards of the well-established film industry. Not until *Lady in the Lake* appeared half a year later did a feature film make use of this technique. In the 1950s, Coe would again make use of the subjective camera with the series *First Person Playhouse*.

On August 11, Coe produced and directed "Something in the Wind," the second episode of *Lights Out*. Coe conceived the story, which was adapted by Ethel Frank. In it, a television director changes a script so that all the color and vitality is drained out of it. The characters materialize and protest, begging the director to restore the writer's original version. He refuses to do so, and they murder him. Coe became legendary among writers for fighting to protect their creative control. Here, in fictionalized form, is evidence of how strongly he felt about the issue.

• • •

During television's infancy, the FCC required stations to remain on the air twenty-eight hours a week. To meet this goal, WNBT ran some unlikely shows. For a while, the lead-in show for Coe's Sunday night dramas was *Geographically Speaking*, hosted by Mrs. Carveth Wells. She narrated travel films shot by her husband, and was accompanied by a pet mynah which chattered during rehearsals, but fell mute on the air. The show was cancelled when Mrs. Wells ran out of her husband's films.

But, *Variety* flippantly reported, a September 1946 story conference involving Coe showed that television was destined for greater things. Coe, NBC head of production Warren Wade, casting director Owen Davis, Jr., and several others were trying to fill an acting slot for a variety show. The name of one veteran vaudeville star came up. Wade favored him; others were opposed.

The argument was moot, Coe said, since the man had died several years earlier. Nonetheless, the argument resumed. "But the guy's dead!" Coe screamed, and participants resumed their search among the land of the living. *Variety* offered this as proof television was hitting the big time, since its story conferences were now as absurd as those of the film industry.

• • •

For Coe's wife, Alice, New York was a jarring change. In Nashville, you lived in a house and had a yard where a child could romp. In New York, you had to take him to the park. But Coe loved the city. With cheerful resignation, Alice realized he was married to the theater—in this case, the electronic theater—and she was married to him.

About 1947, Coe and Alice moved uptown, to a larger, fourteenth-floor apartment at 255 West 88th Street, on the corner of Broadway, and his mother came up from Nashville to live with them. Compared to their previous apartment, it must have looked like Tara to Coe and Alice. There was a large living room, formal dining room, spacious foyer, two bedrooms, maid's room, kitchen, butler's pantry, and two bathrooms.

This was a big move up for them, but Alice's boss, Jack Davies, who helped them find it, had a warning. "A friend of mine just moved out of it," he told Alice. "You may not want to move in, because it's unlucky. It's really the thirteenth floor, not the fourteenth. And my friend just got a divorce." Alice laughed. "That's ridiculous," she said. "Who believes in things like that?'"

• • •

That fall, Coe wrote, produced, and directed *This Time Next Year* for NBC *Television Theater.* A charming romantic comedy which aired September 28, 1947, it contrasts the New South's willingness to be reconciled with the once-hated Yankees with the provincialism and revanchism of the Old South. An early original dramatic script at a time when television adapted most of its dramas from the stage, Coe wrote it while he was delivering hats for John Fredericks. With his customary penchant for self-deprecation, he later called it "rotten," although *Variety's* review said that with some trimming, it might be successful on Broadway.

One can read Fred Coe's glowing reviews from this period and get the impression that staging a live drama was easy, but the premiere of another NBC Sunday night drama series by the prestigious Theatre Guild showed how difficult live TV was.

On November 9, 1947, the Guild lent its talents to television. The occasion was the melodrama *John Ferguson.* Written by St. John Ervine, it had been the Guild's first success on Broadway in 1919. But the play was no evergreen. *Variety's* headline read, "Theatre Guild Makes Auspicious Tele[vision] Bow, Despite Decrepit Script." But *Variety* was kind compared to Jack Gould's scorched-earth review in the *New York Times.*

"The Theatre Guild, venerable doyen of the Broadway stage, ventured out into the strange new world of television last Sunday night and promptly fell on its art," he wrote. In compressing the play from a three-acter to one act in order to fit the show's seventy-minute time limit, director Denis Johnston had removed many of the plot developments, but retained all scenes calling for full-throttle emoting. "The effect," Gould added, "was . . . an unrelieved succession of hysterical outbursts. It was an invitation to scenery-chewing.

"Without any restraining hand on the part of Mr. Johnston, the cast accepted the invitation," Gould added. "The players had a fine and frenzied time, unaware that the television camera magnifies a thousandfold even the slightest tendency to overplay." Gould also noted that there were different sound levels for actors at different positions on the studio floor, a gun was fired on screen without a shot being heard, and a dog was seen barking—in complete silence.

Less than a month after *John Ferguson*, Coe helped to improve the standing of NBC drama somewhat with Tennessee Williams's *The Last of My Solid Gold Watches*, the first of several Sunday night dramas produced by the American National Theater Academy. It aired on December 4, the day after Williams's *A Streetcar Named Desire* premiered on Broadway to critical acclaim.

• • •

On April 22, 1948, NBC added a new live television studio on the eighth floor of the RCA Building. Studio 8G had been a recording studio during World War II (the Glenn Miller Orchestra had made its records there) and a radio studio as well. At just over eighty feet by forty feet, it had nearly three times the space of the cramped and box-like Studio 3H. It also had the new turreted image orthicon cameras.

Along with FCC decisions and popular shows such as the 1947 World Series and Milton Berle's *Texaco Star Theater*, perhaps nothing was more responsible for the rise of television than the image orthicon. It required lower lighting levels and smaller cameras than the iconoscope, and it generated a better picture. Public dissatisfaction with picture quality stymied television's early development; the image orthicon would overcome that.

During the past three years, Coe had been the leading producer and director of live television drama, as well as one of its leading writers. But because there were still so few TV sets, and because of his modesty, even few of those he worked with during the 1950s would know what he accomplished during this period. Still, he was becoming increasingly important to NBC. Perhaps the best sign of his growing confidence was the red Studebaker convertible.

Like many New Yorkers, Coe took a taxi to work, and didn't need a car on a daily basis. But on Memorial Day weekend in 1948, he and Alice took

John to Central Park. They walked down Broadway, and in the window of a dealership was the red Studebaker convertible. For Coe, it was love at first sight.

His first day back at work, Coe asked Alice to accompany him to the Studebaker dealership. "I want that red convertible in the window," he told the salesman." Asked if he wanted to drive it, Coe said he just wanted to pick it up that evening. Alice, in charge of family finances, wrote a check for the entire purchase price. "Well, that was an impulsive thing that he did!" she would say nearly half a century later in a tone of gentle amusement that still implied pride of possession.

Coe's impulses weren't always so benign, though. When John turned three, his parents took him on vacation to Cape Cod. There, Coe threw him in water over his head and urged him to swim. Instead, the terrified child went under and Coe had to rescue him. John later became an all-American swimmer in high school, but it was years before he would go near water again. "I made it without a father," Coe seemed to be telling his son, "and that will be your lot as well."

• • •

When Yale Drama classmate Adna Karns had visited Coe at NBC a few years earlier, he found him grimly laboring away in Studio 3H, directing a vaudeville skit of wallpaper hangers perched precariously on a scaffold. "He was disgusted with what he was doing," Karns says. "He had this crappy little space and nobody knew very much about what television was going to be." But, Karns adds, Coe gave the impression something was going to happen.

"We didn't talk a hell of a lot, because he was in the middle of rehearsal," Karns says. "But I have a sense of him saying, 'I'll put up with this, because it's going to be better some day.'" That day was about to come.

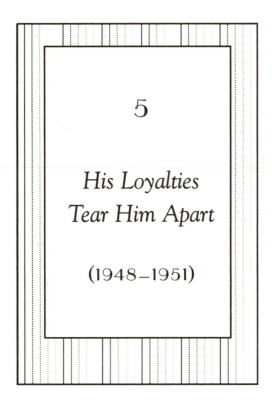

5

His Loyalties
Tear Him Apart

(1948–1951)

In the fall of 1948, Mrs. Ruth Wellborn of Chicago divorced her husband, Orin, a furniture sales manager. The judge awarded Mrs. Wellborn the family television set, prompting *Newsweek* to drily note it was the first recognition of television's role in our culture by the Chicago courts. Had the divorce taken place six months earlier, *Newsweek* added, the family set—assuming there had been one—would not have been contested.

But 1948 was the year television came of age. In 1947, there had been 16,000 television sets in America. Now there were 190,000, and in three years, there would be nearly twelve million. Milton Berle's antics on the *Texaco Star Theater* made him the nation's first TV star. Ed Sullivan's *Toast of the Town*, CBS's response to Berle, was nearly as popular.

Most of the nation turned first to the radio for entertainment. But in the major cities of the Northeast, television was more of a craze than green "chlorophyll" chewing gum, and it would prove far more durable. However, as President Truman's whistle-stop campaign to retain the presidency took shape that fall, the future of the new medium was no more assured than "Give-'em-Hell Harry"'s lease on the White House. The television industry lost fifteen million dollars in 1948, and NBC alone was losing thirteen thousand *a day*.

In 1948, Israel was created, tail fins appeared on Cadillacs, and bikinis appeared on the more daring of the nation's young women. America's postwar prosperity was already in full gear, with unemployment below 4 percent and the net working capital of American corporations at a record high. A year earlier, one of those corporations, Kraft, became the first company to sponsor a dramatic anthology, *Kraft Television Theatre*.

What guaranteed *Kraft's* success was "Imperial Cheese," a dubious and poorly selling concoction one cynic later described as "one of Kraft's fine dairy-related products." Three weeks after being advertised on the premiere of *Kraft Television Theatre*, it sold out at New York City grocery stores. This proof of television's selling power would open the floodgates for sponsored dramatic anthologies such as *Philco-Goodyear Television Playhouse*, *Studio One*, *Robert Montgomery Presents*, and many others.

Television's marketing power was only one reason why sponsored dramatic anthologies flourished: there was also the Petrillo ban. In 1945, James Petrillo, head of the musicians' union, had prohibited union musicians from appearing on television. He didn't want to repeat the experience of radio, where musicians' pay scales were established before radio became a lucrative mass medium. The Petrillo ban lasted until 1948; until then, television could not develop musically based shows. Dramatic shows would help fill the vacuum.

Television was not yet a mass medium, which also favored the development of serious drama. On September 30, 1948, the FCC inadvertently acted to preserve television as an elite medium by imposing "the freeze." In several cases, stations were built too close together, and their signals interfered with each other. The FCC's solution was to stop granting licenses for new stations. Although intended as a temporary measure, it lasted until the summer of 1952, during which television could not grow beyond the 106 stations licensed when the freeze was imposed.

Other major corporations began to follow Kraft in sponsoring dramatic anthologies on TV. (Unlike series, anthologies have no recurring characters and feature a completely different story each time.) In the fall of 1948, *Chevrolet on Broadway* appeared on NBC, while *Ford Television Theater* aired on CBS. Although CBS's *Studio One* at first lacked a sponsor, Westinghouse signed on in early 1949. And the Philco Corporation, which made TV sets, refrigerators, record players, and other durable goods that postwar American consumers clamored for, decided to sponsor a show on NBC. Thirty-three-year-old Fred Coe was chosen as its producer-director.

• • •

Philco Television Playhouse premiered on Sunday, October 3, 1948, at 9 P.M. It was a difficult time slot: Ed Sullivan's *Toast of the Town* was on CBS.

ABC radio featured gossip columnist Walter Winchell and *Theatre Guild of the Air*, and Helen Hayes had her own well-established show on CBS radio. *Philco* countered with *Dinner at Eight*, the 1932 tragicomedy by George Kaufman and Edna Ferber about the inner lives of guests attending a fashionable dinner party at the start of the Depression.

Although *Philco* was one of the first sponsored anthologies, in a sense, it was not a new show. Since 1945, NBC had aired *NBC Television Theater* Sunday nights at or around nine o'clock. But those dramas now had a sponsor, a bigger budget (at $17,000 a week, the biggest of any dramatic program on TV), and the ability to attract name properties and actors.

The show was co-produced by the Hutchins Advertising Company (Philco's ad agency) and Actors' Equity, and its premiere was a breakthrough hailed by Jack Gould in the *New York Times*: "The Equity-Philco presentation of 'Dinner at Eight' was by all odds the most professional production yet to come to the television screen. It had the scope, movement and fluidity of a really matured art. Last week television no longer threatened to bring the theatre to the home; it delivered."

Gould left no doubt where the credit lay. "Chief honors for the Equity-Philco triumph must go to Fred Coe, the director," he wrote. "Mr. Coe arose to [the] opportunity magnificently. He maintained an excellent balance between long shot and close-up, achieving contrasting composition in the image with both assurance and imagination. His work had crispness and subtlety and, perhaps most important, real understanding of the medium in which he was working." Soon, *Newsweek* would call Coe "perhaps the most brilliant of video's new directors."

The next Sunday, Coe directed *Rebecca*, Daphne DuMaurier's romantic thriller, which he had premiered for American theater audiences at the Town Theatre in Columbia, South Carolina. *Variety* praised *Rebecca*, noting "the cast, under the capable direction of Fred Coe, was letter-perfect . . . doubling as producer, Coe handled his cameras without a slip-up." The smooth camera work was remarkable because of all the obstacles Coe had to overcome.

He had to know where cameras and boom mikes were at all times, so they neither cast shadows on the set nor accidentally appeared on camera. His actors had to remember their lines and find their marks precisely so that cameras didn't shoot off the set. If a show was running long or short, he might have to cut a scene or extend it while the show was in progress.

At the end of a scene, Coe had to release actors in time for them to run the length of the studio and appear in the next scene. He also had to release cameras in time for them to shoot the commercials, also done live in Studio 8G. If a camera had to cross over the floor cables of an adjoining camera, it could become tangled in a spaghetti-like web. And because the show was live, there was no chance for a retake if something went wrong.

Coe also had to select properties to perform, cast the actors, and rehearse and stage the play. And because of the weekly schedule, he was working on three shows at a time. The first, for the following Sunday, rehearsed before cameras in Studio 8G. The second, to air two Sundays later, rehearsed without cameras (known as a "dry rehearsal") in the nearby Palladium Ballroom. The third, to air the week after that, was still in the planning stage. This punishing schedule was faced not only by Coe, but producers of other dramatic anthologies as well.

For veteran Broadway director Worthington "Tony" Miner, producing *Studio One* was a terrible grind. "I seldom slept more than four hours a night for close to five years," he later recalled. "And of course, I paid a price. I smoked too much and drank too much. I was a wretched father, an even worse provider."

Many of the denizens of live television paid a similar price. In an article headlined "Is There a Doctor in the House?" *Variety* noted, "It's like nothing before it, in or out of show business. Radio, with its perennial ulcers . . . didn't compare with the hypertensions growing out of TV production. So great is the pressure, that at NBC one of the major requisites for a job is a 'perfect condition' okay from the house medico." Only a few months earlier, someone headed for a key post at NBC had lost out because an NBC doctor was worried about his heart. Fred Coe, with a chronic heart murmur, would surely have been rejected had he undergone such a screening in 1945.

Coe took a physical and psychological beating during the 1948 season. At the Town Theatre, he directed twenty-nine plays in four years. On the first year of *Philco*, he directed twenty-eight plays—under the vastly more stressful conditions of live TV—in little more than six months. "He almost killed himself," says Adrienne Luraschi, Coe's secretary and script girl in his early years at NBC. "That jungle stuff he had came back," she says, referring to his childhood rheumatic fever. "He was almost yellow."

• • •

On January 9, 1949, Coe staged the most ambitious *Philco Playhouse* yet: *Cyrano De Bergerac*. It was one of his most successful productions that year, and produced an incident that would become a centerpiece of the Fred Coe legend.

Cyrano starred Jose Ferrer and a cast of dozens. It featured seven sets, including a surprisingly authentic-looking seventeenth-century Parisian street scene. "A success on all counts" according to *Variety*, "the video play captured all of the [original's] glittering poetry and romantic fragrance . . . Producer-director Fred Coe once again framed the dramatic elements to the need of the TV screen. The long and intricate opening duel sequence was brilliantly executed."

The closing sequence, however, did not go as smoothly. The show ran long and scenes were cut. Hildy Parks, who played a nun, had to make her entrance earlier than scheduled. But because the floor manager was distracted and didn't cue her on time, she made a late entrance. In the control booth, Coe went wild.

"Cue the nun!" he yelled. "Cue the nun! . . . *Cue the Goddamn nun!*"

Under normal circumstances, Coe's remarks would only have scorched the ears of his colleagues in the control booth and cameramen on the studio floor. But because a sound man had taken off his headset and left it near an open microphone on the studio floor, Coe's remarks became a part of the broadcast. This incident would poison Coe's relations with his sound man for some time to come.

Nor did the show help Coe's relations with cost accounting. *Philco Playhouse* was $126,000 over budget two weeks after the broadcast, *Variety* reported, with *Cyrano* a prime culprit, having cost twice as much as budgeted. But if the bean counters and soundman were giving Coe a hard time, that was nothing compared to the Hollywood studios. Fearful of the growing influence of the new medium, they sought to strangle dramatic shows like *Philco* by refusing to let them air kinescopes of their programs.

When *Dinner at Eight* aired on WNBT, NBC's New York station was directly linked with three other stations by coaxial cable (Philadelphia, Washington, D.C., and Baltimore) and three by microwave relay (Boston, Schenectady, and Richmond). But NBC's other eight stations could only air WNBT-produced shows by means of kinescope.

Film studios owning the rights to plays such as *Dinner at Eight* and *Rebecca* blocked NBC from airing kinescopes of them, successfully arguing in court that kines were not delayed broadcasts, as the networks claimed, but films to which studios owned the rights. Movie-studio intransigence would spur the growth of the new medium, however, by forcing it to develop its own writing talent. Given the unavailability of studio-owned plays, Coe would nurture writers like Paddy Chayefsky, Horton Foote, and Tad Mosel. This made the film-company lawyers, in author Max Wilk's memorable phrase, "so many grains of sand, responsible for a multitude of future pearls on Coe's seedbed."

Not that everything Coe produced during the early years of *Philco* was of award-winning caliber. The pressures of making a show from scratch every week guaranteed some rush jobs. As Coe later put it, "We don't know, and it is a blessing never to know, what Shakespeare might have written if he had been a contemporary of 'Howdy Doody' or 'Man Against Crime.'"

Philco's *Becky Sharp*, built around the heroine of *Vanity Fair*, "should have been left within . . . Thackeray's covers," *Variety* said. On P. G. Wodehouse's *Uncle Dynamite*, "Philco tangled with farce and came out in a sad way." And *The Sudden Guest* featured "an unbelievable story and a static production." Television was discovering its "time trap," the huge temporal maw that constantly had to be filled with fresh material.

While some observers claimed the spurt of dramatic shows on TV was evidence of the medium's precocious maturity, there were dissenters. "The networks admit that they have been guilty too often of copying each other," *Variety* noted in December 1949. "The plethora of dramatic programs . . . doesn't represent a pat on the back for the [networks]. Instead, it underlies an overemphasis on dramatic shows." Even at its outset, television's motto could have been "Out of the network, endlessly cloning."

As its first year drew to a close in the spring of 1949, *Philco Television Playhouse* was in trouble. The show was well over budget. Actors' Equity was not delivering the stars and scripts Philco had expected. The show's cancellation was announced in March, with the April 10 broadcast of Budd Schulberg's *What Makes Sammy Run?* slated as its final episode.

But by June, Talent Associates agreed to package the show in place of Actors' Equity. Headed by two young agents, David Susskind and Al Levy, the fledgling talent agency and production company entered into an agreement with the Book-of-the-Month Club that was supposed to provide Philco with a stream of best-selling novels to dramatize. Philco approved, and the show was set to resume in the fall of 1949. It then faced a bigger crisis: Fred Coe left the program.

"By the end of that first year, I was a basket case, a vegetable," Coe later said. "I figured that was enough. I went off on a holiday and came back and took a job in management at NBC, where it was more relaxed." If things were more relaxed for Coe, though, they became more stressful for Philco.

Albert McCleery went on to a successful directing career in television, but his debut was inauspicious. On September 18, 1949, he directed the *Philco* version of Raymond Chandler's *The Little Sister*. The show had only one rehearsal, and no dress rehearsal. The script was six minutes too long. "Desperate cuts were made and a complete shambles ensued," Ira Skutch, who then directed Philco's commercials, later wrote.

Jack Gould of the *New York Times* was contemptuous of the Coe-less *Philco Playhouse*. "Even on the printed page, Mr. Chandler is not always easy to follow," Gould wrote, "but on TV his work was a study in bedlam that could have intrigued only [vaudeville comedians] Olsen and Johnson." In order to keep Philco from cancelling the show, Pierson Mapes, the head of the Hutchins Advertising Company, went to Philadelphia and told them Coe had not done the last few shows. He was persuaded to return.

Another person eager to see Coe back at the *Philco Playhouse* was NBC's new vice president for television, Sylvester "Pat" Weaver. He had come to NBC from advertising agency Young & Rubicam, where he headed the television production department. His faith in television as a culturally beneficial medium made him a rarity among television executives. "In [my] grand design," Weaver later said, "entertainment was used to get the people to watch the medium and get caught by it, but the end would be that we would inform them, enrich them, enlighten them [and] liberate them from tribal belief patterns."

Ever the maverick, Weaver was in the habit of calling RCA chairman and NBC founder David Sarnoff "General Fangs," a luxury he indulged in even in elevators crowded with RCA executives. But one luxury he would not permit Fred Coe was bailing out of *Philco Television Playhouse*. "I called him into the office and gave him a fight talk about what a stupid thing it was for him to go into management when you had his talent for creative work," Weaver recalls. "I told him he should not go into management, a mistake I had already made."

In addition to putting Coe back in charge of *Philco*, Weaver made several programming moves that insured its survival. In the fall of 1949, he changed *Philco*'s lead-in from *Meet the Press* to *The Colgate Comedy Hour*, then one of television's most popular shows. In 1951, Weaver slotted Red Skelton directly after the *Playhouse*. This was not purely pro-*Philco* largesse: Weaver had nowhere else to schedule Skelton that season. An equally important programming move was made by CBS when it switched Ed Sullivan's highly popular *Toast of the Town* from Sunday at 9 P.M., opposite *Philco*, to 8 P.M. For much of its seven-year run, *Philco* only had to contend with orchestra leader Fred Waring and his band, the Pennsylvanians.

With Coe back at *Philco*, the show quickly regained its former prestige. But he was back with a difference. Unwilling to endure the unrelenting stress of producing and directing a live television play every week, he relinquished the director's reins. It was as the show's producer that he would attain greatness, but he regarded the position with ambivalence. "Fred was always a director at heart, and I think—I'm almost sure—that deep down in his soul, he regretted the move that took him out of the director's chair and up into the producer's spot," says Delbert Mann.

• • •

In the fall of 1949, *Philco Television Playhouse* acquired the services of script girl Joyce Beeler. Despite the condescending title (later changed to assistant director), the script girl was an important figure on live dramatic shows. She was the production secretary, keeping records, serving as prompter during rehearsals, noting script changes and getting them to the actors. She kept the director's script up to date, and timed the show to make sure it wasn't running long or short.

The twenty-three-year-old "Beeler," as Philco staffers affectionately called her, was the youngest of three daughters of George Beeler, the postmaster of Bellevue, Iowa. Nestled on the banks of the Mississippi amid a landscape of endless cornfields and rolling hills, Bellevue was a town of two thousand people. After growing up there, Joyce Beeler had attended the University of Dubuque, becoming a campus celebrity for her beauty and singing voice.

About 1947, she had come to New York to study at the Juilliard School of Music with the goal of singing at the Metropolitan Opera. But while the beauty of her singing voice rivaled that of her appearance, becoming a star in New York was more elusive than in Dubuque. While attending Juilliard, and perhaps after leaving it as well, Joyce worked as a church secretary and sang in the choir at Madison Avenue Presbyterian Church, which Coe and Alice attended. Alice had thought Joyce capable and efficient, and recalls recommending her to Coe, who was looking for a script girl. Joyce maintains that she never met Coe or Alice while working at Madison Avenue Presbyterian. In either case, in the fall of 1949, Coe hired her.

Coe was impressed with how well Joyce did her job, and, like many men, was struck by her beauty. But during the fall of 1949, he crossed the line from admiration to infatuation. He started coming home late, sometimes not even calling Alice to say he'd be delayed. In early December, it appeared there was good news for Fred and Alice Coe. For four years, they had been trying to produce a brother or sister for John. Now, Alice's doctor told her they had succeeded. She breezed down to Coe's office and gave him the good news: she was pregnant again.

"Oh," Coe said, looking up from the stack of scripts on his desk with polite disinterest. "Maybe you're not." Stunned, Alice said, "I know I am," and got up to leave. He made no effort to stop her. Not long afterwards, he summoned her to lunch at a Rockefeller Center restaurant. "When this child is born," he said, "I want a divorce."

• • •

As producer of *Philco Television Playhouse*, Coe had to hire one of two directors to replace him. One, Gordon Duff, had been hired during Coe's brief sojourn in NBC management. A forty-year-old of Scottish ancestry, Duff had a dry wit and whimsical nature, much like that of a leprechaun, one colleague observed.

That fall, Coe tried out several directors, finally turning to Delbert Mann, his friend and protégé from the Nashville Community Playhouse. Tall and slender, calm and unflappable with a deep, almost baritone voice, Mann was devoid of flamboyance and show-business affectation. He smoked a pipe and had the studied demeanor of a professor of sociology, which his father was.

Upon Coe's recommendation, NBC hired Mann as a floor manager in June 1949. One of Mann's first efforts at directing television was an episode of *Theater of the Mind*, a half-hour show featuring a fifteen-minute drama on a psychological problem followed by a panel discussion of experts. The show was directed by actor Martin Gabel. For Mann's benefit,

Gabel was supposed to prepare an episode, then allow Mann to put the show on camera, calling the shots during the live broadcast. But instead of giving Mann his chance, Gabel was using him as a glorified errand boy.

When Coe came to watch a run-through and saw what was happening, his temper flared. "Fred went right through the ceiling, and there was an explosive argument between them," Mann recalls. "Martin walked off the show, and was followed by the entire cast." It was patched up over the phone that evening, and under Coe's supervision, Mann got the show on the air. On November 27, 1949, after several practice efforts, Mann successfully directed *The Wonderful Mrs. Ingram* for *Philco*, and Coe hired him on a permanent basis.

Mann would soon—and often—see Coe's temper in action in the *Philco* control room. A frequent target: any stagehand moving or talking, no matter how surreptitiously. Coe would storm up beside Mann during rehearsal, and press the button activating Studio 8G's public address system. In a frothing rage, he would demand the malefactor's name, as his words tumbled over each other, then resolved themselves into a staccato burst: "Who is that moving around?—Get that man's—I—get him out of here! I don't want that man in the studio again!"

Although Coe's protégé, Mann was not afraid to challenge him. *The Symbol*, airing January 7, 1951, was a biography of Jefferson Davis, the president of the Confederacy. The show called for a montage that was difficult to execute under the pressurized conditions of live television. In one scene, as the Confederate flag fluttered in the breeze and "Dixie" played, smoke was supposed to rise in wisps, increasingly obscuring the flag, while the names of Civil War battles flashed on the screen. But on Saturday, the day before the show was set to air, the montage was a bust in rehearsal. In the early rehearsal on Sunday, it flopped again.

"Let's cut it," Coe told Mann before the dress rehearsal Sunday afternoon. "It's not going to work. It's going to be a mess."

"No," Mann said firmly. "I know what I want, and I know I can get it." But at dress rehearsal, the montage, like the Confederacy, went down to defeat.

"Cut the montage," Coe said. "Get rid of the smoke."

"No," Mann dug in, "the smoke is important."

"Pappy, get rid of it."

"No, Goddamn it, I'm not gonna get rid of it."

The show was about to go on live, and Coe's decision hung in the balance. "Alright," Coe said grimly, "do it, then," with an undertone suggesting: If this goes wrong, I know where you live. "And it worked!" Mann recalls gleefully. "On the air it worked, and he apologized afterwards."

• • •

In the fall of 1949, Coe also brought a new writer aboard. David Shaw, thirty-two, had been turning out half-hour scripts for a TV show called

Actors' Studio and writing radio comedy. The younger brother of novelist Irwin Shaw, the good-natured and easy-going Shaw was assigned by Coe, sight unseen, to adapt *Damion's Daughter*, one of many forgettable novels Philco dramatized during the 1949–1950 season.

After sending the script in, Shaw was told Coe wanted to meet him. He called Alex March at *Philco Television Playhouse*. "What's he like?" Shaw asked nervously. "Fred'll scream and holler at you a while," March replied, "after which you'll just go home and rewrite it." But March failed to reckon with Coe's soft spot for writers—especially talented ones. When they met, Coe shook Shaw's hand warmly, asking, "Are you available to do many more of these?"

Shaw would write twenty-seven shows for *Philco*, becoming the show's most prolific writer. He would write comedies, dramas, and thrillers, originals and adaptations. "He's as versatile as a twelve-dollar pencil sharpener," Coe later said of him (at a time when twelve dollars could buy a very impressive pencil sharpener). Shaw, in turn, was impressed with Coe's keen story mind. "He had this marvelous talent," Shaw says. "When you told him an idea, he would ask you, 'How are you going to deal with [some script flaw]?' He would see the problems before I did." As he would do for many of his writers, Coe also fed Shaw story ideas that became *Philco* episodes.

But for all their importance, these skills of Coe's were essentially technical ones. More important was his ability to provide moral support. He often called his writers "Pappy," a nickname many in turn bestowed upon him. It was a sign of fondness on the part of Coe, who had never known his own father. And what Shaw—and almost all of Fred Coe's writers—especially appreciated was his almost blind faith in them.

"He was so encouraging, he would make you better than yourself," Shaw says. And Tad Mosel says Coe had an almost mystical ability to elicit the best from his writers. "I worked with many good producers in television, but none had that quality that Fred had," Mosel says. "He could make you have an idea without telling you what to do. And once you had that idea, he never told you what to re-write, but would talk about your play in such a way that you would suddenly say, 'Oh, I think I know what I should do with this play.'"

• • •

Behind the scenes at the *Philco Playhouse*, the mutual admiration society of Fred Coe and Joyce Beeler was becoming increasingly apparent. "It was pretty common knowledge, although they never acted like friends or lovers," says Larry Elikann, then one of the show's cameramen. But, adds another Philco staffer, they didn't need to. "Joyce was sexy-looking, like Annette Bening, with her hair pulled back," Adrienne Luraschi says. "You could just see the way they looked at each other. There were balls bouncing between them. Everybody knew, and wondered what was going to happen."

By Christmas of 1949, Coe had begun staying out all night. Sometimes he returned home between 3 and 6 A.M., with liquor on his breath. Complicating the situation was the fact that Coe's mother was living with him and Alice. Annette Coe and her son were often at odds. Mornings before he left for his job, one of the most important positions in the high-pressure world of live television, she would infuriate him by asking if he'd remembered to brush his teeth. Annette Coe, who was close to Alice, took an immediate and visceral dislike to Joyce, but since Coe was still rebelling against his mother, this probably worked to Joyce's advantage.

In the spring of 1950, Carol Saroyan, who later married actor Walter Matthau, gave a small party for Charlie Chaplin in the upper floors of a townhouse where she lived on East 76th Street. Among those attending were Fred Coe and Joyce Beeler. Also present was Phyllis Adams, an editor at *Theatre Arts* magazine. Adams was well-connected on the New York social scene, and had been introducing Coe to many of the city's cultural movers and shakers.

Carol Matthau recalls Fred Coe as "very handsome, very decent, and one of the better men one would ever get to meet. And he was in love." But not just with his wife. Later that week, Phyllis Adams had dinner with Coe and Joyce, still thinking their relationship was only that of professional colleagues and that Coe's marriage with Alice was intact. When Joyce was away from the table, Coe turned to Adams. "I am in love," Coe said. For an uncomfortable moment, Adams thought he meant her. But then Coe added, "It's Beeler. I'm in love with Beeler." Adams's dilemma was averted, but Coe's was just beginning.

"He liked and loved Alice and had fallen in love with Joyce," Adams recalls. "It was very painful for Fred. He was very puritanical," she adds. "He was not a philanderer. He was not a guy who played around. He was very serious, very work-oriented. [Joyce] had helped him immeasurably at work. Alice tried to do this, but wasn't in a position to."

In March, Alice, five months pregnant, took John and went to stay with her mother in Nashville. Two weeks later, Coe called and told her it was all right: he was no longer in love with Joyce. Alice returned and gave birth to a daughter, Laurence Anne ("Laurie") Coe, on July 23, 1950. But by September, Coe was again staying out all night. He told Alice again that he wanted a divorce. No, a separation.

People who met Coe during or after the 1950s would speak of his lifelong drinking problem, but that problem dates to this period and his inability to resolve the puzzle of his affections. He would dither over it for years, to the consternation of both women in his life. In *The Symbol*, Jefferson Davis is committed to the irreconcilable goals of allowing the South to secede from the Union and preventing the Civil War which will inevitably follow. "Where does a man go when his loyalties tear him apart, pull him in opposite directions?" he asks plaintively. It's a question Fred Coe must have asked himself many times.

• • •

In December 1949, Alice went to see the Broadway production of Strindberg's *The Father*, starring Raymond Massey. The ingenue role was played by a young actress named Grace Kelly. Impressed by her performance, Alice mentioned it to Coe, who was looking for a young actress to play the lead in *Philco*'s production of *Bethel Merriday*. Coe sent Delbert Mann to see *The Father*, and he was similarly impressed. Grace Kelly's appearance on the January 8, 1950, broadcast of *Bethel Merriday* was her first television role, one that would lead her to Hollywood and, eventually, the role of Princess Grace of Monaco.

That June, another young actor appeared on *Philco*—Charlton Heston. In *Hear My Heart Speak*, he played a World War I veteran who has lost his ability to speak because of shell shock. It was a difficult role: except for one spoken line at the end, Heston had to play the whole show mute, communicating by means of a pencil and pad. But during the live broadcast, the prop man forgot to leave them on the set for one scene. In the control room, Coe howled, "Where's the goddamn pencil and paper on the dining room table?" Heston, wondering the same thing, pantomimed to the actress who played his mother that he was going out to meet his girlfriend.

Although this was one of Heston's two performances for *Philco*, he appeared more frequently on *Philco*'s main competitor: CBS's *Studio One*. Its producer, Worthington Miner, had television roots even deeper than Coe's, having started at CBS in 1941. Although Coe and Miner had the two best dramatic shows on the air, they took completely different approaches to TV drama. Coe built his program around the writers, with everything done to serve the script. Miner built his around the directors, emphasizing imaginative camera work and production methods.

The shows were also distinguished by their attitude toward social class. *Philco* became known for "kitchen-sink drama," which took a piercing and unvarnished look at the real-life problems of ordinary people. Miner took the opposite approach. "It was black tie," Miner later said of his show. "There were no dark alleys nor kitchen sinks on *Studio One*. There were evil souls and dangerous people, but they dressed for dinner. If they were raped, it was in satin." It was a distinction much like that between Warner Bros., with its working-class heroes, and the more refined and elegant films of MGM.

It's an oversimplification to say *Philco* featured nothing but kitchen-sink drama, however. There were comedies, shows which now would be known as docudramas, classic tragedies—and even shows such as Walter Bernstein's adaptation of F. Scott Fitzgerald's "The Rich Boy," where everyone dressed for dinner. But the shows' different attitudes toward social class was real. Asked once by a reporter why more of his programs didn't deal with the problems of the rich, Coe snorted, "There's nothing duller than rich people!"

Philco, Studio One, and *Kraft* were soon joined on the air by dramatic anthologies such as *Robert Montgomery Presents, The U.S. Steel Hour,* and *Pulitzer Prize Playhouse.* The trickle of hour-long live dramatic anthologies became a torrent: the handful of live dramatic shows premiering in the fall of 1948 was followed by another five in 1949, and another eleven in the fall of 1950. Demand for scripts began to outpace the supply.

"The shortage of material became acute," Coe later recalled. "Agents stalked archives, bought rights to stories and novels in umpteen languages, toured obscure libraries here and abroad searching, searching for words to fill the void." As the third season of *Philco Television Playhouse* began in the fall of 1950, this search was producing mixed results. Unlike its first season, which featured plays cut down to one-hour length, or its second, mostly adaptations of books, there was now a blend of the two. But a third factor increasingly appeared: original teleplays.

"When we found no more novels to fulfill the standards we set up, we explored biographies and documentaries," Coe noted. "It was in the course of this phase that we came up with what seemed to be a precedent-shattering idea. Since we were working with research material, why not create an original script based on this material instead of buying a book written from the same material? Out of this very simple notion came *Vincent Van Gogh* by H. R. Hays."

The show aired in *Philco's* second season, on March 5, 1950, and, Coe wrote, "The Van Gogh program cut the umbilical cord for good. We knew at last that television was mature enough to develop its own talent in the writing . . . field." It's a puzzle, though, how Coe could claim the show as *Philco's* first original. Weekly casting lists prepared by staff members read "'Vincent Van Gogh'—By Edward Alden Jewell—adapted by Hoffman R. Hays." And *Variety's* review praised "H. R. Hays's adult and perceptive adaptation of Edwin Alden Jewell's biography of the great Dutch painter." Perhaps Hays's adaptation was so free, it bore little resemblance to the original.

It was equally puzzling to Morton Thompson how *Philco Television Playhouse* could claim *Semmelweiss,* airing two months later, as an original. Thompson was the author of *The Cry and the Covenant,* an account of Dr. Semmelweiss, who developed antiseptic methods for delivering children. Unable to find much original about the broadcast, he sued NBC, *Philco,* and scriptwriter Joseph Liss for plagiarism, although the suit was eventually dismissed.

But even if some of the first "originals" were of dubious originality, it was increasingly clear that television needed to develop its own writing talent. During that first season, film-studio-imposed limitations on kinescoping resulted in *Philco's* having to settle for some second-rate Broadway plays. In the novel-based second season, there was the same problem: if a book had been made into a film, TV rights were unavailable. David Shaw says, "the books they could get rights to were books you never heard of then or since." But the more basic problem was identified years earlier by TV director Edward Sobol: the best play for a given medium is the one written especially for it.

In 1950, *Variety* noted, "[The] shortage of television story properties is still the No. 1 problem confronting video producers." Although well-known screenwriters, playwrights, and novelists were now willing to try their hand at the new medium, the article added, "[The] script shortage is acute, according to one network story editor . . . the [networks] see no solution to the problem."

In July 1950 Charles Underhill, in charge of programming at CBS, announced he was offering writers assignments on a ten-script basis to provide them with regular work, and to assure CBS of a steady source of material. NBC's *Colgate Theater* was already making extensive use of original scripts: In the year and a half leading up to that July, twenty-three of its sixty-nine shows were originals.

But many of these early originals were second-rate efforts from second-rate writers. "The originals we usually get were turned down by theater or the movies," *Kraft* director Stanley Quinn said during this period. The first *Kraft* original, *Alternating Current*, had aired in January 1948. According to author Tom Stempel, it was "a tepid satire of politics, second-rate Hecht and MacArthur."

Coe's solution, like Underhill's, was to give writers multiple-show contracts. But he did more, encouraging them to attend rehearsals (writers were banned from *Kraft* rehearsals) and giving them an active role in casting their shows. Although the script shortage produced a *Variety* headline, "TV Writer Is Today's Kingpin," this was only true on one show: *Philco Television Playhouse*.

Young writers learned that working for Fred Coe, you could give your imagination free rein, do so under supportive conditions, and get up to $1,200 for your efforts, then top dollar for one-hour dramatic scripts. As a result, some of the best writers in New York started contributing scripts to *Philco*. Ironically, the first major writer to join David Shaw in Fred Coe's stable of writers would become a Coe nemesis.

•   •   •

David Swift, thirty-two, was a Los Angeles native who belied the myth of the mellow Southern Californian. A bomber and fighter pilot during

World War II, he had been a radio comedy writer for Bob Hope, Red Skelton, Jimmy Durante, and Jack Carson. Compact, slender, and wiry with a no-nonsense demeanor, he had the physique and temperament of the amateur boxer he once had been.

Swift's first script for *Philco* aired on April 8, 1951. The story of a safe-cracker who plans to pin the blame for his crime on an unsuspecting police reporter, *Routine Assignment* was praised by *Variety* as one of *Philco's* best shows of the season. His second effort, *Operation Airlift*, appeared on June 17. An account of the Berlin Airlift blending fact and fiction, it is an early TV docudrama. The show introduced Swift to the terrors of live television in a way he'd never bargained for.

"On camera day, the star and his agent fell out with Fred over money," Swift recalls. "Fred came to me and said, 'You've got to go on.' I said, 'I'm not going to do it. I'm not an actor. I won't get in front of millions of people.' He said, 'Please, you gotta help us out. You're the only one who knows the words.' Like an idiot, I did it." On the air, Swift appeared smooth and assured, a great improvement from rehearsal.

"It's the only time I ever saw Delbert Mann scream obscenities over a speaker system," Swift recalls. "I was following chalk marks around the stage. They had to mark my path like a map. He'd say, 'Raise your head. You're not speaking into the mike.' I'd come up and get lost and wander off the chalk marks. It was a mess during rehearsal, but we pulled it off."

Although most of Fred Coe's writers approached him with an admiration close to awe, Swift would have none of that. "Fred was a dilettante, a martinet, and a son of a bitch," he says. "But he was a great talent, and he worshipped writers, so the writers all adored him." Swift, however, didn't hesitate to tangle with Coe.

One of his scripts starred Walter Matthau as a recuperating World War II veteran. Swift wanted to call it *Crack Red*, a title which Coe (and the rest of the staff) hated. The two got into a screaming match, and the show aired as *Tour of Duty*. It was an omen that Coe and Swift would fight over a title, though, since several of their confrontations would take on the quality of title fights.

The next writer to become a *Philco* regular was Robert Alan Aurthur. Bright and outgoing, the native of Freeport, Long Island, was a marine lieutenant during the war. He had worked as a longshoreman and short story writer, and liked to hang out in jazz clubs. His first effort was *The Birth of the Movies*. Airing on April 22, 1951, it was the story of pioneer film director D. W. Griffith. Aurthur co-authored the show with Hoffman Hays.

Based on the memoirs of Lillian Gish, who narrated the show, the script was a scathing indictment of the film industry for neglecting, in his later years, the man who transformed films from a sideshow amusement to a major art form. For Coe, it was not only a good show, but perhaps a way to pay Hollywood back for attempting to stifle *Philco* at its outset.

In a prominently placed review which doubled as an editorial, *Variety* tore into the program. "Philco Playhouse took an unfair slap at the film industry," it said. Acknowledging Griffith's many important contributions, it added, "the Philco scripters painted their story in black and white tones exclusively. They built Griffith into a superman, at the same time caricaturing his successors in Hollywood as a group of money-grubbing businessmen who sacrificed any creative ideals to the all-important box office."

Birth of the Movies is important both as an early *Philco* original and for the debut of one of its top writers. It is a prime example of Fred Coe's willingness to offend the powers that be in order to put on a good show ("the program won't help cement relations between the film and TV industries," *Variety* sniffed). And it's the only one of his hundreds of TV shows where Coe appears on camera. *Birth of the Movies* features opening and closing segments in which Coe interviews Gish about Griffith. It isn't clear how much he identified with the show's subject, but Gish told Coe that *Philco* reminded her of Biograph, implying Coe was the D. W. Griffith of television. It's a surprisingly apt comparison.

Both Griffith and Coe were tall, angular youths who discovered the theater and wanted to be playwrights. Each was the most important dramatic pioneer in his medium. Interviewed years later for a documentary on Griffith, Gish said, "He didn't do everything the first time, like a closeup, but he gave us the grammar of filmmaking: the cutting, the handling of humanity before a camera, and [he] understood the psychic strength of a lens." Substitute "television" for "filmmaking" and you have Fred Coe's role in the development of early television drama.

Both disliked excessively clever camera work, both inspired intense personal loyalty among their creative staff, and both trained the next generation of film directors, actors, and writers. Both would start drinking in response to personal crises in their lives. And both turned to their work with a preternatural intensity and concentration. Speaking of Griffith, actress Zita Johann said, "He shut out the world. He shut out whatever was unpleasant and gave his best to his work." As did Fred Coe.

• • •

By the 1950–1951 season, *Philco* was not only an artistic success, but popular as well. In February 1951 it was No. 6 in the Trendex ratings and No. 4 in the Hooperatings, beating Arthur Godfrey, *Your Show of Shows* with Sid Caesar and Imogene Coca, and *The Colgate Comedy Hour*. In October 1950 a new system, the Nielsen ratings, reported *Philco* as No. 3 among all TV programs for number of homes reached in the U.S., although only No. 9 for percentage of homes reached in the reception area of stations which carried it.

As television grew, this discrepancy would bode ill for *Philco Television*

Playhouse and other live dramatic anthologies: because of their prestige, most stations carried them, but variety shows had more mass appeal. Still, on its list of 100 most highly-rated programs in American television history, the 1995 *Complete Directory to Prime Time Network TV Shows* ranked *Philco Television Playhouse* above all its live dramatic competitors, as well as such popular subsequent fare as the sitcom *Green Acres* and game show *The Price Is Right*.

As the head of TV's premier dramatic show, Coe inspired future producers such as Bud Yorkin, a floor manager on *Philco* and eventually producer, with Norman Lear, of films such as *The Night They Raided Minsky's* and the landmark TV sitcom *All in the Family*. "He was really the model we all hoped to be some day," Yorkin says of Coe. "It was overwhelming to be around him." Fresh out of Smith College, Rhoda Rosenthal was so eager to get a secretarial job with Coe that she bluffed and said she knew stenography. She soon learned to her relief that Coe's Southern-accented speech came pouring out so slowly she didn't need speedwriting. "You could write his memos in three languages, never mind steno," she says.

With *Philco* gaining in public acceptance, its writers became increasingly bold in their scripts and the special effects they called for. While primitive by today's standards, those effects still produced a lot of anguish for the professionals who had to create them. "That show used to drive me wild," says makeup artist Dick Smith. "The scriptwriters kept taking greater and greater liberties."

Max Wilk's *The Fast Dollar* was about an aging Wall Street financier who wants to make one last killing. Airing on June 10, 1951, it featured Vaughan Taylor as the financier. In order to age Taylor, Smith experimented with a vinyl mask, instead of the more traditional latex rubber. Vinyl allowed for a more expressive mask, but as Smith realized too late, it was completely non-porous. "Vaughan had been working hard, and he accumulated a certain amount of perspiration underneath," Smith says. "It didn't have much place to go."

By the end of the first act, Smith could see on the studio monitor that the chin and lower lip were starting to come loose. In the second act, Taylor, a highly demonstrative actor, would have his longest and most histrionic scene.

During the short commercial break between the first and second acts, Smith hustled Taylor into the makeup room, located next to Studio 8G. He pulled off Taylor's chin piece. Some of the sweat ran off. Smith grabbed a blow dryer to dry off Taylor's real chin. The air got under the upper part of the mask, ballooning its cheeks out, and causing Taylor's sweat to pour forth in rivulets. There was less than a minute before Taylor was due back on camera.

Smith put more glue on the chin piece, slapped it back on, squirted adhesive around the edges and started to wipe off the excess. The stage manager stuck his head in the door. "Vaughan, you're on!" he said.

Taylor dashed out, with Smith close behind. As the actor waited for his cue, Smith said, "Vaughan." Taylor turned around, Smith wiped off a dab of goo from his mask, and Taylor made his entrance.

"He's sitting down, looking up at someone. He's stretching his neck, putting the worst possible stress on this thing, and he goes on for at least five minutes of strong dialogue," Smith recalls. "I'm sweating and I'm praying. I've got all my fingers crossed." To his horror, Smith realized the mask was loosening.

"I was thinking with all that sweat, it will come loose and fall with a plop! in front of the camera. Thank God, it didn't happen," he adds. "I don't think I ever used that material again. It was the scare of my life."

Eight months later, *Philco* aired *Crown of Shadows*, about the ill-fated rule of Emperor Maximilian and Empress Carlotta in Mexico. Its makeup challenges would dwarf those of *The Fast Dollar*. Carlotta was played by Felicia Montealegre, who began the show as the aged and mad Carlotta, flashed back to her youth, became an old hag again, and then regressed a second time to her youth. "This is absolutely the end," Smith said, and went on a vacation timed to ensure he would miss the show.

• • •

As the new television season loomed in the fall of 1951, the young medium was starting to attain critical mass. The coaxial cable carrying TV signals now crossed the United States, making television a truly national medium. When President Truman addressed the Japanese Peace Treaty Conference in San Francisco on September 4, 1951, it was the first television broadcast seen simultaneously all over the country.

In allowing the construction of the cable, Hollywood's studio heads ignored the advice of mogul Samuel Goldwyn, who was said to have advocated forming a posse to halt its advance in the Utah desert. "Why should anyone pay to see a bad picture in a theater," he reportedly asked, "when he can see one for nothing at home?"

The following summer, the FCC would lift the freeze on licensing new TV stations, and cities across the country would have television for the first time. Many who would work in television felt its allure for the first time. "I don't know what the hell it was all about," says Bob Costello, later Coe's unit production manager on *Mr. Peepers*. "We were so trusting in our leaders and in ourselves. It's what the time was all about. A bunch of us went to school on the GI Bill, then we fiddled around. I rattled around Europe and the States and did some theater. And then suddenly, we all believed that television was invented to give us a job. It came along just when all this talent was waiting to seize the opportunity."

The curtain was about to go up on the most stunning burst of literary creativity in American television history. Robert Lewine, then an NBC vice president, described television drama between 1948 and 1951 as "the gathering of energy and experience and the calm of adapting others' works before the storm of original creations." When that storm cloud burst, Fred Coe would be the chief rainmaker.

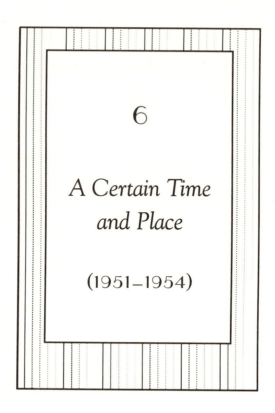

6

A Certain Time and Place

(1951–1954)

Despite the whipsaw turbulence of his personal life, Coe showed no signs of distress on the job. There were still the occasional screaming jags, but *Philco* staffers regarded them as part of the landscape, much like the towering Christmas tree that appeared every December in Rockefeller Plaza. Coe's wintry blasts were surrounded by the springlike geniality and supportiveness he showed his creative staff, the summery warmth of his hospitality at the home he soon bought in East Hampton and the autumn-like melancholy which few who worked for him ever saw. But when he blew, it was memorable.

Sunday nights at 9:00, *Philco* aired live from Studio 8G in the RCA building. Delbert Mann, who directed more than 100 episodes of the show, knew the routine when something went wrong on the air. Directly across the hall from 8G's control room was the executive viewing room, where Coe watched the broadcast, ready to spring into action if a camera shot was missed or if there was a wayward sound in the studio.

Through the closed door of the control room, Mann could hear the door on the other side of the corridor slam. He would count one . . . two . . . bang! The back door of the control room slammed open and Coe would stride in, right behind Mann and the others at the control panel. "It was never to interfere, never to give us the feeling he was chastising us, but just in case he could rectify the emergency of the moment," Mann adds. "I used to joke with Gordon Duff, 'Goddamn it, some day I'm going to lock the back door of the control room and he'll impale himself on it.'"

Although Mann accepted Coe's intervention in the intended spirit, that wasn't always the case with the other denizens of the control booth. Adrienne Luraschi selected the show's music and gave sound cues when she worked with director Gordon Duff. An elegant and composed woman, she tended to lose that composure when Coe came flapping into the control room like a great flightless bird. "He would be hollering, and we were all trying to say, 'Go away. Take four. Get ready for the music.' The hollering would continue. I could feel myself shaking, and I thought, 'If he doesn't leave, I am going to take a pencil and stab him to death!'" she recalls. "Finally, O. Tamburri would say, 'Sit DOWN, Fred!'"

Orland Tamburri, *Philco*'s unflappable technical director, whittled his first name down to "O" at Coe's suggestion so it would fit more easily into the show's closing credits. It was said Tamburri never pushed the wrong button on the primitive 20-button control panels of that era. But even he became frayed around the edges when Coe came storming in.

Toward the end of one show, Tamburri was performing a complicated series of dissolves between live action, slides, and title cards when something went wrong with one of the slides from the projection booth. As he recalls: "Fred came barreling in and stood between the director and me, saying 'What happened? Get the guy's name [in the projection booth]! He'll never work here again!'" Asked to wait until the show was off the air, Coe continued to sputter. Tamburri was so upset that as soon as the show faded to black, he took his headset off and threw it at the floor in Coe's direction, forgetting it was still clipped to his belt. "The headset flew towards Fred as far as it could go, then shot back past my face at what seemed like 100 miles per hour. That joke was on me," Tamburri admits. "Later, we all cooled down at Hurley's Bar and had a good laugh."

But the pressures on the show were no laughing matter. The normally placid Delbert Mann became a two-pack-a-day chain smoker. And for Arthur Penn, who joined the show two years later, directing live television held the same terrors as Kurtz's trip up the Congo in *Heart of Darkness*. "Incredible," Penn says in a dark and harrowed voice. "It was incredible. It was simply beyond belief." Sometimes a camera would break down while the show was on live, and a technological bucket brigade of TV engineers would charge onto the studio floor with spare parts, trying to fix it before it was needed on the air again. "It was a devastating job," Penn adds. "It's almost impossible to describe to people now."

The producer of the *Television Playhouse* still expected his directors and cameramen to use those bulky image orthicon cameras as if they were Rembrandt's brushes. "Ah want to see their eyes!" was his standard refrain if a shot of an actor's face was taken from too high. "Can't you get any lower?" While he didn't believe in closeups for their own sake, Coe knew live TV didn't do action or exteriors well, and that much of its drama took place in actors' faces.

Getting lower could be a problem, though. The crane camera, used to take shots from overhead, had to be hand-cranked down, and sometimes got stuck. For closeups, Coe had directors use 75-mm lenses. They produced less facial distortion than standard 50-mm lens, but the longer lenses were more sensitive and prone to lose focus than the shorter ones. "The 75-millimeter is tougher because the focus changes more rapidly," says Jack Coffey, a *Philco* cameraman and later noted soap opera director. "The longer the lens you go to, the bumpier the ride is. He liked long lenses."

• • •

Philco Television Playhouse began its fourth season in the fall of 1951 with two important changes. First, Philco brought in Goodyear Tire & Rubber as an alternate-week sponsor because of rising production costs. Fred Coe was now the producer of the *Philco-Goodyear Television Playhouse*.

To the writers, actors, and directors working for Coe, this appeared to have no practical effect. But as the drumbeat of McCarthyism grew louder, Young & Rubicam, Goodyear's advertising agency, would insist on using *Red Channels* as a casting guide. A year and a half earlier, *Philco* had rebuffed "Counterattack," which promoted the blacklist in television and radio. But with Goodyear and Young & Rubicam, it would return.

A more artistically important change involved the show's scripts. With the start of the fall 1951 season, *Philco-Goodyear* increasingly became a show where original scripts, rather than adaptations, were the rule. Coe was the first producer of a dramatic anthology to commission original scripts on a regular basis. (Six of *Philco-Goodyear*'s first eight shows in the fall of 1951 were originals at a time when most other dramatic anthologies were still adaptation-based.) He cosseted writers as few producers do. And he paid them top dollar: when $600 to $750 was a standard scriptwriter's fee on hour-long dramatic shows, Fred Coe's writers received $700 to $1,200. These would prove powerful lures: one by one, writers with prodigious talent but few or no credits appeared in his small, cluttered office on the fourth floor of the RCA Building. They would coalesce into the most impressive writing staff in 1950s live television drama.

• • •

In the spring of 1951, Coe had already moved out of their West 88th Street apartment. Soon after, unable to face her, he wrote to Alice asking her to take the children and move to Florida, which lacked New York's strict divorce requirements. As in so many other matters, Alice complied with his wishes, moving to Fort Lauderdale that September with five-year-old John and one-year-old Laurie. It appeared the endgame was at hand, but as both Alice and Joyce soon discovered, things were never that simple with Fred Coe.

Although Alice had moved to Fort Lauderdale to get the divorce Coe sought, by December he was still wavering. For Christmas of 1951, he came down with his mother to visit Alice, John, and Laurie.

"I don't want you to get a divorce," he told her the night before he went back to New York. "I want you to come back." Relieved and overjoyed, Alice packed her bags for the trip to New York. But when Coe woke up the next morning, he had changed his mind. The divorce was finalized in January of 1952.

Alice had waited patiently in Nashville when Coe went off to Yale. She'd served as business manager of the Town Theatre, and provided Coe with the logistical and emotional support that allowed his genius to bloom. As the one who recommended Joyce as a script girl for the *Television Playhouse*, she realized somewhat grimly that she'd also hired her own replacement.

Coe and Joyce had been involved for more than two years. He and Alice were now divorced, but in emotional terms, he was still going back and forth between the two women, and continued to drag his feet about marrying Joyce. A field marshal in the world of live television, he was wracked by indecision in his personal life. In May, drunk, he said to Alice, "It would seem from your letter and our last telephone conversation that 'you don't know how you feel.' I guess it could go on like that for any number of years, and I guess you are very wise, or at least you think you are, to have it such. You certainly must know by now that I always leaned on someone, mostly you, when such a decision was to be made," he added, "and I guess that you have now decided that you will have nothing to do with the making of *this one*. So be it! Or does it not even come down to that anymore? Maybe you're not even—well, maybe you don't give a damn. I can't blame you." Just below the surface of his drunken meandering is a cry for help. "What should I do?" he nearly asks. "What should I do?"

That spring, the rumor at the *Television Playhouse* was that Joyce, fed up with Coe's indecision, was going to leave the show. "I heard Joyce felt that she could not stay and was going to leave the company or go back to Iowa," script girl Adrienne Luraschi recalls. "And he didn't want her to go. I don't know how it came to a head, but he realized, 'No. You can't go.'"

In July 1952 Coe asked Alice to meet him with the children for a few days in Washington, D.C. At his request, they came back to New York: he had rented a house for them in East Hampton. Perhaps there's still hope,

Alice thought. But shortly after midnight, Coe drove up alone in the red Studebaker convertible and announced: "Joyce and I are going to be married."

The marriage would be at Andrews Air Force Base in Maryland, where Joyce's brother-in-law was stationed. Remarkably, Coe asked Alice to drive him to Penn Station so he could catch the train to Washington. Even more remarkably, she agreed. But when Alice arrived at 88th Street, she learned Coe had changed his mind again, and had taken a cab. Fred Coe and Joyce Beeler were married on Friday, August 1, 1952.

· · ·

Back in New York, Coe had a simple definition for his job: "Reading scripts, hiring directors, actors and writers, holding meetings and screaming and tearing my hair to put out a good show." Given all that could go wrong in live television, it's a wonder he didn't go bald. For example, Coe's script *This Time Next Year*, which aired on September 2, 1951, featured a live remote from Grant's Tomb. An NBC car was supposed to take actor Frank Sutton (who played the ghost of General Grant) there, but the car was delayed. Sutton was given cab fare and, in full General Grant uniform and makeup, raced onto Sixth Avenue, jumped into a cab, and yelled "Take me to Grant's Tomb!" The startled driver overran the curb, but got Sutton to Grant's Tomb in time.

Unlike his literary creation, Fred Coe was inconspicuous when he walked around his adopted city, looking every bit like *Homo conformicus*, or 1950s man, with his crew cut, horn-rimmed glasses, and J. Press ties. "I'd see him on the street sometimes," said E. G. Marshall, a frequent actor on *Philco*. "We'd talk and he'd say, 'Well, I've got to go get a haircut.' And I'd look at his hair and almost see skin."

Although he became a devotee of Brooks Brothers, Coe's style of dressing is often described as "rumpled" and "careless." One of his writers said he always looked as if he were dressed by J. C. Penney. In his early days at NBC, *TV Guide* observed, Coe had looked like an Ivy League student. Now, it said, he looked like an Ivy League professor. As his daughter Laurie later put it, "He dressed like Banana Republic before there was a Banana Republic." At 6'1, he was hardly a giant, although it is a measure of his forcefulness that many remember him as not only tall, but towering.

That forceful quality comes through in a memo Coe wrote to the *Philco-Goodyear* staff at the start of the fall 1952 season. The show was already one of the most prestigious on television. But, Coe felt, this was not enough: "As a razor-backed producer I am still not satisfied with the results I see and hear on Sunday night from 9 to 10." He added that there would have to be a ceaseless effort to make each script, each scene, each word better during the coming season. The *Television Playhouse* had to achieve a new level. With Fred Coe in charge, it would: the 1952–1953 season was its greatest yet.

• • •

Soft-spoken Horton Foote was from the town of Wharton, near the Texas Gulf Coast. He was one of the few members of his family ever to leave the state, and one of the few *Philco* writers to achieve stature as a playwright before joining the show: his first play, *Only the Heart*, opened on Broadway in 1945. Foote, like many others, appreciated Coe's attitude toward writers. "He was terribly supportive," Foote says. "He felt the writer was the center of the universe. Writers like to hear that."

On March 1, 1953, one of the most critically acclaimed *Philcos* aired: Foote's *The Trip to Bountiful*. It was the story of an old woman, living with her henpecked son and his shrewish wife, who escapes from their Houston apartment and revisits the town of her childhood in an attempt to regain her lost dignity. Coe decided to cast Lillian Gish in the starring role as the elderly woman, while Eileen Heckart played Gish's viper-tongued daughter-in-law, John Beal her weak son, and Eva Marie Saint a young woman she meets on the bus.

Bountiful produced an avalanche of calls to NBC. "People were just overcome by Lillian Gish's performance," says Foote, who with characteristic modesty doesn't mention the script. "William Paley, the head of CBS, called her and told her that television had come of age that night." Soon after, Fred Coe decided to make it the first play he would produce on Broadway, and when it opened at Henry Miller's Theatre on November 3, 1953, for an all-too-brief run, it would mark Coe's first time on Broadway since acting in 1944's *The Day Will Come*.

The Trip to Bountiful was part of a cycle of four teleplays Foote wrote for Coe based on an incident from Foote's youth, in which he heard about a man and woman who loved each other, but were forbidden to marry by their families. *Bountiful* examines this incident from the point of view of the disappointed woman looking back at the end of her life. *The Midnight Caller*, which also aired on the *Television Playhouse* and is even more powerful than *Bountiful*, takes place just several years after the marriage has been frustrated: the woman survives, the man's spirit is broken. *Tears of My Sister*, airing on *First Person Playhouse* in the summer of 1953, is seen from the poignantly uncomprehending point of view of the woman's younger sister. And, on *Flight*, airing three years later on *Playwrights '56*, the couple secretly marries, but when the young woman goes to join her husband in Houston, she learns he has betrayed and abandoned her.

Expectant Relations, about members of a greedy family waiting for the father to die, showed Foote also had a gift for comedy, but most of his scripts for the *Television Playhouse* were known as Southern mood plays.

Gore Vidal has called Foote's work of this period "allusive, delicate and elegiac," similar to the early Tennessee Williams, while Coe was the first to call Foote "a Chekhov of the Texas small town." Foote's teleplays are soaked in the regional authenticity of the Texas Gulf Coast right down to their stage instructions: In *A Young Lady of Property*, starring Kim Stanley and Joanne Woodward, "Miss Martha gives a peal of laughter that sounds as if she thought Mr. Russell Walter the funniest man in five counties."

Bringing Foote's scripts to life was director Vincent Donehue. Quiet but intense, the Albany, N.Y., native had worked with Foote in the theater for years before coming to the *Television Playhouse*. He would go on to direct Mary Martin in the television version of *Peter Pan* and, on Broadway, *The Sound of Music*, also directing Broadway and film versions of *Sunrise at Campobello*. Donehue was no stranger to Coe: they had been in summer stock together in 1935. Donehue's pairing with Foote was a good one: he highlighted and dramatized moments that Foote wrote well, but would flatten out, left to his own devices.

Foote's *Television Playhouse* scripts tend to be dramatically understated: in *Bountiful*, when Lillian Gish tears up the Social Security check her daughter-in-law is eager to cash in, it's one of the most highly charged moments in the script, yet it's easy to miss because it's played on almost a throwaway basis (Foote eliminated the scene entirely from the Broadway and film versions.) Authors Barbara Moore and David G. Yellin note that in rewriting *Bountiful*, Foote pared away the more obviously dramatic scenes, replacing them with more stoical ones. In a sense, Foote is the Mies van der Rohe of the modern American theater, a man to whom less is always more.

• • •

Sidney Chayefsky, a young Jewish writer from the Bronx, was known as Paddy because he tried to avoid kitchen police ("K.P.") duty during wartime military service by claiming he had to attend Catholic mass. Influenced by Arthur Miller's *Death of a Salesman*, he had been writing serious, verbose plays no one wanted to produce. Coe encouraged him to write in his own voice, in a more natural and economical style. He took Coe's advice so well that Bernard Kalb later wrote in the *Saturday Review*, "Chayefsky's works are as authentically Bronx as a rush-hour subway bound for the Grand Concourse."

His first *Philco*, *Holiday Song*, was about a cantor who loses, then regains his faith on the eve of the high holy days. First airing on September 14, 1952, it was loosely based on a *Reader's Digest* article Coe had given Chayefsky to read. But while Coe was away getting married during the summer, David Susskind intruded into the production process of *Holiday Song*.

Susskind told Chayefsky the script was "too Jewish" and urged him to rewrite the central character as a priest or minister. The young writer reluctantly complied. When Coe returned from vacation, he was uncomfortable with the script. "This is a nice story, Pappy," Coe said. "But shouldn't it be one of those, like, rabbi people?" Chayefsky eagerly switched it back.

Ron Simon, curator of television for the Museum of Television and Radio, says Coe's supportiveness and encouragement released the creative spark that illuminated the Golden Age. "You get a sense that Coe helped create the golden moments by helping to give a voice and a sensibility to his young writing staff," he says. "What was that inner strength he had that could draw work out from others? Paddy Chayefsky, for example. If you look at his early career, you don't get a sense of a man who could create something unique for television. But Coe encouraged Chayefsky to go within himself. I think he did that with his other writers as well."

On Monday morning, May 11, 1953, Coe read one of the few genuinely wretched scripts ever submitted to *Philco*. Rehearsals were due to begin on Friday for the show that would air a week from the following Sunday, and there was no usable script. Coe knew Chayefsky was working on a story about two lonely people who meet in a dance hall, and called him at home. Delbert Mann, in Coe's office at the time, recalls the conversation.

"How's it going with that script"? Coe asked.

Chayefsky said he'd finished the first act, was writing the second, and had outlined the third. (On *Philco*, a show's three acts were separated by commercials twenty and forty minutes through the show.)

"When can you have it done?" Coe asked.

"Give me a couple of weeks," Chayefsky said.

"How about Thursday?" Coe shot back.

"I don't know, Fred," Chayefsky replied. "I'll give it to you the best I can." Chayefsky turned in a complete script by Saturday. Originally called *Love Story*, its name was changed at the last minute to *Marty*.

Marty had its origin in the rehearsal of a previous Chayefsky show for Philco, *The Reluctant Citizen*, about an immigrant from Central Europe afraid to apply for U.S. citizenship, fearing it would subject him to the same governmental oppression he had fled. It rehearsed for a week in the ballroom of the Abbey Hotel on 53rd Street before being brought into Studio 8G for two days of on-camera rehearsal. Coe always had the writer in rehearsal in case there were script problems. On *The Reluctant Citizen*, though, Chayefsky had little to do because rehearsals were going smoothly.

"Paddy got to wandering around the ballroom," says Delbert Mann, who directed most of Chayefsky's *Philco-Goodyear* teleplays. "At night, it was used as a kind of lonely hearts club where singles could come and dance to juke-box music and have a Coca-Cola. There were little hand-printed signs all around the hall with suggestions for behavior, suggestions how to dress. One of them said, 'Girls: Dance with the man who asks you. Remember—Men have feelings, too.' Paddy was wandering around the hall, looking at the signs and thinking.

"At a break in rehearsal, he came up to me and said, 'Hey, I've got an idea. I want to do a show about a girl who comes to a place like this.' As much to get him out of my hair as anything, I said, 'Yeah, Paddy. That's a great idea. Wonderful. Go do it.' And he wandered off."

By the next rehearsal break, Chayefsky had changed his mind. Now he wanted to write about a *guy* who came to a place like that. Caught up in overseeing the rehearsal, Mann repeated his perfunctory, distracted approval. Chayefsky disappeared into a hotel bathroom, put on his thinking cap, and came up with the idea for *Marty*.

Starring Rod Steiger as a plain, lonely butcher and Nancy Marchand as the equally plain and lonely girl he meets and falls in love with, *Marty* electrified the nation when it aired on May 24, 1953. The next day, Chayefsky's dialogue was on everyone's lips. Marty's immigrant mother attempting to sound colloquial, saying "Why don't you go to the Waverly Ballroom? It's loaded with tomatoes." Marty's crude but heartfelt love call, "So you see, you're not such a dog as you think you are." And the show's most famous—and most frequently misquoted exchange—between Marty and his pal Angie, "What do you feel like doin' tonight?" "I don't know. What do you feel like doin' tonight?"

Among the show's many fans was Jack Gould. In an unusual move, he devoted the bulk of his *New York Times* column to a single show. "Dramas that undertake to study the lives of 'little people' more often than not are tedious stuff," he wrote. "But the Television Playhouse avoided most of the pitfalls and offered a theatrically valid and moving hour in its production of 'Marty.'" He had a mixed reaction to Steiger's performance, however, noting, "While at times sounding uncannily like Wally Cox in "Mr. Peepers" [the new situation comedy Coe was producing about a mild-mannered schoolteacher], Steiger brought a controlled spontaneity to the part that was unusually effective."

The morning after the show aired, Steiger, who lived in midtown Manhattan, went out to a neighborhood coffee shop. When he went downstairs, a woman said, "Hi, Marty, what do you feel like doin' tonight?" Playing along, Steiger said, "I don't know. What do you feel like doin' tonight?" As he walked along the street, a garbage truck went by and a man inside yelled, "How ya doin', Marty?" When Steiger got to the coffee shop, the man who took his order said, "Whaddya want, Marty? What are ya doin' tonight?" "I don't *know* what I'm doin'," said Steiger, beginning to weary of the joke. "Gimme a corn muffin and tea!"

Other Chayefsky teleplays such as *The Catered Affair*, *The Mother*, and *The Bachelor Party* frequently dramatized the dilemmas of immigrant families such as his own and solidified his reputation as one of the best writers of the Golden Age.

While *Marty* is the best live drama in the history of television, Horton Foote's *Philco-Goodyear* teleplays, taken as a whole, are those of a more mature playwright with greater command of his narrative voice and dramatic structure. With the exception of the enduring *Marty*, future generations will read Chayefsky's teleplays to gain insight into 1950s America. They will read Foote's to gain insight into their own time and place.

• • •

The next writer to join Coe's stable at the *Television Playhouse* was N. Richard Nash. Although he had been writing screenplays in Hollywood, he says that when Coe recruited him, he had already left writing. "You don't write in pictures," he says sardonically. "You do what they tell you." One of Nash's *Philco* teleplays, *The Rainmaker*, about an amiable charlatan who promises drought-stricken towns he can make it rain, became the basis of the Broadway hit and the film version starring Katharine Hepburn and Burt Lancaster.

Nash was impressed not only with the creative freedom Coe gave his writers, but with the way he could make a snap decision as to whether an idea would result in a worthwhile script. One Saturday night, Nash called Coe with a story idea. "Give it to me in a sentence," said Coe, on his way to a party with Joyce.

"It's the story of two sisters in love with the same man who is a plumber and pretends not to be," Nash said.

"Fine," Coe replied. "That's a commitment," and dashed out to the party. Nash's sentence aired on the *Television Playhouse* as *The Brownstone*.

• • •

Fred Coe had started going to East Hampton with Alice as a guest of Hoffman Hays, one of the *Philco* writers, who had a house there. Only two hours from mid-town Manhattan, East Hampton's tree-shaded lanes and remoteness from the fast pace of New York appealed to Coe, and he and Joyce bought a house on Baiting Hollow Road in September 1952.

At first, it was little more than a gardener's cottage with weathered shingles and a greenhouse attached. But by the summer of 1953, they had refurbished it, adding a new section two stories high. Coe would expand the house many times over the years and it would become the hub of an active social scene involving the show business people who swirled around the Coes. Joyce was an excellent hostess and cook; Coe loved to hold court for his dramatic artists.

Among the many frequent guests on Baiting Hollow Road were Coe's agent Priscilla Morgan, *Mr. Peepers* unit production manager Bob Costello, and writers David Shaw, Sumner Locke Elliott, Tad Mosel, Joe Liss, Hoffman Hayes, and their families and friends. Arguments and discussions about the Korean War, McCarthyism, and new president Dwight Eisenhower went on long into the night. And although they were far from Radio City, the conversation frequently returned to what linked them all: work.

For most of the Coes' houseguests, there was good fellowship, camaraderie, and good-natured ribbing. "We didn't sit in reverence of Fred," Bob Costello says. Eva Marie Saint adds, "I've never been with a repertory theater, but as I think back, *Philco-Goodyear* was a repertory group. It was all one big theatrical group, and Fred was in charge."

Even as he presided over the conviviality at his East Hampton vacation home, Coe always stood to some extent apart. As close as he was to his writers, he still kept them at a distance. "In a strange way, he was our friend, but at the same time he wasn't that close," JP Miller says. "He was a very lonely man, enigmatic, capable of tremendous affection and tremendous hostility."

• • •

Eager to move beyond his role as agent and co-owner of Talent Associates, David Susskind served as producer of *Philco-Goodyear Playhouse* during the summer of 1953. Meanwhile, Coe worked on a summer replacement for *The Life of Riley*. In a display of the network's confidence in him, Coe was given carte blanche to develop the show.

What he had in mind was an experimental program based on first-person short stories in which the narrator is also the principal character. The series, called *First Person Playhouse*, premiered on July 3 and ran on Friday nights until September 11. Although largely forgotten, it is a classic example of how Coe could stretch the medium of television for dramatic purposes. To direct most of the shows, Coe chose an ex-Army infantryman he had known in Columbia, South Carolina, during World War II.

In the spring of 1953, Arthur Penn had recently been promoted from floor manager to associate director for NBC in Los Angeles, where he helped to build sound effects and prepare the set of the *Colgate Comedy Hour*. It was work he did well, but he wanted to direct drama. He remembers the phone call that changed his life.

"I got a call one day, and it was, 'Hey, Pappy! This is Fred Coe. You 'member me?' And I said, 'Oh, Christ, yes!' I had been watching *Philco* like crazy and seeing all this wonderful work. And he said, 'How do you feel about coming East and directing an experimental show I want to try?' I left California in the greatest rush you've ever seen."

In effect, the camera was the main character on each episode of *First Person Playhouse*. Creating the aesthetic ground rules was a challenge. "I remember talking with Fred and asking, 'What are you looking at when it's a "first person" telling a story?'" Penn recalls. "If the story said, 'It was a hot day and nothing was moving,' what was the viewer looking at?" Answering his own question, Penn reasoned, "If you say, 'It was a hot day and my dress was sticking to me,' there's something for the camera to capture. We developed a kind of visual language designed to create the atmosphere, the climate, and the given circumstances."

As with the *Television Playhouse*, the shows on *First Person* ranged from serious drama to light comedy. On each show, an off-screen actor would speak the lines attributable to the camera's point of view, either as an expression of the narrator's thoughts, or in dialogue with the on-screen actors.

The first show, Robert Alan Aurthur's *Desert Cafe*, focused on the conflicts between a poor widower and his insecure young son, with the camera playing the role of an employee in a desert cafe where the two spend the night. On David Shaw's *Comeback*, the camera's point of view represented a talent agent trying to get a TV acting role for a has-been actress (irritatingly, the agent keeps appearing on camera, causing the viewer to wonder whose point of view he's being seen from). Horton Foote contributed the tragic *Tears of My Sister*, and Harry Muheim the comic *I'd Rather Be a Squirrel*, featuring the voice of Wally Cox.

Despite its limited run, *First Person* was a success. "Fred Coe, one of TV's bright young veterans, has come up with one of the most imaginative program ideas of year," *TV Guide* raved. "The series represents one of the few summer replacements which should remain on the air through the regular season." But Coe and his troupe had enough on their plate as it was. Although *First Person* didn't remain on the air, its director did. That fall, Coe moved Arthur Penn into the directors' rotation on *Philco*, along with Delbert Mann and Vincent Donehue, while director Gordon Duff moved up to associate producer.

• • •

George Ault Mosel, Jr.'s, father liked neither his own name nor the fact that his wife insisted on giving it to his son. One day when he came home, he asked "How's the little tad?," and George Ault Mosel, Jr., became Tad Mosel. The native of Steubenville, Ohio, had a few television credits, but was still working as a ticket clerk for Northwest Airlines near Grand Central Station when he met Fred Coe in the spring of 1953. Mosel came to Coe's attention through *The Haven*, a play which touched on three subjects then taboo for television—alcoholism, adultery, and suicide—and which Coe would nonetheless produce.

When they met, Coe didn't grill Mosel about his limited television credits. Instead, impressed by *The Haven*, he simply asked how many shows Mosel wanted to write for the upcoming season. "Can you imagine being asked something like that?" Mosel says. "It was like I'd died and gone to heaven." Mosel told Coe he'd do six shows, although he now acknowledges, "Nobody's that facile—not even in those days, when people were turning out things left and right."

Instead of blanching, Coe readily agreed, telling Mosel, "You can sit at your typewriter and write 'ABCDEFG,' but let me tell you, I am going to put it on the air." Spurred on by Coe's faith in him, Mosel turned out dramas such as *Ernie Barger Is 50*, starring Ed Begley as a man coming to terms with his own aging, which aired on August 9, 1953, and *Other People's Houses*, which aired on August 30, with Eileen Heckart and Rod Steiger as a couple torn by the prospect of having to put the wife's aging father in a nursing home.

Although *Ernie Barger Is 50* and *Other People's Houses* marked Mosel's arrival as a member of Fred Coe's stable of writers, both shows were produced by David Susskind. When Coe recruited Mosel, he intended to open *Philco-Goodyear*'s fall 1953 season with one of his plays. But Susskind, wanting to make a name for himself as a producer, took two of Mosel's plays and in effect produced them while Coe was busy with *First Person Playhouse*. Coe and Susskind clashed on this point, and it would not be the last time they did so.

As with many *Television Playhouse* writers, Mosel was more interested in developing character than complex plots. His teleplays usually take place in the Midwest he left as a child, and many of the strongest scripts feature a strong father-daughter relationship. *The Lawn Party*, which aired on May 23, 1954, is Mosel's variation on Sinclair Lewis's *Main Street*. India, the exotically self-named housewife who is the main character, is reminiscent of Carol Kennicott, trying to bring beauty and culture to a small Midwestern town that strenuously resists it. Mosel turns this theme on its head, though.

Carol Kennicott's spirit is crushed by the philistinism of Gopher Prairie. But India is an aesthetic bully who doesn't care that the beautiful lawn party she's planning will damage her husband's health, prevent her daughter from getting her boyfriend a birthday present, and alienate her neighbor. In the end, she realizes these relationships are more important to her than the superficial beauty of the lawn party.

When Mosel is at his best, which he usually is, his quiet stories have a galvanizing intensity and an almost surgical ability to dissect character. He has a talent for choosing just the right word and no more; or, as the *Saturday Review* put it, "his writings have a naked lyrical quality." On those occasions when he isn't at his best, though, his little people are, well, too little. Reviewing Mosel's teleplay *The Morning Shirt* several years later, the London *Times* wrote, "With the best will in the world we could not accept Mr. Mosel's molehill as a mountain."

• • •

JP Miller was a hulking 6′3 Texan with a rich Texas twang who had studied at the Yale School of Drama, but had no writing credits. The veteran of a brief boxing career under the name Ted Frontier, he lived in Jackson Heights, Queens, where he was writing scripts and failing to make a living selling air conditioners.

Miller's story shows how Coe could give substance to a frightened writer's aspirations. "I sold a script to *Philco* in kind of a miraculous way," he says. After watching and admiring the show, he wrote a script for it and took it up to NBC and gave it to Yale Drama classmate Bob Costello, who passed it along to NBC script editor Terry Lewis. She called Miller a few days later.

"Who's your agent?" she asked.

"I don't have one," Miller said.

"We don't accept unsolicited manuscripts," Lewis replied, "but now that I've read it, I want to buy it."

Soon afterwards, Coe called him in. Miller feared it was to reverse the script editor's decision. "He was the guru of live television at the time, the ultimate, the top of the mountain," Miller recalls. "So a writer like me who had no credits—I was terrified, and thought I was going to get dismissed peremptorily.

"Instead, I walked in and here he sits with these Coke-bottle glasses on, staring at me. He said, 'Listen, Pappy. You got any other stories?' And I said, 'Oh, yeah.' And he says, 'Well, tell me one.' I was so nervous, I was stuttering. I thought of a story that had been going through my head and told him about it and he said, 'I like it, Pappy. Write it.' That was our contract."

The play Miller timorously pitched to Coe aired on April 25, 1954, as *Old Tasselfoot*, the moving tale of an aging blacksmith who lives along a saltwater marsh on the Gulf Coast of Texas. He keeps vigil over the disappearing whooping cranes, and every year greets Old Tasselfoot, a wounded, aging crane, on its flight north. Then one year, it doesn't return . . .

Old Tasselfoot so moved Coe, he directed it himself, something he rarely did anymore. Reflecting upon Coe's ability to stimulate writers, Miller comes up with an earthy metaphor. "Fred understood that you don't get milk out of a cow by beating the cow," he says. "You get milk by caressing the cow's tits and squeezing them gently. Fred knew that writers were like cows, so he caressed writers' psyches."

Coe later produced a Gore Vidal script on *Playwrights '56*, leaving only two major Golden Age writers he didn't work with: Reginald Rose, author of *The Remarkable Incident at Carson Corners* and *Twelve Angry Men* (both for *Studio One*) and Rod Serling, who wrote *Patterns* (*Kraft Television Theatre*) and *Requiem for a Heavyweight* (*Playhouse* 90). Looking at why Coe never worked with them throws into relief the kind of writing he sought to air.

Both Rose and Serling were capable of drawing fully-realized characters, but their work during this period emphasizes plot or social commentary at the expense of character. One of Rose's teleplays, *An Almanac of Liberty*, is a blistering attack on McCarthyism. Describing it, Rose wrote, "The protagonist . . . is the force for good and its antagonist is the force for evil. The people in the play are merely instruments to stir those forces into movement." Similarly, Serling's *Patterns* is a strong critique of the corporate jungle, but its characters are stock figures.

Coe was more interested in probing character, in illuminating the dark corners of the human heart. His philosophy for the *Television Playhouse* was best summed up by a remark Horton Foote once made about himself. "I'm not per se a social writer," he said. "In other words, I'm not out to overthrow anybody or anything. Really I'm trying to report on the human condition as I see it."

Live television drama was an art form as unique to its time and place as the miracle and mystery plays of the medieval era. When live TV is remembered at all, it's usually for its frenetic production pressures and the seriocomic errors that resulted, or for the famous actors and directors whom it launched. More easily forgotten is that this period gave rise to a significant and distinctive body of original dramatic literature, and that Fred Coe was the main purveyor of it.

· · ·

Whether he knew it or not, JP Miller had had superb timing. Live television was at its peak, but its decline was already in motion. With the West Coast now connected to the east by the coaxial cable and Los Angeles serving as a point of origination for national programming, a flood of filmed programs would overwhelm live drama. The networks, sponsors, and ad agencies increasingly took control of the medium, and maverick producers such as Fred Coe, Worthington Miner, and Herbert Brodkin, who regarded television more as a cultural than a commercial medium, would find less room to operate. McCarthyism was enveloping New York television. *Red Channels* enforced the blacklist against entertainers who had engaged in, or were rumored to have engaged in, activities unacceptable in the increasingly chilly Cold War atmosphere. "It was a hysterical period," Eli Wallach recalls. "Sometimes you'd sit down to a rehearsal [of a TV show] and you'd read, then there would be a break for twenty minutes.

You'd come back, and there would be two empty places. They'd checked on someone's 'credentials.'"

Careers were hampered or destroyed, and sometimes worse. Phil Loeb, who appeared in *Dinner at Eight*, the premiere episode of *Television Playhouse*, lost his role as Uncle Jake on the sitcom *The Goldbergs*. His star waned, and a few years later, beset by health and career worries, he checked into New York's Taft Hotel and took a fatal overdose of sleeping pills.

On the *Television Playhouse*, Young & Rubicam, Goodyear's advertising agency, served as enforcers for the blacklist. "Young and R. put a lot of pressure on us," casting director Bill Nichols recalls. "Scripts had to be sent to them. And they wanted to know which actors we were considering for different roles." This task was oppressive logistically as well as morally: time was at a premium in live television, and pulling that information together took time. Coe instructed his staff to use controversial actors and writers in the alternate weeks when Philco sponsored the *Television Playhouse*.

But by 1953, not even Philco and Hutchins, its advertising agency, were immune to the pressures of the blacklist. Pierson Mapes, who headed Hutchins's New York office, kept a copy of *Red Channels* in his desk. However, given his long association with the show, he was more likely to approve a politically suspect artist than Young & Rubicam was. "If we had a particularly good script and we wanted one special person on, an actor who was controversial, we'd put them on Philco," Nichols says. "That continued for quite a while."

Several times, Coe had to talk Delbert Mann and Gordon Duff out of resigning over their exasperation with the blacklist and their inability to get the actors they wanted. He understood and shared their frustrations, but said he intended to work against the blacklist from the inside. The case of Judy Holliday shows he was as good as his word.

Coe wanted to get Holliday for David Shaw's script *The Huntress*, but she was blacklisted, and Young & Rubicam refused to approve her. In January 1954, the Y & R executive who had been Goodyear's liaison with the show since 1951 retired. He threw a three-martini lunch at The Twenty-One Club for the show's top creative staff. Well into his third martini, the executive, who was sitting next to Coe, gushed expansively about how great it had been to work with him and asked if there was any way he could show his gratitude. There was, Coe said. Clear Judy Holliday for *The Huntress*.

"Well," the executive said, sobering up a bit, "I don't know . . ." Nothing more was said, and the luncheon ended. Two hours later, the phone rang in Coe's office. It was the grim, outmaneuvered account executive from Young & Rubicam. "Use her," he said.

The Huntress aired on Valentine's Day in 1954. The witty and beguiling story of a young woman scheming to get a rich husband, it is played superbly by Holliday, with Tony Randall as Richard Beekman (a man so rich that when his father tries to arrange a marriage for him to a suitably wealthy woman, Randall sniffs, "It would probably be annulled as a violation of the Sherman Anti-Trust Act").

Randall's father has the room clerk in a hotel where Holliday is staying give her a check for a million dollars. With all that money, he figures, she'll no longer want to marry his son. Holliday asks the clerk who would give her a million, but the room clerk only replies, "Let's just say I'm an intermediary." Randall suspects his father's machinations and urges Holliday to tear up the check.

"Do you really think a room clerk would give you a million?" he asks. "It wasn't him," Holliday replies with perfectly timed Judy Holliday loopiness. "He was an interplanetary." This bravura show was made possible by Fred Coe's principled guile. "Fred's attitude was 'Get 'em on the show, get 'em on the show, get those actors on the show and let the advertising agencies scream about it later,'" Arthur Penn says. "For a guy from Alligator, Mississippi, he had a great sense of what was honorable among people."

There were limits to what he could do, however: after Walter Bernstein adapted *The Rich Boy* for *Philco*, he was blacklisted. Coe would not let him work for the show, not even through a front, a practice in which banned writers submitted their work under the name of someone else. "I think that, like a lot of producers, he was scared," says Bernstein. "If NBC had known he was doing this, he could have gotten fired."

Coe's blacklist battles with Young & Rubicam weren't the end of his conflicts with them. He felt strongly that artists should be shielded from the intrusion of commercialism. In the studio, he drew a line between the show's artistic and commercial sides, especially when ad agency executives tried to insinuate themselves into the creative process.

"If anyone came from the sponsor or the agency, they were allowed to go to a small viewing room and watch the rehearsal of the actual show," recalled Sumner Locke Elliott, whose sharply observed modern comedies of manners made him a valued member of Coe's writing stable. "Fred would go in and speak to them for a minute or so, but if one of them set foot on his set, there would be an explosion."

Goodyear's new ambassador to Coe from Young & Rubicam soon got a taste of this. During the dress rehearsal of a JP Miller show in the spring of 1954, the Y & R man left the executive viewing room and crossed the hall to the control room, where he began to make suggestions about the script. As far as Coe was concerned, he might as well have crashed through Berlin's Checkpoint Charlie.

"Fred screamed at him so loud that everyone jumped," Miller recalls. "He said, 'What the fuck are you doing in here? Get your ass outa here!

Get back to your fucking office!' The guy turned white and backed out of the control room. It was like, 'My God, what did I do to deserve this?'" As Coe put it to writer Harry Muheim in a calmer moment, "The sponsor *pays* for this show, but *I* run it."

Aware of the pressure Goodyear was putting on Coe and the *Television Playhouse* through Y & R, *Variety* ran an editorial that month urging Goodyear to back off. Its dealers around the country were asking for more light and airy shows of the "boy meets girl" variety rather than kitchen-sink dramas and the full range of thoughtful plays from Coe's writers. But acquiescence to such a move would be a blow to television as a mature and intelligent medium, *Variety* noted.

There was also pressure on Coe from the Philco side. On Horton Foote's *The Midnight Caller*, a man in a small Southern town, spiritually broken by his parents' refusal to let him marry the woman he loves, becomes a drunkard. A Philco distributor wrote to corporate headquarters saying several people told him that after seeing the show, they would not buy Philco products. A woman wrote to the president of Philco complaining, "Not one person in the cast was a normal American. They were all neurotics for one reason or another. It is a shame with so many fine stories available such trash is forced on the public." These letters always found their way to Fred Coe's desk, but he never mentioned them to the writers.

Despite these brickbats, in April the *Television Playhouse* won the prestigious Peabody Award and *Variety*'s Showmanagement Award (the trade weekly called the show the "Phil-Coe" Hour). In its citation, *Variety* noted, "In a business where the race is to the swift, 'Television Playhouse' seems always gifted with a yen to get there slowly, but to get there." While this is a tribute to the thoughtful and mature (if sometimes slow-to-develop) plots of Fred Coe's writers, it also reflects the personality of the show's producer.

It's an enduring irony that the most successful producer in the fast-paced, high-pressure world of live television was a man whose speech and actions were highly deliberate, a man of almost Oblomovian lassitude. "Fred drove all the writers mad because he wouldn't get on with the reading of the script," says Mary Phipps, wife of writer Thomas Phipps. "But once he did, he was brilliant."

In an article for the June 1954 issue of *Theatre Arts*, Coe concluded, "We are confident that the next five years of *Television Playhouse* will be just as restless, perplexing and magical as the first five. Tune us in and you'll see." Although written in the spirit of a manifesto, the article, "TV Drama's Declaration of Independence," would prove to be more of an elegy: in August, Coe was forced out as the show's producer.

According to *Time* magazine, the advertising agency—unnamed, but probably Young & Rubicam—was displeased by the number of shows with unhappy endings. An anonymous adman complained, "One week there'd be a story about a blind old lady in Texas, and the next week a story about a blind young lady in Texas." It's also easy to imagine the new Y & R account executive beseeching his supervisors, "For God's sake, get this maniac off my back!" With *Philco's* ratings having slipped over the summer, he was in a position to get his wish.

If Y & R thought they would solve their problems by dispatching Coe, however, they were mistaken: Gordon Duff, Coe's associate producer, took the helm and continued to use the same writers Coe had. And as Pat Weaver flippantly observes, "I'm sure Fred was still the controlling monster over at the *Television Playhouse.*"

Nonetheless, Coe's ouster showed that sponsors and advertising agencies were increasingly asserting control of the new medium. As Robert Alan Aurthur wrote wistfully only two years later, "One of the reasons it was fun, probably the main reason, was because of Fred Coe. He was Big Daddy, Southern accent and all, and we were the family, and while we were growing up we had ourselves a ball. . . . [W]e were a family in a certain time and place and then the time and place passed by, and we were no longer a family."

• • •

For Coe, leaving *Philco* was not a demotion, but a promotion: NBC president Pat Weaver had a new assignment for him. The timing was fortunate, as Weaver was soon kicked upstairs by David Sarnoff to the largely ceremonial position of chairman of the board.

Producer's Showcase was one of the last of Weaver's inspired program ideas at NBC. During the mid-1950s, the notion of specials (or spectaculars, as they were then called) had not yet entered television's lexicon. Audacious for its time, Weaver's idea was to get Broadway and Hollywood stars, many of whom would still have nothing to do with TV, paying them top salaries to star in major shows with quality production values.

Coe would mingle with the most powerful and famous figures of Broadway and Hollywood. He would be responsible for only one live show a month, instead of four on Philco. "I think he was glad to be rid of *Philco,*" Delbert Mann says. "He was probably exhausted, physically and emotionally. And there was increasing pressure from the sponsors, not all of it having to do with the blacklist."

There were clouds on the horizon, but they seemed small and distant. Television was beginning to move toward film and Los Angeles. In 1952, CBS had opened its mammoth Television City complex, described as "a complete motion picture studio designed especially for the electronic medium." For someone as committed to live television as Coe, these were not good developments.

But as he moved to take the reins at *Producer's Showcase,* Fred Coe was still a rising star, one of the most important producers in network television. He was concluding a six-year-plus run as producer of one of its best dramatic shows, had begun producing *Mr. Peepers,* one of its top situation comedies, and had taken over at the helm of its greatest marquee program.

When he was hired by NBC in 1945, Coe was making $270 a month; he was now earning about a quarter of a million dollars a year. Many of his troupe of leading writers, directors, and actors were still gathered around him in a kind of extended family. He had a gorgeous new young wife who adored him. Fred Coe was thirty-nine and still on his way up. The producer and director of *Old Tasselfoot* had no way of knowing that in a few short years, the world of live New York television would not be like the whooping crane, which is making a modest comeback, but like the dodo, which is extinct.

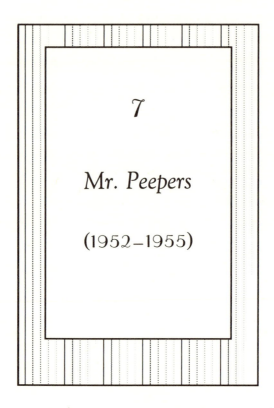

7

Mr. Peepers

(1952–1955)

Six years after the end of World War II, David Swift was still a white-knuckle flier. During the war, he had been shot down over Russia at the helm of a B-17 bomber. A P-51 fighter he was piloting over Germany was struck by anti-aircraft fire and he struggled back to France, where he crash-landed. On November 19, 1951, he was a passenger on United Airlines' noon flight from New York's Idlewild Airport to O'Hare in Chicago. There was no reason to feel jumpy, but he felt jumpy.

To distract himself, he turned to the assignment Fred Coe had given him that morning: figuring out what to do with Wally Cox. Three weeks earlier, *Philco-Goodyear Television Playhouse* had aired Swift's comedy *The Copper*. Directed by Delbert Mann, it starred Cox as a bumbling policeman who could do no right, and it was immensely popular. NBC executives had called Coe and said they wanted a show built around Cox. Coe called Swift and told him to think one up. Now, en route to Chicago, where his wife, Maggie McNamara, was appearing in *The Moon Is Blue*, Swift puzzled it out.

There wasn't much you could do with Cox. No one would confuse him with an action-adventure hero. He was a walking encyclopedia, a storehouse of trivia on everything from the internal combustion engine to birds and insects (walking across a lawn as a youth in Evanston, Illinois, Cox purportedly once startled a companion by calling for silence, saying "An ant lion is poised to attack"). By the end of the flight, Swift decided Cox would be a teacher, and *Mr. Peepers* was born on United's noon flight from Idlewild to O'Hare.

The show's pilot episode, simply called *Peepers*, aired from Studio 8H in the RCA Building on May 15, 1952. Directed by James Sheldon, it starred Cox as Robinson Peepers, "Jefferson City's most popular general science teacher." Featured players were Joseph Foley as Mr. Gurney, the principal; Norma Crane as Rayola Deen, the music appreciation teacher and Mr. Peepers's girlfriend; and Leonard Elliott as Mr. Wadd, the malevolent science teacher who briefly serves as Mr. Peepers's antagonist.

Although the role of Coach would later be played by David Tyrell, followed by Jack Warden, he was played in the pilot by Walter Matthau. In a sign of growing tension between Coe and Swift, Coach, an amiable bonehead, calls everyone "Pappy," Coe's standard greeting. When Mr. Wadd steals Mr. Peepers's seat in the cafeteria, Coach says, "Aw, look, Pappy, he's the new teacher. Let him sit here and get acquainted." It was, Swift thought mischievously, a little constructive criticism.

In the sixty-minute pilot, Mr. Peepers mistakenly shows up several months early for his teaching job at Jefferson Junior High. The principal tells him to assist the prissy and autocratic Mr. Wadd, who has complained about not having a teaching assistant. But Wadd, threatened by what he perceives as a competitor for his job, assigns Peepers a series of menial and degrading tasks, such as sharpening so many pencils that his fingers are covered with bandages.

Mr. Peepers doesn't have a malicious bone in his body, but he defeats his nemesis in the school cafeteria when a strategically placed fork on his lunch tray accidentally lifts Mr. Wadd's hairpiece to reveal his baldness. The vain and now-humiliated Mr. Wadd flees, allowing Mr. Peepers to take over as science teacher.

The pilot not only impressed NBC, but Ford, which agreed to sponsor *Mr. Peepers* as a Thursday-night summer replacement series for *The James Melton Show*. The premiere, a trimmed-down half-hour version of the pilot, aired from Radio City's cavernous 2,500-seat Center Theater at 9:30 P.M. on July 3. As airtime neared, Coe, along with the cast and crew, was nervous. "Ah think we better hear that theater rock at the end of the first act," he told Jim Fritzell, who wrote the show along with Swift. In addition to his nerves, Coe's trademark perfectionism and temper were increasingly apparent as the afternoon wore on.

One of the key gags on the show involved a science-class experiment with a balloon that goes awry when Mr. Peepers is distracted by Mr. Wadd.

The balloon expands to gargantuan proportions, then bursts, leaving Mr. Wadd looking like he's been hit by incoming shellfire. Following the afternoon rehearsal, Coe decided the balloon was too small. "We had a weather balloon from the prop department at NBC, the biggest one they could find," says Bob Costello, the show's production manager. "But Fred didn't think the balloon was big enough."

Costello called every conceivable government agency, including the New York Police Department and the National Weather Service. Late in the afternoon, he reached a Coast Guard station on Long Island. The Coast Guard had a slightly bigger balloon, but could not get it through Fourth of July holiday traffic to Radio City in time for the show. They would have to make do with the balloon they had.

"I think we can get away with it," Costello told Coe as they stood on the expansive stage of the Center Theater, with its ninety-foot proscenium. "We can come around the side and shoot past the balloon toward Wally, and it will look bigger." But Coe wasn't buying. "Ah want to see the vice president in charge of bal-LOONS!" he thundered as engineers and stagehands scattered for the wings, leaving Costello alone with the enraged Coe at center stage.

"Fred was a very demanding guy, and that was his way of saying that NBC had fucked up," Costello says. "I was young in the business, and hadn't learned that you don't tell the boss what's right and what's wrong." Having caught the first of many public earfuls from Coe, though, Costello soon learned something else about his boss: that his rages passed quickly; he was not a man to nurse a grudge like an expensive drink.

The theater *did* rock at the end of the first act. Fans lined up to get into the Center Theater on Thursday nights at 9:30. Although *Mr. Peepers* was originally set for an eight-show run, NBC ordered five more episodes. Viewers increasingly tuned in. "In a dull season of summer TV replacements, one new show last week was giving viewers a pleasant tingling in the funny bone," *Time* wrote. "The program: 'Mr. Peepers.'" *The Hollywood Reporter* said the show was "a lead-pipe cinch for a regular fall spot if ever we saw one."

At the center of this commotion was the unlikeliest of television stars. The mild-mannered twenty-seven-year-old Cox was 5'6, weighed 130 pounds, and, according to the *New York Times*, "is dreamy-eyed, moves in vague motions and usually wears a tired expression implying that his mind is a thousand miles away." He was born in Detroit, where his father was an ad agency copy editor, his mother a mystery story writer. Following their divorce, his mother took him to Evanston, Illinois, then to New York. After high school, he was drafted, but the army turned him away because he was susceptible to heatstroke.

In a classic odd-couple arrangement, Cox became the roommate of Marlon Brando, a friend from his Evanston days. He used their apartment in Greenwich Village as the base for a less-than-thriving business as a silversmith, making tie-clips and cuff links. But there would be more silver in his offbeat world view. Brando took him to parties, where his monologues about a mythical hapless boyhood friend named "Dufo" so amused partygoers that he decided to try his luck at The Village Vanguard, a popular nightclub.

At the same time, Fred Coe and David Swift were looking for an actor to play Timothy Trundle, the milquetoast starring role of *The Copper*. Bill Nichols, the casting director for *Philco-Goodyear Playhouse*, made the connection. "He took me and Fred down to the Village Vanguard, and there was Wally Cox doing his act about 'Dufo,'" David Swift recalls. "I knew immediately that was our guy."

Their guy was the man *TV Guide* called "probably the most non-aggressive man in show business." Despite this lack of aggressiveness, Cox was soon earning a salary that would make him the envy of men with higher testosterone levels: during the first season of *Peepers*, he earned $1,500 a week (in 1953 dollars). By the end of the show's run, that would rise to $2,500.

And Cox would earn that money. Like the show's other regulars, he had to memorize a half-hour script every week. Sometimes he fell victim to outrageous sight gags. "We had one scene where he got caught in a basketball net, and was supported by a sling running through his crotch," Bob Costello says. "He was in total agony and never said a word. It wasn't until after the show was over we realized he was really bruised up a little bit."

Swift and Fritzell would build on Cox's lack of aggressiveness to turn Mr. Peepers into a comic icon. After losing his seat in the cafeteria and his chance to sit next to the pretty Miss Deen on the show's pilot, Mr. Peepers takes his tray to a solitary corner of the cafeteria. But every time he goes back to get an item he forgot, like napkins or a utensil, his tray—and his food—get cleared away. This happens until the food lines close, and a cafeteria worker brusquely informs Mr. Peepers he's out of luck. All he has salvaged is a glass of water. He pours some ketchup in, swirls it around and sadly drinks it, a paradigm of forlorn nebbishness, much like Charlie Chaplin trying to eat a boiled shoe in *The Gold Rush*.

During the summer, Bill Nichols also found Tony Randall to play history teacher Harvey Weskit, as hearty and extroverted as Mr. Peepers is shy and diffident. Then came Marion Lorne as English teacher Mrs. Gurney. A master of the befuddled stutter, she was second only to Cox in popularity among the show's stars. And when the show was still on its shakedown cruise, she may have been even more important.

"She couldn't remember her lines, but that was part of her charm," Bill Nichols says. "She really saved that show in the early days, because it was live from a theater and she kept the audience laughing. It was an odd show, and it took people time to get used to Wally and his funny characteristics." But Lorne's backing and filling, her comic trademark, almost spelled her demise. "When she was first on, she'd come in and say, 'I was down there— uhh—uhh—uhh,' and we'd say, 'What is this?'," David Swift says. "She was searching for her line. It became such a trademark that the audience became hysterical. We were going to fire her, but Bill said, 'Give her an- other week.' She was getting better laughs than anybody."

Although Cox and the other faculty members of Jefferson Junior High were a gentle bunch of eccentrics, the same could not be said of their creators, Fred Coe and David Swift. That two such high-powered, domi- nant, and aggressive men in conflict could create and nurture such a whim- sical and gentle show has to rank high in the annals of show-business alchemy. The two, however, were increasingly getting on each other's nerves.

"David wanted to make a more stand-up comic kind of show out of it," Bill Nichols says. "Fred was very much opposed to that. He wanted to make it more meaningful, a sort of deep, warm comedy kind of thing." In one case, Nichols says, Swift wanted a scene where Wally Cox shakes someone's hand while holding a fish. "David thought it was terribly funny, Fred didn't think it was funny at all," Nichols adds. "David wanted more of an emphasis on slapstick, Fred wanted a quiet, gentle humor."

Although Swift doesn't remember that exchange, the show where the conflict broke into the open did involve a fish story. The episode of Sep- tember 18, 1952, was written by David Shaw and Robert Alan Aurthur while Swift and his wife were on vacation. On the show, Mr. Peepers is faced with a problem student. "Roscoe, it's good to see you back in school again," Cox tells one of his students in chemistry lab. "The pool room was closed for alterations," the budding juvenile delinquent replies, pouring chemicals down the sink which disable the school's plumbing system.

With school closed for the day, Mr. Peepers takes Roscoe fishing in an effort to build his character. It was the sort of quiet, gentle comedy not favored by Swift, who returned from vacation in time to view the dress rehearsal. Never one to underestimate his own talents, he felt the show wasn't up to his standards. And always the bucking bronco in Fred Coe's stable of writers, he had no hesitation about challenging the boss.

"I shouldn't have done this, but I said 'Goddamn it, it's awful, Fred! I don't want my name on it!'" Swift recalls. "He went sky-high and started screaming at me, and I told him to take the show and shove it. There we were in the Center Theater, screaming at the top of our lungs." Swift stalked out of the theater. He and Coe could no longer work together. It didn't matter, though, because *Mr. Peepers* had reached the end of its sum- mer run.

Fred Coe's father, Frederick Hayden Hughs Coe, and his mother, Thursa Annette (Harrell) Coe, in pictures probably taken in Memphis around the time of their marriage in 1909. *Courtesy of John Coe*.

Coe's birthplace, the residence of Dr. Samuel and Sue Wells in Alligator, Missisippi. This simple one-story house served as home to Coe and his widowed mother until he was seven or eight. *Courtesy of Kate Wells*.

Fred Coe on a tricycle in Alligator, in a photo taken about 1917, when he was two years old. Despite his healthy appearance, he was a sickly child. *Courtesy of Laurence Anne Coe.*

As a sophomore at Peabody Demonstration (High) School in Nashville in 1931. *Courtesy of Kate Wells.*

Hillsboro Presbyterian Church in Nashville. Fred Coe's career as a producer and director began here when youth minister W. F. Christopher suggested he start an amateur theatrical group. The Hillsboro Players performed in the basement, in room whose window tops are visible at lower left. *Courtesy of Edmund W. Meisenhelder III.*

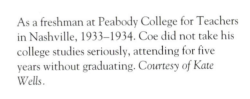

As a freshman at Peabody College for Teachers in Nashville, 1933–1934. Coe did not take his college studies seriously, attending for five years without graduating. *Courtesy of Kate Wells.*

A performance of Maxwell Anderson's *Winterset* at the Nashville Community Playhouse in 1937. Coe played Garth; Alice Marie Griggs, whom he had secretly married several months earlier, played Miriamne; and Billy Burroughs was Mio. *Courtesy of Delbert Mann.*

As director of the Town Theatre in Columbia, South Carolina, during World War II, Coe also acted in several of his shows. Here he is as Darcy in 1942's *Pride and Prejudice*, with Madeline (Cate) Buford as Elizabeth. *Courtesy of Ellen Nagy.*

With Jose Ferrer during rehearsals of Philco Television Playhouse's *Cyrano de Bergerac*, airing January 9, 1949, on NBC. *NBC photo/Courtesy of Dick Smith.*

On vacation at Myrtle Beach, South Carolina, in spring or summer of 1949, after the first season of *Philco Television Playhouse*. A rare moment of repose for a man whose restless nature and many projects kept him in constant—if slow—motion. *Ira Skutch photo.*

Too many cooks spoil the broth, but Coe was always the master chef on his shows. This picture was taken at a *Philco Playhouse* banquet at the end of the show's second season in the spring of 1950. Seated, from left, are Pierson Mapes, head of the Hutchins advertising Company, Philco's ad agency; Fred Coe; floor manager Ira Skutch; and the art director, Tom Jewett. Standing, from left, are Hutchins executive Eugene Schiess, technical director O. Tamburri, Hutchins executive James Burton, and director Delbert Mann. *Courtesy of Libby and Ira Skutch.*

Alice Coe with son John in the late 1940s. *Ira Skutch photo.*

Joyce Beeler worked as a script girl and assistant to Fred Coe at NBC before becoming his second wife. *University of Dubuque Yearbook photo.*

At *Philco-Goodyear Television Playhouse*, Coe discovered and nurtured an extraordinarily diverse and talented stable of writers, who were at the heart of the show's success. Coe is in front at right, along with associate producer Gordon Duff. From left are writers Harry Muheim, Tad Mosel, Sumner Locke Elliott, Robert Alan Authur, Paddy Chayefsky, David Shaw, Thomas Phipps, and N. Richard Nash. Not shown are Horton Foote, David Swift, and JP Miller. *NBC photo/Courtesy of Delbert Mann.*

Rod Steiger and Nancy Marchand in an emotionally charged scene from Paddy Chayefsky's *Marty*. Directed by Delbert Mann on May 24, 1953, the *Philco-Goodyear* show about a lonely Bronx butcher who finds love in a dance hall galvanized the public, and is the finest example of live television drama. *NBC photo/Courtesy of Delbert Mann.*

Although Horton Foote was noted for Southern mood plays, his work sometimes had a light side as well. *A Young Lady of Property* starred Kim Stanley (at right) and Joanne Woodward in the tale of a young woman who has to come to terms with her father's decision to remarry. Airing on *Philco-Goodyear Playhouse* April 5, 1953, it was directed by Vincent Donehue. *Wisconsin Center for Film and Theater Research*.

Just as Paddy Chayefsky's *Philco-Goodyear* stories focused on the Bronx and Horton Foote's on the South, Tad Mosel's teleplays featured the unadorned lyricism of his native Midwest. *Ernie Barger Is 50*, starring Ed Begley and Carmen Matthews, was directed by Delbert Mann on August 9, 1953. *Wisconsin Center for Film and Theater Research*.

Amid the chaos and unrelenting pressure of live television drama, Fred Coe projected calm and confidence, inspiring writers, directors, actors, and support personnel. At the same time, he had a dark and brooding side that he rarely showed them. *Courtesy of John Coe; NBC photo.*

In a script conference with writer Sumner Locke Elliott (left) and director Delbert Mann (right) on *Philco-Goodyear Playhouse*. Coe's superb literary sense and ability as a story editor enabled him to spot script flaws others missed and to provide solutions others failed to imagine. *Courtesy of Delbert Mann.*

Coe was highly adept in the many production aspects of theater and television, helping to make *Philco-Goodyear Television Playhouse* the best live dramatic anthology of the 1950s. Here he is (at far right) behind the scenes with (from left) production supervisor Milt Myers, set designer Otis Riggs, prop man Matty Kronyak, and director Delbert Mann. *NBC photo/Courtesy of Delbert Mann.*

David Swift's *The Copper*, a *Philco-Goodyear* episode airing October 28, 1951, starred Wally Cox in the comic tale of a bumbling police trainee, with Pat Carroll as his wife. Directed by Delbert Mann, the show was so popular that NBC asked Coe to build a show around Cox. Coe told Swift to think something up, and Swift thought up *Mr. Peepers*. *NBC photo/Courtesy of Delbert Mann.*

In rehearsal for the pilot episode of *Mr. Peepers*, Wally Cox accidentally lifts off the wig of his nemesis, science teacher Mr. Wadd, with the help of a strategically placed fork. Sitting in as Mr. Wadd during this rehearsal was David Swift, the show's creator and writer. *Courtesy of David Swift.*

Everett Greenbaum (left) and Jim Fritzell with Fritzell's mother in a picture taken during the 1970s. Greenbaum and Fritzell wrote *Mr. Peepers* for the bulk of its three-year run (1952–55) after David Swift left the show. *Courtesy of Everett Greenbaum.*

ABOVE: *Peter Pan*, starring Mary Martin as Pan and Cyril Ritchard as Captain Hook, was directed by Clark Jones and first aired on *Producers Showcase* March 7, 1955. Although it was a critical success and the most-watched program in television's brief history, Coe regarded it as just "a song-and-dance thing." *NBC photo*. RIGHT: Frank Sinatra, Paul Newman, and Eva Marie Saint starred in the live musical version of Thornton Wilder's *Our Town* on *Producers Showcase*. Directed by Delbert Mann, it was adapted by David Shaw and aired September 19, 1955. *NBC photo/Courtesy of Delbert Mann*. BELOW RIGHT: *The Plot to Kill Stalin* aired on *Playhouse 90* on September 25, 1958, and featured (from left) Oscar Homolka as Khrushchev, Melvyn Douglas as Stalin, Thomas Gomez as Malenkov, and E. G. Marshall as Beria. One of Coe's first shows for CBS after leaving NBC, it was written by David Karp and directed by Delbert Mann. The show created an international incident at the height of the Cold War. *NBC photo/Courtesy of Delbert Mann*.

Coe and director John Frankenheimer on the set at *Playhouse
90*. The two turned out several
memorable shows (*Days of Wine
and Roses*, *Old Man*, *Journey to
the Day*, and *For Whom the Bell
Tolls*) for *Playhouse 90*, the last
important live dramatic anthology of the 1950s. *Courtesy of
John Coe*.

With the death of live television,
the focus of Coe's career shifted to
Broadway. *The Miracle Worker*,
which he produced in 1959, was
written by William Gibson and
directed by Arthur Penn. Patty
Duke starred as Helen Keller,
Anne Bancroft as social
worker Annie Sullivan, and
Torin Thatcher as Captain
Keller. *Photofest*.

Arthur Hill as Jay Follet, the father whose life is
cut short in a car crash, and John Megna as his
son, Rufus, in *All the Way Home*. Adapted by Tad
Mosel from James Agee's novel and directed by
Arthur Penn, the 1960 play won the Pulitzer
Prize for Drama. *Photofest*.

With Paul Newman and son John Coe on the set of *The Left-Handed Gun* (1958). *Photofest.*

With Arthur Penn on the film set of *The Miracle Worker* in Red Bank, New Jersey, in 1961. *Courtesy of Arthur Penn.*

Directing Jason Robards in the film version of *A Thousand Clowns* in New York, 1964. *Wisconsin Center for Film and Theater Research.*

Zero Mostel (left) as Tevye and Michael Granger as Lazar Wolfe the butcher in *Fiddler on the Roof*. Coe was the show's original producer and assembled key elements of its creative package. *Photofest.*

Coe's son John (center) and daughter Laurie (far right) with friends about 1970. *Courtesy of Laurence Anne Coe.*

Sue and Sam Coe, Coe's children with Joyce Coe, his second wife, in a picture taken about 1965. *Courtesy of Laurence Anne Coe.*

Eleanor Cogbill with the now-obese Coe in a picture taken about 1977. *David Lohman photo.*

Marion Hooper (Gilmer Mc-
Cormick, left) and Henry Adams
(Peter Brandon) are married in
the twelfth episode of *The Adams
Chronicles*. Coe produced and di-
rected this and three other
episodes of the 1976 PBS series.
*Carl Samrock photo/Courtesy of
Michael Shepley Public Relations*.

Fred Coe shortly before his death, in Simi Valley, California, on location for
the 1979 telefilm *The Miracle Worker*. *Eleanor Cogbill photo*.

Public reaction to the show's departure, however, would yoke them together again. During the show's last week, NBC logged 15,000 calls and letters of protest. But NBC had fixed its fall schedule, and Ford had pulled out as the sponsor. *Mr. Peepers* would return, however, when *Doc Corkle*, an insipid sitcom, was quickly chased from NBC's fall lineup by scathing reviews and public indifference. The Reynolds Metals Company, makers of Reynolds Wrap, signed on as a sponsor and *Mr. Peepers* moved into the 7:30 P.M. Sunday time slot vacated by *Doc Corkle*.

Coe now had to contend with Swift again, as well as Sunday nights in which he had only sixty minutes between the end of *Mr. Peepers* and the start of *Philco-Goodyear*. After the dress rehearsal for *Peepers*, he and several members of the cast and crew repaired to Hurley's Bar for a few drinks. After *Philco-Goodyear Playhouse*, he would return to Hurley's with the Philco crowd for a few more drinks. Coe was now working two shifts every Sunday at Hurley's Bar.

The creators of *Mr. Peepers* had to scramble to put the show back on the air. Tony Randall, for instance, had no interest in returning to the show. "For me, being on the show was just an accident," he later said. "I was much more interested in directing, and when they called me back, I was very busy directing something, and I tried desperately to get out of doing 'Peepers' again. But Fred Coe wouldn't let me out of it, and that was the turning point in my career."

When *Mr. Peepers* returned to the air on October 26, 1952, there were several new faces. Coe replaced director James Sheldon with the more forceful Hal Keith. Norma Crane, who had muffed too many lines and failed to do so as colorfully as Marion Lorne, was replaced as Mr. Peepers's girlfriend by Pat Benoit as nurse Nancy Remington. Benoit's wispy and there-but-not-quite-there nature made her a perfect counterpart for Mr. Peepers. Her parents were played by Ernest Truex and Sylvia Field. As Mr. and Mrs. Remington, Truex was blustering but affable, Field calm and benevolent but not to be trifled with—one of those marriages where father knows best but mother calls the shots.

The next personnel change, and perhaps the one most to Coe's liking, involved David Swift. Although he co-authored the first five shows of the fall season with Fritzell, it was common knowledge that Swift and Coe weren't getting along, and that Swift would leave the show as soon as a replacement writer could be found. But events would speed his leavetaking. The climactic confrontation between the tall, ramrod-straight Coe and the shorter, pugnacious Swift took place in the 52nd Street offices of Talent Associates in late fall.

Each had an ownership stake in *Mr. Peepers* and it was time to settle accounts. (In yet another hallmark of a bygone era, they wound up splitting ownership 50-50, with NBC getting nothing. "In those days, the network didn't take a percentage," Swift says. "They didn't know what it was worth.") David Susskind and Al Levy, who ran Talent Associates, would serve as referees, although Swift felt that because Coe was one of Talent Associates' most important and powerful clients, Susskind automatically sided with him. As for Coe, Swift had pushed him to within several degrees of his easily reached boiling point.

"Fred had a tendency to tower over people and glower at them," Swift says. "I didn't like the money they were offering me. And he said, 'You just better by God take that money, Pappy! And be thankful! You hear me? You take it and be thankful, 'cause you're just a kid!,'" the thirty-seven-year-old Coe told the thirty-two-year-old Swift. "I blew," recalls Swift, who had done amateur boxing in the 160-pound weight class. "I stood up. I was going to deck him, I think. Al Levy grabbed me and Susskind grabbed Fred, or we would have tangled right there. The whole thing was settled, but not graciously."

With Swift gone, Coe drafted Robert Alan Aurthur to help Fritzell turn out *Peepers* scripts on a temporary basis. The search for a new writing partner for Fritzell lasted through Christmas, and led to the toy-frog concession at Macy's.

. . .

Everett Greenbaum was from Buffalo, N.Y., where he had a comedy radio show called *Greenbaum's Gallery*. His budget was so small that he had to find sound effects on hand and write material to fit them, rather than the other way around. Now living in a Greenwich Village cold-water flat, Greenbaum was working in Yiddish radio, acting, and taking odd jobs to support himself.

During the Christmas season, he was working for a concessionaire selling toy frogs at Macy's. "Have fun with Freddie the Frog," Greenbaum wearily intoned to passersby in the toy department for hours on end. He hated the job and the man he worked for. The exact point on which Greenbaum and his employer came to grief is unclear. In an interview years later, Greenbaum said the concessionaire came around one day and told him to up his dollar volume, with Greenbaum responding, "Up yours, too." But in his memoirs, Greenbaum says a producer at NBC learned of his job and delivered a batch of live frogs to his work station at Macy's, creating a commotion.

In any event, Greenbaum was fired. To compound his misery, his last paycheck was drawn on insufficient funds. Furious, Greenbaum returned to Macy's and grabbed his former boss by the throat, determined to strangle him. Realizing Greenbaum was one toy-frog salesman not to be trifled with, the concessionaire threw several twenty-dollar bills on the floor. Greenbaum picked them up and left.

Out of work, Greenbaum walked aimlessly through the falling snow, finding himself at Talent Associates, where he had gone several times seeking work. "We've been looking for you all day," said Julian Claman, whose portfolio included acquiring literary properties and hiring talent. "We're going to try you on a writing job for two weeks. Get in that office and write with Jim."

"Jim" was Jim Fritzell. Not only would he and Greenbaum write *Mr. Peepers* for most of its three-year run, they would remain writing partners, with one interruption, for twenty-seven years, writing for *The Real Mc-Coys*, *The Andy Griffith Show*, and *M*A*S*H*. Like Brando and Cox, Fritzell and Greenbaum were the unlikeliest of pairings. Greenbaum was a gregarious Jew from Buffalo, Fritzell a shy and almost reclusive Scandinavian from San Francisco. Greenbaum was drawn to science and the arts, while Fritzell's cultural tastes ran to watching sports, playing poker, smoking and drinking.

Greenbaum had an even disposition (so long as his checks didn't bounce), while Fritzell had more phobias than a porcupine has quills. He feared open spaces, strangers, doctors and dentists, and, especially, heights. One time Greenbaum learned Fritzell never voted, although he was keenly interested in politics. "Why not?" Greenbaum asked. "Because that's how they get your name for jury duty," Fritzell responded. "And the courts are on the ninth floor."

What Fritzell and Greenbaum had in common, though, was a knack for the small-town humor that would bring Jefferson City to life. Although both were from good-sized cities, they came from outlying neighborhoods. "It's good that we weren't from New York or Chicago, because we were able to write Americana," Greenbaum says. "We were able to get into small-town American life."

The first show written by Fritzell and Greenbaum aired January 4, 1953. Using the frequent storms from Greenbaum's Buffalo boyhood as a source of inspiration, they wrote an episode in which Mr. Peepers's desire to throw a surprise birthday party for nurse Nancy Remington is almost thwarted when a snowstorm traps everyone at Jefferson Junior High. Fritzell and Greenbaum worked with a series of other writers through the winter as Coe looked for just the right combination. Finally, in March, he settled on them to write the show exclusively.

While grateful for the job, the chatty Greenbaum was not sure at first that Coe represented a step up from the toy-frog concessionaire. "At first I was very afraid of him," he says. "I thought he was being mean to me, but I was talking unnecessarily, and every minute had to count in his office. There were people lined up waiting to see him all the time."

Every Monday, Fritzell and Greenbaum dropped by Coe's office to discuss the script they would write that week. Usually, they arrived with several ideas. When they drew a blank, Coe would start talking about one of the secondary characters on Mr. Peepers. Helped by Coe's musings, Fritzell or Greenbaum would devise a problem for Miss Gurney, Nurse Remington, or Harvey Weskit, and find a way to relate it back to Mr. Peepers. They would cobble out a rough story line and leave to write it.

Once they turned their script in, Coe was remarkably adept at finding structural flaws without being discouraging. "'Why don't you change the guy's attitude *here?*'" Fritzell later recalled him saying. "And that would be the root of the whole problem. He'd put his finger right on it, and we couldn't wait to get back to the office at eight or nine at night and start to redo the whole damn script."

Coe also consoled Greenbaum once when he drew a blank on the air. Knowing of Greenbaum's interest in acting, he encouraged him to write himself a good part on one show, which Greenbaum did. He then froze on camera. "I became very nervous and drew a complete blank," he says. "Afterwards, I tried to get out the back door so I wouldn't run into Fred, because I thought he would kill me. And there he was in the hallway. He came up and put his arms around me and said, 'It's alright, Pappy.' He knew what I was going through."

It was another case of Fred Coe as father figure to his writers, actors, and directors. What makes this benevolent paternalism so poigniant in the context of Mr. Peepers is that the forceful Coe and the gentle Robinson Peepers were both fatherless children. There was a Mom Peepers, played by Ruth McDevitt, but there was never a Pop Peepers on the show.

David Swift, who formulated most of the show's characters along with Jim Fritzell, says Coe had no input into this aspect of the story line. "I suppose we brought Mom in because we were heavy with men: Wally, Tony, the principal [who was phased out and replaced by Mrs. Gurney]," he says. But it must have given Coe an extra sense of identification with the show, and an added pleasure at exchanges like one that Peepers has with a British relative, who says he knew Peepers's father in America before Peepers was born. "Of course," Cox replies. "I knew I knew you from somewhere."

The substitution of Greenbaum for Swift shifted the show's emphasis from mechanical sight gags and broad, slapstick-style humor to the more character-focused personal humor Coe wanted. This was not a case of black and white: while Swift was there, there were some wonderful character bits, and after Greenbaum came in, the sight gags and slapstick were not dispensed with. But there was a change in tone.

An admirer of the silent film comedians, Swift felt television was too talky. Sight gags were his remedy. At the school dance in the gym, an iced-tea dispenser won't stop dispensing. Mr. Peepers pours the iced tea into as many cups as he can find. Running out of them, he connects the dispenser to the gym's fire hose, which winds up pouring the iced tea into a tuba held by one of the members of the band.

A Swift sight gag of Rube Goldberg proportions would become the show's trademark. Like so many things at Jefferson Junior High, Mr. Peepers's hallway locker was always slightly askew. To open it, Cox had to take a hammer from the top of his locker, tap it briskly several times, jiggle the handle, go to the end locker with a yardstick, measure off a certain spot, kick that spot and watch the door to his own locker fly open. *TV Guide* ran an article explaining to enthusiastic fans how several of the *Peepers* sight gags worked, but Jack Gould of the *New York Times* sniffed, "Mr. Peepers should be more than a prop caddy."

With Greenbaum on board, Wally Cox developed his slightly off-center Peepers persona to the fullest. In one almost zen-like exchange with Pat Benoit, he tries to describe his Aunt Lil, who is coming for a visit:

NANCY: What's she like?
PEEPERS: Well, there are aunts who are aunts. But then there are aunts
            who are aunts.
NANCY: That's very true.
PEEPERS: And Aunt Lil's one of those.

It was dialogue like this which caused *TV Guide* to wonder whether *Mr. Peepers* was "too high-brow, too low-brow or too neither brow," while *Variety*, on a note of befuddled approval, said, "Appeal of 'Mr. Peepers' is difficult to pin down, but is definitely there."

Greenbaum was also more inclined than Swift to "punnish" viewers. On one show, Mr. Peepers goes to hear the will of his uncle read—a man who has made "a killing" in insecticides. In true Peepers fashion, he's more interested in the old man's rare insect collection than his fortune. But he worries that other relatives will also covet the collection, noting "a lot of people have been bitten by the insect bug."

As the show's first year progressed, it was decided to marry off the Tony Randall character. A striking blond actress named Georgiann Johnson came on board in December 1952, to play Marge Bellows, who would become Harvey Weskit's bride at season's end. Unlike Fritzell and Greenbaum, she came from a real small town.

But one look around the set told her she wasn't in Decorah, Iowa, anymore: Hal Keith, the director, idly tossed a penknife into the floor of the stage to relieve tension during rehearsals. Wally Cox was shy, elusive, and difficult to talk with ("Don't touch Wally at any time," Keith once startled her by saying. "He doesn't like to be touched"). Marion Lorne fussed around, trying to remember her lines. Tony Randall amiably swaggered around, and Pat Benoit was preternaturally calm and quiet. These people aren't acting, Johnson thought. "I felt like I was the most straight, regular person on the show," she says. "Everyone was sort of off in little orbits. They kind of fell slightly into the categories they were playing."

Coe attended dress rehearsals, where he usually stayed in the background. It's a testimony to how low his profile was that Johnson doesn't even recall his being there. Tony Randall, however, had no difficulty picking Coe out at Center Theater rehearsals. "Coe was marvelous for actors," he has said. "He'd come to a rehearsal, and the way he would laugh! You thought you were the funniest person who ever walked." And as airtime approached, Coe could make his presence painfully obvious if things weren't working. "Sometimes during rehearsal on Sunday, he would really start screaming if something offended him," Greenbaum adds. "He would scare the hell out of everybody."

On Sunday night, April 26, 1953, the first season of Mr. Peepers ended with the marriage of Harvey Weskit and Marge Bellows. For Tony Randall's character, it was not an easy step: the morning of the wedding, he appears so morose that a coffee-shop waitress cracks, "What time do they throw the switch?" But there was little to be morose about: ratings were high and NBC was happy.

• • •

As the second season of Mr. Peepers got under way, Coe again took charge of *Philco-Goodyear Playhouse*. In addition, he was now serving as the executive producer of *Bonino*, a situation comedy NBC asked him to design for opera star Ezio Pinza. Conceived by Thomas Phipps, one of Coe's *Philco* writers, and written by David Shaw and Robert Alan Aurthur, it was produced and directed by Gordon Duff, Coe's associate producer on *Philco*. Pinza played opera singer Babbo Bonino, the widowed father of eight who cuts back on his concert career to spend more time with his children.

Premiering on September 12, 1953, the show lagged in the ratings and was off the air by December 26. After an unbroken string of successes, it was Coe's first failure in television. Some argued, though, that he didn't have much to work with. "Ezio Pinza was not a sitcom actor," David Shaw says. "He enjoyed doing it, I think, but he was stiff." Modestly, Shaw adds, "I don't want to lay it all on him—the scripts weren't very good." David Swift thought Bonino wasn't likeable, all gusto and bravado. *Variety* said the show's theme was "interesting but not earth-shaking."

Broader social trends may have worked against *Bonino* as well. In *Honey, I'm Home!*, Gerard Jones's study of TV sitcoms, he notes that as America headed into the Eisenhower fifties, ethnic sitcoms were increasingly replaced by all-American, white-bread shows such as *The Adventures of Ozzie and Harriet* and *Leave It to Beaver*. *The Goldbergs* (Jewish) and *Mama* (Norwegian), would soon follow *Bonino* into oblivion, and the ethnic sitcom would not return until the late 1960s.

• • •

Despite the success of its first year, ratings began to decline during the second year of *Mr. Peepers*. In an effort to reverse the trend, Coe instructed Fritzell and Greenbaum to heat up the ongoing flirtation between Mr. Peepers and nurse Nancy Remington. Although Peepers was in the habit of saying, "When I see something I like, I snap it right up," he was taking his time on this one.

Since Pat Benoit first appeared as nurse Nancy Remington on September 11, 1952, she and Cox had been performing the slowest of mating dances. On the episode of January 4, 1953, she says her sister was married in white silk. "You'd be beautiful in white silk," Mr. Peepers says dreamily. And on the broadcast of October 18, 1953, Mr. Peepers tells Nancy he comes from a large family, with seven children. She reacts with enthusiasm:

PEEPERS: Do you like large families?
NANCY: Uh, huh. Very much. Why?
PEEPERS: Well, I just thought (pause) if you like large families (pause) you and I—
NANCY: Yes?
PEEPERS: Uh—could go and visit my family some time.

As laughter erupted in the Center Theater, Peepers fans could be justified in thinking no wedding was imminent. Like Fred Coe, Robinson Peepers was indecisive in matters of love. But if a Peepers marriage would bring viewers back, he was willing to try it.

Nancy accepted Peepers's proposal on the broadcast of April 18, 1954. Their marriage was set for May 23, the final broadcast of the show's second season. In *TV Guide*, Coe teased viewers about how it would happen. "The advantage of live TV over film is that nothing happens until the minute it happens. . . . When the time comes, Mr. Peepers will—or he won't."

No longer the eloping kind (as he and Alice once had been), Coe went along with the writers' decision to give Peepers and Nancy a traditional church wedding. But Fritzell and Greenbaum then developed writers' block. "Jim, who always had terrible luck with ladies, wanted to be happily married in the worst way," Everett Greenbaum recalls. And Greenbaum knew the fate of the show was riding on that episode. "The show was my whole life," Greenbaum adds. "I was a nervous wreck."

As the ceremony approached on the Peepers wedding episode, Ernest Truex, the father of the bride, repeatedly fretted, "She's all I've got." When the show ended, though, he turned to Wally Cox and said, "She's all *you've* got." With 40 million viewers for the wedding episode (making it one of the highest-rated broadcasts in the show's history), *Mr. Peepers* had something else: renewal for another year. It also had the enthusiastic support of *TV Guide*, which wrote, "*Mr. Peepers* comes close to being the perfect TV show."

Perhaps inspired by Mr. Peepers, Jim Fritzell soon followed in his footsteps, marrying in the fall of 1954 a beautiful young Swiss model named Micheline he had known in California. The earthy Fritzell moved out of his second-floor midtown apartment, and into an uptown luxury apartment tower on East End Avenue with his elegant new wife. But the marriage quickly fell apart. It was an inauspicious sign for the show's third year. The wedding episode would prove a temporary anodyne. The show's ratings started to fall off again, and with no more leading characters to marry off, there was no quick-fix solution this time.

• • •

Things were starting to go wrong behind the scenes as well. Everett Greenbaum had opposed the Peepers marriage, feeling a timorous character like Mr. Peepers would never marry and that the show would lose much of its distinctiveness. And Jim Fritzell, who had wanted to be married in the worst way, was.

The show's new address was also working against it. Shortly before the wedding episode, *Mr. Peepers* had moved out of the Center Theater and back into Studio 8H. While 8H was a large broadcast studio, it was small compared to the Center Theater. "In the Center Theater, the laughs would start in the balcony and roll down toward the stage. It was terrific," Greenbaum says. "But in a flat room, sitting on folding chairs, it was miserable. Half the people couldn't see anything in 8H."

Not only were the sight lines more limited in 8H, so were the acoustics: it could hold only 200 to 300 people. Mahlon Fox, the show's audio director, had to make that comparative handful sound like a multitude, scattering extra microphones above the studio audience in a futile effort to achieve the bigger sound of the Center Theater crowd. Since microphones alone would not do the trick, the audience was salted with unemployed actors who were paid $5 a head to laugh. Coe either formulated or approved this plan. For its last year, *Mr. Peepers* in effect had a live laugh track.

Unlike the belly laughs most sitcoms aimed for, *Mr. Peepers* was geared more toward the knowing chuckle or even the amused nod of agreement. For two years that had worked, but it no longer seemed enough. "It's possible that *Peepers*'s quiet humor doesn't appeal to the average viewer," said David Shaw, now working with Fritzell and Greenbaum as a script consultant. During the show's run, the number of television homes in America had doubled, from 15 million to 30 million. While *Mr. Peepers* was not an elite entertainment, it had an intellectual tinge, and intellectuals were not the ones buying all those new TV sets.

The third dilemma faced by *Mr. Peepers* was the growing popularity of Los Angeles–based filmed situation comedies, especially *I Love Lucy*. Rather than Robinson J. Peepers's comic sensibility, it was Lucy Ricardo's that was increasingly winning public favor. *Mr. Peepers* and *I Love Lucy* were polar opposites: one was broadcast live from New York, the other was filmed in Los Angeles. One was built around a diffident, somewhat abstracted male, the other a zany, rambunctious female. It was a show in a minor key versus one in a major key, bittersweet versus sweet. Both had their place, but the audience—and increasingly, the critics—were voting with their dials. Even as early as 1953, when *Mr. Peepers* won the Peabody Award, Jack Gould of the *New York Times* felt that constituted a snub of *Lucy*.

At the start of the show's third season, *Variety* indicated it was starting to wear out its welcome. While still finding *Peepers* charming, it added, "Practically all of the characters in the script are of obsessive understated sweetness. . . . The danger ahead lies in equating charm with fuzzy-mindedness and having too incredible a population of adorable eccentrics."

With *Peepers*'s ratings dropping, as *TV Guide* put it, like a barometer before a storm, desperate measures were taken. Guest stars such as Cyril Ritchard were trotted out. There were new plot lines, including one where Mr. Peepers sails to England. Perhaps the oddest was the musical-variety format used on several episodes in the show's last two months. Artificially maneuvered into situations where he had to sing, that dubious songbird Wally Cox belted out "There Is a Tavern in the Town" and "Basin Street Blues." Jack Gould was not amused. "Much of the style and mood of 'Mr. Peepers' was compromised without compensating values in terms of the fresh approach," he wrote.

Reynolds informed NBC it was pulling its sponsorship, and there was no replacement sponsor in sight. The last episode of *Mr. Peepers* aired on June 12, 1955. Would Mr. Peepers leave Jefferson Junior High for a better-paying job at a nearby military academy? Tony Randall urged him not to, saying it would reduce their friendship to "a brief encounter at the canoe racks at Lake Tehachacopi." But Nancy was pregnant (as Pat Benoit now was in real life), and Peepers had no choice. The school board met in special session and approved Mr. Peepers's request for a raise. But it wasn't the school board that counted, it was the Reynolds Metals Company, and they were not so easily swayed.

While lamenting to *TV Guide* that "Mr. Peepers is one of everybody's favorite shows and nobody watches it," Fred Coe retained a buoyant optimism that it would return. There had been a "fatigue quotient," he told the magazine, and "with a new time spot, we'll pick up a whole new audience." *TV Guide* noted there was talk of bringing the series back as a fifteen-minute show five days a week.

But no new sponsor could be found, and there would be no more meetings at the canoe rack of Lake Tehachacopi. Coe offered to sustain Fritzell and Greenbaum by signing them to adapt the novel *The Ghost and Mrs. Muir* for Broadway. But Fritzell, having just been divorced by his wife, wanted to try a divorce from his writing partner as well.

Viewers tuning in to NBC at 7:30 P.M. Sunday the next season would find a western called *Frontier*. *Mr. Peepers* was not the only show displaced by a western, though. The vogue of live dramatic anthologies was starting to crest. The appetite of the television viewing audience for filmed westerns would prove insatiable, and westerns would ride live television off of the range. Television's center of gravity was shifting from New York to Los Angeles. Fred Coe, that die-hard advocate of live New York TV, would reluctantly follow in its wake.

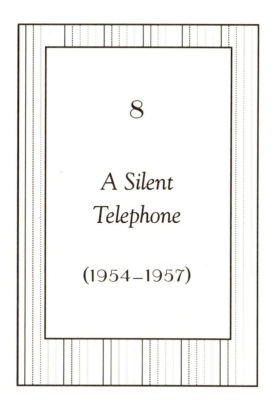

8

*A Silent
Telephone*

(1954–1957)

By the mid-1950s, the portents were increasingly grim for live dramatic anthologies. First, there were too many of them. "Television's vicious programming cycle—the same cycle that flooded the networks with substandard crime shows, half-hour filmed dramatics and latterly situation comedies—now appears to have finally caught up with the hour-long dramatic showcase, once the creative darling of the industry," *Variety* wrote. "The hour dramatics, it's the growing feeling, are currently at a new high in quantity and a new low in quality." (Exempted from this judgment were *Philco-Goodyear*, *Studio One*, and *Kraft Television Theatre*.)

Sponsors and advertising agencies, uncomfortable with controversial topics and downbeat endings, were also becoming increasingly assertive about shows' contents. In the *Saturday Review*, Robert Lewis Shayon wrote about one ad agency's style guide for television writers: "We are reaching out for serious plays with great impact," it noted, adding, "We present . . . a 'family show' which all may view without offense to any age group. . . . We usually want a happy ending, either accomplished or implied." Shayon sneered at this formula. "'Serious plays with great impact' vs. 'the family show with the happy ending and without offense to any age group,'" he wrote. "Here is a play which the author of the communique ought to write and sell to himself."

While the Army-McCarthy hearings in the spring of 1954 and Senator McCarthy's subsequent censure by the Senate destroyed him as a political figure, McCarthyism was still alive in TV, with ad agencies routinely checking the names of actors, writers, and directors to make sure they weren't listed in *Red Channels*. Audience members sometimes got into the act as well: On November 8, 1954, CBS's *Studio One* aired *An Almanac of Liberty*, an impassioned defense of such American liberties as the rights to free speech and a fair trial. Shortly after the broadcast, writer Reginald Rose answered a call on one of the studio phones. "I'm a college graduate, so you can't fool me with that stuff," the anonymous caller said. "Why don't you *Studio One* Commies go back to Russia?"

Sponsors, leery of offending potential customers in the South, also didn't want blacks on their shows. *Variety* described "blandishments and pressures" from national TV sponsors. "From all accounts . . . dealers holding southern franchises . . . are growing more and more fearful of boycott repercussion from potential white customers if Negroes are showcased on the sponsor's show," it reported. "At one major agency the word has gone out: 'No Negro performers allowed.'"

By now, the television audience had expanded from a core of well-to-do adults in East Coast cities to all classes and age groups around the country. Sponsors felt the appeal of dramatic anthologies was to the elite, rather than the blue-collar workers increasingly able to afford TV sets as prices came down. But they may have underestimated their new audience—as late as December of 1954, three years after the coast-to-coast coaxial cable made TV a truly national medium, four of the top ten rated shows were dramatic anthologies.

Technology was also working against live drama: videotape, in a crude form, was demonstrated as early as 1951. By the spring of 1956, a videotape whose quality equalled that of a live broadcast was demonstrated, and the next year would see CBS and NBC begin to tape parts of their shows. Networks, advertisers, and sponsors had limited control of live shows: even if they reviewed a script, there was always the potential for surprises at airtime. Videotape removed that potential.

Although film was not new, it was new to television in two ways: the Hollywood studios were starting to sell old movies to the networks, providing them with a cheap form of programming that could be used repeatedly. Secondly, adopting an "If you can't beat 'em, join 'em" philosophy, the studios were setting up subsidiaries to produce filmed shows for TV. They lacked the literary quality and topical themes of live New York shows, but would prove increasingly popular with networks and audiences.

• • •

By the fall of 1954, NBC was consistently running behind CBS in the ratings. NBC President Pat Weaver wanted to pull NBC back ahead and shake up the week-in, week-out grid of regular series programming. To accomplish both goals, he decided that on one Saturday, Sunday, and Monday night every month, there would be high-budget specials, known as "spectaculars," in color: the FCC had just approved RCA's system of color TV, and RCA corporate chairman and NBC founder David Sarnoff was eager to cash in.

Pat Weaver's choice to head the Monday night specials, airing under the title *Producers Showcase*, was Leland Hayward, Pulitzer Prize–winning producer of *State of the Union* and *South Pacific*. But in mid-September, a month before the premiere of *Producers Showcase*, Hayward became ill. Weaver turned to Fred Coe as a last-minute replacement. At the start, Coe would serve as executive producer, supervising the work of other producers. As *Producers Showcase* evolved, however, he would increasingly turn into the hands-on producer he had been at *Philco-Goodyear*.

Because NBC was staking so much on the spectaculars, the pressure was enormous. That pressure increased when the first one, put together by Max Liebman (producer of Sid Caesar's *Your Show of Shows*), aired on September 12, 1954, and was spectacular only in the magnitude of its failure.

A musical called *Satins and Spurs*, it starred Betty Hutton as a rodeo performer who falls in love with a *Life* magazine photographer. Both its ratings and critical esteem were low, and despite its being billed as an original, critics noted a strong resemblance to *Annie Get Your Gun*. Liebman's next effort, an adaptation of *Lady in the Dark*, eked out a narrow ratings win, but did so at a cost of half a million 1954 dollars. *Variety* reported "everyone was having second thoughts" at NBC and that there were "plenty of worries."

Producers Showcase aired from Brooklyn One, NBC's huge new studio in the Midwood section of Brooklyn, which was equipped for color broadcasting and had much more space than Studio 8G in the RCA Building. For Fred Coe, the biggest change in moving from *Philco-Goodyear* to *Producers Showcase* was not the heightened pressure, but the greater marquee value of its stars. It was a much bigger show, with more rehearsal and preparation time and larger budgets. There were three weeks of rehearsal for an hour-and-a-half show, instead of ten days for an hour show. And NBC was spending a lot of money on *Producers Showcase*. "It was very luxurious," says Dominick Dunne, an assistant director on the program. "We went out to the Brooklyn studios in limousines and things like that."

But if NBC put a lot of money into Brooklyn One, it was still pinching pennies on rehearsal halls. The high-priced stars of *Producers Showcase* rehearsed in the ballroom of the Capitol Hotel, on 51st Street and 8th Avenue, across from the old Madison Square Garden. The Capitol was shabby and rundown, and served as the base for a ring of call girls. Jane Wetherell, a bright and charming assistant director on *Producers Showcase* fresh from exclusive Skidmore College, learned about the hotel's skin trade during a cab ride to rehearsal one day. "You look like a nice girl," the cabbie said in a tone of paternal disapproval, "what are you going there for?" Cheerfully and innocently, she replied, "I work there!"

With *Producers Showcase*, Fred Coe reached the apex of his career at NBC. He was in charge of its most expensive, heavily publicized and prestigious show. By assuming its leadership, he was in effect promising to help NBC overtake CBS in the ratings. This brought him power, a probable hefty salary increase, and a corner office on the twenty-eighth floor of the RKO Building with a commanding view of Manhattan and its surroundings.

Not everything about *Producers Showcase* was to Coe's taste, though: for example, it featured adaptations of well-known works, rather than the originals he developed on *Philco-Goodyear*. He would do some of his best-known television work on *Producers Showcase*, but, in a purely literary sense, not his most important.

As major domo of *Producers Showcase*, Coe also had to relinquish some of the control he enjoyed at *Philco-Goodyear*. In Studio 8G, Fred Coe's word was law. He respected his creative professionals and acceded to their wishes when he felt they were right—and even sometimes when he felt they weren't—but his decisions were obeyed. On *Producers Showcase*, with its big-name stars and correspondingly large egos, he would have to adapt.

• • •

The premiere episode of *Producers Showcase* was *Tonight at 8:30*, airing on October 18, 1954. A series of three short plays by Noel Coward starring Ginger Rogers, it was panned by the critics. "The color technicians went wild," Philip Hamburger wrote in *The New Yorker*. "Unfortunately, the performances didn't have quite the same brilliance."

Worse, from NBC's point of view, the show's three half-hour segments fared increasingly worse in the Trendex ratings against CBS, beating *The Burns and Allen Show* 27.4 to 20.4, losing to Arthur Godfrey's *Talent Scouts* 27.6 to 19.6, then getting trounced by *I Love Lucy* 40.8 to 19.6. Two days later, *Variety* reported NBC would probably write off the spectaculars as a "one-season wonder."

State of the Union aired a month later on November 15. Guest producers Howard Lindsay and Russel Crouse updated their 1945 Pulitzer Prize–winning Broadway play about a politician faced with compromising his convictions in order to win election. Arthur Penn directed, with Joseph

Cotten starring as the politician, Margaret Sullavan as his wife, and Nina Foch as his mistress. Writers Lindsay and Crouse were well-established, having written for Broadway since the late 1930s. Director Penn, on the other hand, was a Young Turk who a year earlier had been associate director of *The Colgate Comedy Hour*. Lindsay and Crouse didn't like some of his ideas.

Sauter-Finnegan was a band doing unusual arrangements, a somewhat advanced, not purely melodic use of the big band sound. Penn decided to use their music in *State of the Union*. But when Lindsay and Crouse first heard the music in rehearsals, they reacted as generations of elders unable to understand the musical tastes of the young have done: they didn't like it, they didn't understand it, and they wanted it out of the house. Coe had to step in between them.

"Fred came into the control room and started his basic, 'Hey, Pappy, listen . . .' And not with my complete pleasure, got me to say, 'Okay, I'll change it.'" Penn says. "That was always the way with Coe. He was very reasonable. For a guy who had a terrible temper, he also had very good diplomatic skills." When they ran crosswise of the literary, theatrical, and Hollywood stars of *Producers Showcase*, Coe and his *Philco-Goodyear* family members lacked that show's creative carte blanche. Paradoxically, though, this incident reaffirmed a basic tenet of Coe's method: the writer gets the last word.

One of Coe's responsibilities on *State of the Union* was keeping its stars, jumpy about the pressures of live television, as calm and focused as possible. "Maggie Sullavan and Joe Cotten needed a great deal of diplomatic stroking and cajoling and generally keeping them in a benign state of mind," Penn says. Apparently, Coe succeeded: *State of the Union* was the first spectacular to win critical praise. While saying Penn's direction was ragged in spots, Jack Gould of the *New York Times* called it "a fine production," adding "for 90 minutes, the best of Broadway was over at Radio City." *Variety* called it a "stunning TV production."

Suddenly, the spectaculars were no longer the object of derision. Not all of the credit went to Coe and his creative minions, though: In October, a new ratings service, the A. C. Nielsen Company of Chicago, came out with numbers indicating the first few spectaculars had higher viewership than the more quickly-compiled Trendex indicated. "It's no longer considered in bad taste to mention the word spec[tacular]," *Variety* reported. Still, his virtuoso skills as a producer made Coe the ideal man to lead the spectaculars to respectability.

If spectaculars were no longer a dirty word, their standing at the end of 1954 was still precarious. At first glance, Sidney Howard's *Yellow Jack*, airing on January 10, 1955, did not seem calculated to raise that standing. Its protagonist is not so much Walter Reed, who discovered that yellow fever is spread by mosquitos, as the scientific method. The enemy, transmitted by mosquitoes at a turn-of-the-century U.S. Army camp in Cuba, is a microbe, a non-visual adversary for the most visual of mediums. Jack Gould of the *New York Times* saw Howard's play as "a little dated," while theater critic Brooks Atkinson would call it "a reticent, abstract play."

Coe was under pressure to put on a good show and bring the spectaculars up in the ratings. When he received JP Miller's script for *Yellow Jack*, he knew it would do neither. Rather than re-imagining the play for television, Miller, awed by the center-court prominence of *Producers Showcase*, had done a cut-and-paste job of Howard's play. After the first rehearsal of *Yellow Jack*, Coe called a script conference in his twenty-eighth-floor office with Miller and director Delbert Mann. Under the circumstances, a producer under the gun could be expected to chew Miller out, but that wasn't Coe's way.

"What's your image of the play?" Coe asked him.

Miller tried to explain.

"Well, that's not what you have here," Coe said calmly.

"I was trying to adapt the play," Miller said.

"Forget about adapting," Coe replied. "Try to create your own experience, based on what you have here. And think of the medium we're working in."

Once again, Delbert Mann was impressed by Coe's kid-glove treatment of a writer. "Fred quietly tore JP's script apart without discouraging him or dictating what he should do to re-write it," Mann recalls. "He inspired JP. It was the most extraordinary event in terms of watching a creative producer at work with a writer he trusted." As the afternoon wore on and twilight fell, something clicked for Miller. "I had never done an adaptation," Miller says. "I suddenly realized I could create characters, create scenes, I could do what I wanted. I started all over. I threw out Howard's stage dialogue and did filmic dialogue."

When the revised show aired on January 10, 1955, *Variety* praised Miller for his "expertly wrought adaptation," calling the show "an exciting drama of tension and suspense." Despite his reservations about the play, Jack Gould called it excellent, although he must have thought Howard adapted his own work, since he neglected to give Miller credit for it. Noting that NBC's showcase for color TV had produced an essentially monochromatic show, though, Gould added, "As an example of good color, 'Yellow Jack' wasn't."

Bill Nichols, Coe's chief lieutenant at the time, agrees. "Otis Riggs, the set designer, came up with sets that were very pale and gray and yellow. Sarnoff called up the next morning, screaming [at Coe], 'I'm trying to sell color televisions and you give me a show like this. I want *color*!'" Mike Dann, then a top executive at NBC, doubts it happened that way. "That would be total nonsense," he says. "The General would never call a producer. He was much too high up." But there may have been something about NBC's—and RCA's—high-stakes gamble on color that led General Sarnoff to descend from his station. "When we were blocking *State of the Union*, there was a feed going back into Manhattan, into General Sarnoff's office," Arthur Penn says. "And every once in a while, we would get a communication from there saying, 'That dress is not bright enough.' He wanted more color. So suddenly there would be this great scramble to get another dress for Maggie Sullavan."

Instead of passing along any bile Sarnoff may have dispensed, Coe was lavish with praise for his staff. "I just want to thank you for your polished and eloquent direction of *Yellow Jack*," Coe wrote to Delbert Mann a week after the broadcast. "It was a source of great pleasure and satisfaction to me to witness the quiet authority and instinctive good craftsmanship and taste with which you imbued this production."

Coe would write no such mash notes to Shelley Winters, a star of *The Women*, which aired in February. Clare Booth Luce's satirical portrait of New York society women was adapted by Sumner Locke Elliott and directed by Vincent Donehue. It had an impressive all-female cast featuring Paulette Goddard, Ruth Hussey, Mary Astor, Mary Boland, Valerie Bettis, Cathleen Nesbitt, Bibi Osterwald, Pat Carroll, and Winters, who proved one of Coe's sternest tests as ego manager to the stars.

While the show was in rehearsal, Winters's marriage to actor Tony Franciosa was unraveling. Winters, who played the femme fatale Crystal, lacked Coe's ability to separate personal traumas from professional life. "Nothing ever suited her," Bill Nichols recalls. "She was always late, and demanded extra attention of all kinds. Her dressing room was a mess. There was Kleenex and lipstick and all kind of junk all over the floor. She was a slob." Winters later acknowledged her on-set misbehavior, writing, "I had been so preoccupied with Tony and so terrified of playing the beautiful Crystal that I gave Mr. Fred Coe, the producer, a very bad time indeed."

But Coe never had a completely bad time when Sumner Locke Elliott was on the set. As Dominick Dunne has observed, "Before camp, he was camp." A gay man with a sharp sense of humor, he excelled in impersonations of the show's stars. "Sumner could do an imitation of every woman in 'The Women,'" Dunne says. "And he could carry on not just their dialogue from the show, but improvise conversations between them. He would have Fred on the floor screaming with laughter. Fred was the first guy I ever knew—the most solid man, man, man—who found camp humor hilarious."

In light of the reviews, perhaps Elliott should have done his imitations on the air. While saying the show was uncommonly interesting, the *New York Times* found it lacked the substance of the Broadway version, with *Variety* adding that none of the stars brought their characters to life. But

Coe's next effort for *Producers Showcase* would galvanize the public, win over the critics, and lay to rest any remaining doubts about the viability of spectaculars.

. . .

Peter Pan, starring Mary Martin as Pan and Cyril Ritchard as Captain Hook, had played for months at Broadway's Winter Garden Theater. Choreographed by Jerome Robbins, J. M. Barrie's story of a group of children from Victorian London transported to the magical world of Neverland was adapted by Sumner Locke Elliott and directed by Clark Jones, with Martin and Ritchard repeating their Broadway roles.

Airing on March 7, 1955, little more than a week after it ended on Broadway, *Peter Pan* charmed the nation, but didn't make much of a first impression on its producer. "Fred kind of sloughed it off," says Larry Elikann, the show's technical director. "He loved the show, but to him a musical was a song-and-dance thing. He was into heavy drama, basically."

Across the country, between 65 and 75 million viewers saw *Peter Pan*, making it, at the time, the single most-watched program in television history. As of this writing, only three subsequent shows have been watched by a higher percentage of the American viewing audience: the final episode of M*A*S*H, the "Who Shot J.R.?" episode of *Dallas*, and the final episode of the original *Roots* mini-series.

Because there were only about fifteen thousand color TV sets in the country, *Peter Pan* parties were held in the homes of those who had them. Traffic thinned on the nation's roads, and some schoolchildren got out of homework by promising to watch *Peter Pan*. Not only did *Peter Pan* beat top-rated *I Love Lucy* in the Trendex ratings, it knocked it out of the Top 10 for the first time in years.

Critical response matched the public's. In the *New York Times* the next day, Jack Gould wrote, "Surely there must be a trace of fairy dust from coast to coast this morning," calling *Peter Pan* "an unforgettable evening of video theater." In an unusual step, Gould wrote a second review five days later, praising Mary Martin for a glorious performance, Jerome Robbins's dances, and the style of Cyril Ritchard, calling them all jewels. But one man had pulled it all together. "Television's role was to take these cherished gems and hold them forth for a nation, not a handful of persons to see," Gould wrote. "Under the guidance of Fred Coe, NBC did just that."

There would be no more *Variety* headlines asking "Spec[tacular]s Just '1-Season Wonder'?" Spectaculars, or specials, would not only survive, but flourish. Pat Weaver, who conceived the series, gives Coe the credit. "Fred was really the genius that made *Producers Showcase* come to flower," he says.

• • •

After such a rousing triumph, a letdown was perhaps inevitable. *Reunion in Vienna*, a tale of faded Austrian nobility which aired on April 4, was dismissed by *Variety*, which noted: "Seldom has so much coin, lavish and painstaking production and particularly fine talent wasted itself on such antiquated theatre."

Darkness at Noon, however, would find Coe and company in top form again. Airing on May 2, 1955, Robert Alan Aurthur's script was adapted from Arthur Koestler's novel about Rubashov, an idealistic Bolshevik revolutionary, who helps to foment Communism in Russia, only to be arrested on trumped-up charges, imprisoned, and executed by the revolution he helped to create. Directed by Delbert Mann, it featured Lee J. Cobb as Rubashov, Oscar Homolka as the good cop who interrogates him, David Wayne as the bad cop, and in the flashback sequences, Ruth Roman as his secretary/girlfriend. But the real star of the show was scene designer Otis Riggs's sets.

One of the most common criticisms of live television drama was its restriction to cramped indoor quarters, with transitions between scenes slow and awkward as actors scrambled from one set to another. Otis Riggs's work on *Darkness at Noon* shows how set design might have evolved if the networks hadn't abandoned live drama. The Communist prison consisted of a two-tiered set looking so authentic that *Variety*'s reviewer wrote, "The cavernous stone corridors and cells were cold and dark and dank."

This almost palpable sensory effect was not the most remarkable aspect of Riggs's sets, however. For the flashback scenes in which Rubashov returns to his pre-imprisonment life, Riggs designed two prison cells for Cobb: one, in the large, two-tiered set, established that he was surrounded by cells of fellow inmates. A second free-standing cell, a near-duplicate of the first, was located nearby and used only in closeups. Cobb would get to it while the camera was on other inmates.

This second cell had only two walls, with the other two sides opening onto scenes from Cobb's past. A camera placed at one angle to this cell made it appear Cobb was in prison, while a camera perpendicular to the first made it appear Cobb was back in his past—even though he hadn't moved an inch.

Saying "television viewing is not often so stimulating," Jack Gould praised the show for "truly inventive stage craft," adding that "the transitions back and forth between the cell and the flashback scenes were achieved almost by magic." The only shortcoming Gould found was the filmed insert at the end, in which Vice President Richard Nixon praised the show for its anti-Communist content. "The effect," Gould wrote, "was a little like following an impressive symphony concert with a harmonica solo."

Airing four weeks later on May 30, *The Petrified Forest* was the first live dramatic show in color broadcast from NBC's Burbank studios, another sign of television's move west. Directed by Delbert Mann, it starred Humphrey Bogart, Lauren Bacall, and Henry Fonda, and featured Jack Klugman, Morris Buchanan, and Richard Jaeckel as inmates who break out of prison along with Bogart to menace customers at a roadside restaurant in Arizona. The show marked Bogart's only appearance in live television drama, and Tad Mosel, who adapted Robert Sherwood's play about an idealist (Fonda) forced to confront the human savagery of Bogart's Duke Mantee, thinks Bogart may have done it for his wife, Lauren Bacall.

Before this show, Bacall had only been in films, never acting a role from beginning to end in one session, much less on live television, where any mistake would be instantly broadcast to millions of viewers around the country. But it won critical praise and high ratings ("'Forest' Petrifies CBS Competition," *Variety* wrote), and served as a springboard to her successful stage career.

While Coe's productions were doing well with the public and critics, however, he was increasingly at odds with Saul and Henry Jaffe, the powerful entertainment attorneys who headed Showcase Productions, which owned *Producers Showcase*. It isn't clear why: the Jaffes may have wanted to increase the number of shows devoted to classical music and ballet at the expense of serious drama; they may have wanted more West Coast–based productions than Coe did; or he may simply have regarded them as an infringement on his right to produce the show as he saw fit. In any case, they decided to fire him. On September 7, twelve days before the *Producers Showcase* musical version of Thornton Wilder's *Our Town*, *Variety* reported that Coe was not only leaving the show but might quit NBC.

Mike Dann, then NBC vice president for program sales, says there was nothing the network could do about it. "Fred Coe was looked up to by me and my associates as [being as] close to a Mr. NBC, as far as producers went, as possible," he says. "Fred wanted to stay, and he was doing important work. On the other hand, the Jaffes had the legal right to exercise certain decisions. There was a constant battle." The Jaffes prevailed, but after the many aggravations of *Our Town*, Coe might have been glad they did.

• • •

Thornton Wilder's tale of life in a small New Hampshire town at the turn of the century was staged in Hollywood. It starred Frank Sinatra as the stage manager, a one-man Greek chorus, and Paul Newman and Eva Marie Saint as young lovers who go through the life cycle from youthful infatuation to marriage and parenthood to death. Its songs (including "Love and Marriage") were written by James van Heusen and Sammy Cahn. *Our Town* was already a classic, and the decision to make it a musical was a risky one.

Coe's biggest problem, however, was Frank Sinatra. At the height of his stardom, he acted arrogantly even by Sinatra standards. During rehearsals, Sinatra complained to J. P. Shanley of the *New York Times* about rehearsals lasting almost four weeks, adding, "They're going to have to devise a method of cutting down on rehearsals." Always one to do things his way, Sinatra devised a method of his own: he skipped many of them, including the all-important dress rehearsal.

"He came to rehearsal so few times that we had a stand-in for him, with whom I blocked the show," Mann says. "Then Frank would come in, and we would show him the moves. He would go through it a time or two and depart with his entourage. It did not harm the show since the character, with few exceptions, does not get involved in playing scenes.

"But came the dress rehearsal the day before the show went on the air, and Frank didn't show, and he made no explanation. We did not know whether he was going to even appear for the air show. We went through the dress rehearsal with the stand-in doing the show and put in a call to Johnny Desmond, who was singing in Las Vegas, to get him to come in." Dominick Dunne, the show's assistant director, recalls the effects of Sinatra's erratic behavior on Coe and Mann. "I think Fred almost lost his mind on *Our Town*, as did Del Mann," he says.

After the dress rehearsal, Sinatra sent word that he would appear for the air show. At a meeting for final director's notes to the cast on the day of the show, Mann, quietly livid, refused to speak to him and never did again. Coe would have fired an actor on *Philco-Goodyear* who acted like Sinatra, but he told everyone after dress rehearsal not to bother Sinatra about it, or to ask where he had been.

On the eve of the air show, Coe and Mann realized they had another problem: the lighting, done by an NBC lighting man they'd never worked with before, was inadequate. After dress rehearsal, they sent him home, then, with the lighting crew, worked all night to relight the entire production.

Their success can be seen by watching a kinescope of the show. As Sinatra sings "Love and Marriage," Paul Newman and Eva Marie Saint, silhouetted in the background, pantomime a courtship ritual. Not only is it lit effectively, it's an inspired bit of direction on Mann's part: otherwise the song would have seemed staged and artificial.

And in the last act, following Emily Webb's premature death, Eva Marie Saint appears as the newest resident of the graveyard of Grover's Corners. As she talks with the others, no longer one of the living, yet not fully one of the dead, the lone spotlight on her simultaneously underscores both her solitude in death and her still-radiant quality. The scene's haunting mood is effectively highlighted by a series of lap dissolves, shots in which an image of Saint taken from a camera at one angle slowly and magically blends into an image taken from another.

Despite all the pre-production aggravation, the show jelled. David Shaw's script adeptly blends Wilder's meditations on human destiny with flip asides to the viewer. When the show's first half hour is over, Frank Sinatra's stage manager muses, "Babylon had two million people and all that we know are the names of the kings and some wheat contracts. . . . It's the end of the first act. You can grab a snack—those of you not on a diet." (Executives at Ford and RCA, both of which paid several hundreds of thousands of dollars for their commercials, were probably not happy to hear this.)

While Frank Sinatra and Paul Newman came in for their share of praise, most of the acting honors went to Eva Marie Saint. "Eva Marie Saint was responsible for a major share of the production's fine quality," J. P. Shanley wrote in the *New York Times*. "She performed brilliantly." Similarly, *Variety* called her performance "stunning." Even *The New Republic* gave the show its grudging approval, with Wendell Brogen writing, "Given the dubious decision of musicalizing a classic of dramatic prose, television displayed a good deal of artistic integrity." These reviews failed to change the Jaffes' minds, however, and Coe was out of *Producers Showcase*.

• • •

At the same time the curtain came down on Coe's involvement with Pat Weaver's spectaculars, it also descended on a show whose passing *Variety* marked as "the end of an era": *Philco-Goodyear Television Playhouse*. The show had become so identified with Coe that *Variety* described him as "Mr. 'Philco Playhouse' himself."

But with the show's ratings slipping, Philco pulled its sponsorship. *A Man Is Ten Feet Tall*, airing on October 2, 1955, and starring Sidney Poitier as an idealistic and courageous dock worker, was slated as the final episode. Among *Philco-Goodyear's* many successful shows in 1954–1955 were Paddy Chayefsky's *The Catered Affair*, JP Miller's *The Rabbit Trap*, and Gore Vidal's *Visit to a Small Planet*. Although Duff was credited as *Philco-Goodyear's* producer that last year, Coe's associates still dispute whether he retained control.

Casting director Everett Chambers and assistant director Jane Wetherell, asked about Coe's involvement in 1954–1955, both say, "None that I know of." Delbert Mann says Coe made a clean break from the show, and Gore Vidal affirms that Duff was the producer. But there is a significant chorus of dissenting voices.

David Shaw, a frequent writer until the show's end, says "Fred was calling the shots when I did that show. Nobody else. I can't believe he left in '54." Arthur Penn adds, "Fred never relinquished a proprietorship in *Philco*. He just never did. With all due respect to Gordon Duff, who's a very sweet guy, Gordon was not a real producer. He was a guy who kept the equilibrium, and he was charming and a great guy to have a drink with."

After October 2, 1955, though, neither Coe nor Duff would produce NBC's Sunday night nine o'clock dramas. *Philco-Goodyear Television Playhouse* would go out with a bang rather than a whimper, however. *A Man Is Ten Feet Tall*, written by Robert Alan Aurthur, was a searing and realistic study of corruption on the waterfront. It had something unprecedented for television drama: a black in the starring role. The process by which Gordon Duff and Robert Alan Aurthur got Sidney Poitier on the show would itself have made a good television drama.

After getting out of the marines at the end of World War II, Robert Alan Aurthur worked as a stevedore on the New York waterfront. There, he was befriended by a black dockworker named Tommy who refused to be worn down by racism. One night several years later, Aurthur and N. Richard Nash went to see *The Blackboard Jungle*, with Sidney Poitier as one of its stars. Poitier reminded Aurthur of Tommy, and he wrote a script in which Poitier could play the lead.

Duff approved the script, but couldn't recall a single case where a black had played the lead in a live television drama. "Write it without describing the guy as a Negro," he told Aurthur. "Then, after we cast Poitier, it'll be too late for anyone to complain." When Philco announced it was pulling its sponsorship, Duff decided to make *A Man Is Ten Feet Tall* the last *Philco Television Playhouse*.

Philco reacted calmly to Poitier's casting, but NBC didn't. Ironically, the network's stated concern was not that Poitier was black, but that he had associated with political activists such as Paul Robeson and Canada Lee. At a meeting with network lawyers, Poitier was asked to sign a document repudiating his relationship with them. Torn between his desire to advance his career and preserve his integrity, he exploded in tears. "Not only is this unfair, but I have nothing but respect for Paul Robeson—and that's the truth," he reports saying in his autobiography. "And if you see my respect for him as un-American, then I *am* fucking un-American!" Poitier stormed out of the meeting, and only extensive efforts on Aurthur's part (including paying him $2,000, twice what any other actor on the show had received) brought him back.

The show, directed by Robert Mulligan, was a smash, winning seven awards, leading to a movie version, and providing a critical boost for Poitier's career. *A Man Is Ten Feet Tall* was not met with universal praise, however. Two Southern newspapers called Aurthur a Communist. Six

Philco distributors, unaware they no longer sponsored the show, threatened to cancel their franchises. A petition from Jackson, Mississippi, with six thousand signatures swore the signers would never watch *Philco Television Playhouse* again. But far outweighing these criticisms was a call Aurthur received at home around eight o'clock the night after the show. It was from Poitier, being followed around Harlem by an adoring crowd. He ducked into a drugstore in a vain effort to escape them. The crowd's noise was obvious to Aurthur. "I'm talking to the guy who wrote it," Poitier told the throng. "Tell him what you think." Aurthur heard a loud cheer go up.

Whether he was there or not during the show's last year, at *Philco-Goodyear*, Fred Coe presided over and played an active role in shaping—both in literary and production terms—the writing tradition variously called the Fred Coe School, the Paddy Chayefsky School, the kitchen-sink drama or, by Madison Avenue, the work of the Unhappiness Boys. As Tad Mosel has observed, though, the diversity of its writers makes it hard to describe that body of work with any precision.

"*Philco-Goodyear* writers were different," he says. "And yet there was a quality that may have been what Fred gave us, a quality that made a *Philco-Goodyear* play recognizable in the sense that you might hear people talk about a *New Yorker* short story." By this measure Coe was not only the D. W. Griffith of TV's Golden Age, but its Harold Ross as well.

• • •

In the fall of 1955, Coe took charge of a new hour dramatic anthology. But before it went on the air, he had to help Alice extricate herself from a too-hasty remarriage. Although she was still grieving over the breakup of her marriage to Coe, it was an outwardly festive year for her: Donald Phillips, Coe's best friend from Nashville, was getting married and there was no end of parties. At one of them, Alice met Ford McNeill, a real estate developer.

Alice married him in October 1955. Then it hit her: She didn't love him, and it was a dreadful mistake. She turned to Coe, who flew to Nashville immediately. Mustering a decisiveness on her behalf he had been unable to summon on his own, Coe told her to return to Fort Lauderdale and file for divorce, which she did, ending a marriage that had never really begun. Although he had now been married to Joyce for four years, it was another example of Coe's ongoing commitment to Alice.

• • •

Back in New York, Coe started work on his new anthology, sponsored by Pontiac. Pontiac and its ad agency wanted to call it *Pontiac Theatre*, but Coe held out for *Playwrights '56* to honor the show's writers. Unfortunately for Coe and the fading hopes of live TV drama, it drew the worst possible time slot.

In April of 1954, the U.S. Supreme Court had ruled that the FCC's ban on quiz shows awarding cash prizes was illegal. When assistant director Jane Wetherell vacationed in Jamaica in May of 1955, she met a friend from CBS, telling him Coe's new show would air every other Tuesday night at 9:30.

"It's going to die," he said.

"Why?" Wetherell asked.

"CBS is putting on a show called *The $64,000 Question*, and everyone's going to watch it," he said.

He was right. Premiering on June 7, 1955, *The $64,000 Question* became the top-rated show by August 10, deposing *I Love Lucy*. When *Playwrights '56* opened on October 4, it was already in trouble.

For Coe and his crew, *Playwrights '56* was a homecoming, but not a completely happy one. It aired from the first-rate Brooklyn One studio, but rehearsals were held in the Palladium Ballroom, the rehearsal hall from *Philco's* early years. The aroma of beer and cigarette smoke still lingered the morning after, and, if anything, seemed to have gotten stronger. To Dominick Dunne, this reflected the loss of status from the spectaculars. "It didn't have the glamor of *Producers Showcase*, the stars," he says. "I never truly enjoyed *Playwrights '56*."

The show featured many of what *Variety* called "the Coe-terie of tip-top dramatic boys," but this did not mean Coe was just going to repeat the *Philco-Goodyear* glory days. On the show's premiere, a new writer, David Davidson, adapted Philip Wylie's *The Answer*. Directed by Delbert Mann, it was the conceptual opposite of kitchen-sink drama.

The Answer is a fantasy in which military radar records an unidentified flying object near an atomic bomb test. Once the bomb is exploded, the UFO is identified as an angel observing the blast and killed by it. Jack Gould of the *New York Times* said it was not successful, perhaps because TV's literal cameras were not the ideal medium for such a theme. But he praised the producer for tackling it. "In doing 'The Answer,' Mr. Coe quickly re-affirmed that he is not one to settle for the ordinary in TV drama," Gould wrote. "Mr. Wylie's work is anything but easy to translate to the screen, and Mr. Coe deserves every credit for undertaking it."

However, there was a sense in which Coe did repeat himself from *Philco-Goodyear*. In an interview, he later said Paddy Chayefsky's *Marty* spawned too many imitation *Martys*. But *Playwrights '56* was guilty of Creeping Martyism: *Adam and Evening*, airing March 13, 1956, is *Marty* as a cat-owning construction worker (he even has to stop off at a butcher shop on the way home), while *Nick and Letty*, airing June 5, 1956, is *Marty* as a mid-level officer on a World War II cargo ship transporting a group of nurses.

Still, *Playwrights '56* featured a wide range of genres and writers' voices.

Now, though, Coe would pick the shows with an eye to counter-programming *The $64,000 Question. Sometimes You Get Rich* was a satire of quiz shows. And *The Battler*, airing from Hollywood on October 18, 1955, was going to star James Dean as a broken-down, has-been boxer in a story by Ernest Hemingway.

A. E. Hotchner, biographer and friend of Ernest Hemingway, was in Italy when he got a cable from Coe saying he was being battered by *The $64,000 Question*. They then spoke by phone.

"Can you do a Hemingway and cast it well?" Coe asked.

"Fred, all the really good Hemingway, things that can be done in an hour, have already been sold to film."

"There must be something you like."

"I like this short story 'The Battler,' but it's only a few pages long," Hotchner replied. A few pages was enough for Coe. Hemingway sold it to *Playwrights '56*, and Hotchner's adaptation was his first television play. But on September 30, Dean was killed in a car crash near Paso Robles, California.

"We had two weeks before rehearsal and Fred tried desperately to get a name to play the part, but nobody was available," Hotchner says. "I guess it was Fred who, on Arthur Penn's recommendation, put Paul Newman in the lead. It was a great character part, and at that point Newman wasn't a character actor. But Fred talked him into it. And the first rehearsals were terrible."

Coe told Newman about a YMCA downtown, next to a fighters' gym, encouraging him to go down there and familiarize himself with the people. As a result, Hotchner says, Newman developed a terrific portrait of *The Battler*, which led to his career-making role in *Somebody Up There Likes Me*. "It was really Fred's guidance that got Newman the part and made this thing go," Hotchner says. "He was very persuasive."

It wasn't just Newman who found Coe persuasive on the set of *The Battler*. Rehearsals were conducted in the anteroom of a mortuary near NBC's Burbank facilities, and while a rehearsal was under way, Coe was approached by two men wearing black suits, black ties, and white shirts. They were not morticians, but officials from Continuity Acceptance at NBC, also known as the censorship department. But as far as Coe was concerned, they were trying to bury his show.

"They came in and asked to speak to Fred," Hotchner says. "They wanted to point out some objectionable things in the script. It had a couple of 'hells' in it, and a 'damn,' I think. Fred took one look at them, and I could see the color rising in his face. He said, 'You sons of bitches come in here and interrupt rehearsal in order to tell me I can't use a "hell" and a "damn"? Well, get the hell out of here!' And he just barked them right out the door," Hotchner says. "The script went in as ordered."

But *The $64,000 Question* was Coe's main problem. When *Playwrights '56* aired *The Sound and the Fury* on December 6, 1955, it was the night Dr. Joyce Brothers correctly answered the $64,000 question. Jack Gould gave the Faulkner adaptation the measured praise of someone who's been told to eat his spinach because it's good for him, adding that it took a lot of discipline not to peek at *The $64,000 Question*. Most viewers lacked that discipline. "In the shadow of that giant," *Newsweek* observed, "Fred Coe has done a commendable job of getting 'Playwrights' on its feet." But shows that would have basked in the spotlight on *Philco-Goodyear* were getting lost.

One of the most critically acclaimed episodes of *Playwrights '56*, Tad Mosel's *The Waiting Place*, aired December 20, 1955, and was trounced in the ratings, pulling 18 percent of the audience to *The $64,000 Question's* 69 percent. The few viewers of *The Waiting Place* saw a well-crafted and moving story about a young woman's coming of age, directed by Arthur Penn and starring Kim Stanley in an audacious bit of casting.

"For about the first 10 minutes of last week's 'Playwrights '56' presentation of Tad Mosel's 'The Waiting Place,' it looked as if producer Fred Coe had flipped his lid," *Variety* reported. "Imagine casting Kim Stanley as a 14-year-old. But after those first few minutes, they could have called him Canny Coe, for Miss Stanley was not only completely believable in the part, but delivered one of the stunning virtuoso performances of this or any other season." *Variety* was also lavish in its praise of director Penn, and Frank Overton, who played Stanley's father.

As part of his efforts to champion *Playwrights*, Coe made himself more available to the media than he had been on *Philco-Goodyear*. In a January 17, 1956, interview with Sid Shalit of the New York *Daily News*, Coe said, "Everybody's interested in gimmicks and gadgets,and 64 G's is in that category. It's a phenomenal success, but it's a gimmick nevertheless, and the public eventually tires of gimmicks, and in the long run they decide on substance," leading Shalit to muse, "The quixotic Mr. Coe might be accused of wishful thinking, but never of poor taste."

Despite his head-on competition with the ratings behemoth, Coe continued to use *Playwrights* to experiment with the very nature of television as an electronic theater. Airing on January 17, 1956, *Lost* was written by Arnold Schulman and directed by Arthur Penn; it is the story of an amnesiac (Steven Hill) attempting to regain his identity. A superb example of what can only be called *TV noir*, it features dark, abstract sets and stream-of-consciousness narration as Hill tumbles through a variety of urban settings in search of himself. Bill Klages, the show's lighting director, would learn how seriously Coe took the show's somber, moody lighting.

During on-camera rehearsals at Brooklyn One, Klages decided that a sequence where Hill winds up in a hospital ward should be lit brightly, to contrast with the darkness enveloping the rest of the show. The scene was re-lit—until Coe saw it. "We're doing the run-through, and all of a sudden, the control-room door opens with an enormous bang," Klages recalls. "Fred comes in and says, 'When ah want *Howdy Doody* lighting, ah will get the *Howdy Doody* lighting director!'" The hospital sequence was re-lit to make it dark again.

Languishing opposite *The $64,000 Question*, *Playwrights '56* would soon go dark as well. In March, Pontiac announced that it would not sponsor another season. Soon after, NBC moved the show from Brooklyn One back to Studio 8G in the RCA Building. Along with the return of *Playwrights* rehearsals to the Palladium Ballroom, things were coming full circle for Fred Coe at NBC. The network hoped to find a sponsor for a summer version of *Playwrights*, but none was found, and Gore Vidal's *Honor*, airing on June 19, was the series' farewell.

A Civil War drama directed by Vincent Donehue and starring Ralph Bellamy, *Honor* had an appropriate theme for a series finale: What constitutes honorable conduct in the face of defeat? As a plantation owner given to bellicose anti-Yankee rhetoric, Ralph Bellamy urges his neighbors to burn their mansions to deny sustenance to the invading Union army. After they do so, he loses his nerve and refuses to burn his own, earning the scorn of his neighbors, wife, and son. In the end, he sets fire to his mansion after all.

While the scene makes for moving television, fire marshals objected to it during rehearsals, fearing the fire might get out of control. Director Donehue couldn't budge them. During the impasse, Coe called Jane Wetherell, the show's assistant director, from his aerie atop the RKO Building.

"How are things going?" he asked.

"We're having a little trouble with the fire marshals," Wetherell said.

"Would it help if I came over and screamed?"

"Yes, it would."

Coe came down, yelled at the fire marshals, and saved the scene. The series was lost, but he fought well and with honor. He also gave Jane Wetherell new insight into him. "He was well-known for yelling, and [until then] I always thought it was sincere yelling," she reflects. She learned a lesson Larry Elikann had already learned on *Philco-Goodyear*. "Fred would take chairs and throw them across the studio," he says. "He was very volatile. Some of it was bullshit, though. I'll never forget his screaming at someone, going crazy. Then he turned to me and said, 'How did you like that?'"

Paradoxically, after *Playwrights '56* received its pink slip, its ratings began to improve. The *New York Times* reported on April 25 that *Playwrights* had higher ratings than six other one-hour dramatic shows, a remarkable accomplishment, as most of them had been on longer and faced weaker competition. While the ratings of *Playwrights* still did not approach those of *The $64,000 Question*, it was an impressive vote of confidence for Coe and his playwrights from the television public. "Fred was just caught," Mike Dann says. "*The $64,000 Question* was a hit. But he didn't know that was going to happen. It was a tragedy, because it helped kill original drama."

Playwrights '56 was replaced on NBC's Tuesday night schedule by *The Kaiser Aluminum Hour*, produced by Worthington Miner. But early in the 1956–1957 season, Miner quit after an adaptation of John Galsworthy's *Loyalties*, about anti-Semitism in England, was blackballed by Kaiser. After Miner left, a variety of shows on controversial themes by leading writers was killed by Kaiser and Young & Rubicam. Finally, the show's leading directors, Franklin Schaffner, Fielder Cook, and George Roy Hill, were personally fired by Henry Kaiser, who said they refused to produce plays that were non-controversial and more "Americana-oriented."

The final postscript to *Playwrights* came in 1958, when the quiz show scandal erupted. First on *Dotto*, and then *Twenty-One* (the celebrated Charles Van Doren case), evidence surfaced of answers supplied in advance to contestants who were attractive to the public and therefore good for ratings. One after the other, prime-time quiz shows were discredited, and the November 9, 1958, broadcast of *The $64,000 Question* was its last. Fred Coe's prophecy about the ephemeral nature of quiz shows had come true, but too late to do him any good.

• • •

Just as *Playwrights* was going off the air, Coe got a highly public pat on the back from his *Philco-Goodyear* gang. "An Appreciation of Fred Coe," spearheaded by Bill Nichols, Everett Chambers, and Chuck Weiss, a publicist for *Playwrights '56*, appeared in *Variety* on May 23, 1956. It was the first *Variety* tribute to a figure from television.

One of the most literate issues in *Variety*'s history, it serves as a stylistic Rosetta stone for the writers Coe developed at NBC, bringing together the genial macho and Hemingwayesque cadences of JP Miller, the lyrical conciseness of Tad Mosel, the intensity of Paddy Chayefsky, the self-effacement of Horton Foote, and the good-natured humor of David Shaw.

Variety editor Abel Green said *Philco-Goodyear* had been the "No. 1" dramatic show on television, and the leader in terms of having its shows adapted by Broadway and Hollywood. Directors Delbert Mann and Vincent Donehue, writer Robert Alan Aurthur, and musical director Harry Sosnik also contributed articles. The tribute filled two pages of *Variety*, along with twenty pages of congratulatory ads from a Who's Who of the entertainment industry.

Most figures of Coe's stature in the entertainment industry would have basked in such acclaim, but "Fred was very unhappy about it," Bill Nichols recalls. "I said, 'Oh, come on, Fred, grow up. You're important!' He really did not like being in the public eye." It was much like Coe's reaction when author Frank Sturcken read him Tad Mosel's observation that, for his writers, Coe was a combined father, friend, buffer, psychiatrist, and newspaper critic. "A composite of that guy would look pretty funny, wouldn't he?" Coe said tersely.

• • •

With *Playwrights* over and—for the first time in his career at NBC—no shows assigned for the fall, Coe went to East Hampton for the summer of 1956. While he and Joyce were in residence on Baiting Hollow Road in East Hampton, he rented a farmhouse in nearby Watermill for Alice, John, Laurie, and his mother. Coe was still spending a lot of time with Alice, even taking her to dinner on her fortieth birthday. Meanwhile his position had been deteriorating at NBC, and it dramatically worsened in the fall of 1956 with the resignation of Pat Weaver as NBC chairman of the board. Weaver was an advocate of live TV drama in general and of Coe in particular. NBC's new top programming executive was Robert Kintner, a man committed to filmed programming and buying shows from outside producers. Both tendencies boded ill for Coe.

As visionary executives and pioneers like Weaver disappeared, they were replaced by businessmen and market researchers, men whom *Variety* called "the slide-rule boys." With their ascent, the values that made the Golden Age possible would soon vanish. Whether 1950s television drama constitutes a Golden Age, though, is an idea that has passionate and articulate detractors.

In Tom Stempel's book *Storytellers to the Nation*, E. Jack Neuman, who subsequently wrote several episodes of *Wagon Train* and the 1982 miniseries *Inside the Third Reich*, says:

> The best of it was really a third-rate movie, the very best. [On] "Playhouse 90," I was always thinking about what I could do on a movie set, and how terribly awkward and limited [it was]. The people who were running it at the time, mostly New Yorkers, [had theatrical] aspirations or actual theatre background. They wanted to preserve that "spontaneous" horseshit. I had no use for them. . . . [I]t was a boring medium, in my estimation.

And in a 1956 article in *Theatre Arts* magazine, Gore Vidal wrote about several leading teleplays of the period:

> I have not deluded myself, nor will I try to delude others into thinking these plays are among the treasures of the world drama. They are not. . . . Considering the difficulties and restrictions under which these . . . plays were

written and produced, they are excellent; but one could not, with a straight face, compare them to *Hamlet* or even to *The Member of the Wedding*, to name a good small play.

Neuman's critique is more notable for its vitriol than its substance. Yes, the facilities of 1950s television were inadequate. While a limitation, though, the cramped quarters were also a challenge to the imagination of its writers, a challenge to which many rose admirably. It makes no more sense to criticize live television drama for its inadequate production facilities than to criticize the ancient Greek or Elizabethan stages for their lack of production values or to criticize Egyptian tomb art because its characters are two-dimensional stick figures that lie flat on their sides like beached flounders.

As for Vidal's comments, it is worth noting that in the introduction to his own collection of teleplays, he also wrote, "Television has, for all its limitations, created what is, I suspect, a golden age for the dramatist."

Many leading broadcast historians feel this period was indeed golden. Writer and broadcaster Jeff Greenfield observes, "Television drama through the first decade of its existence was, by present standards, astonishingly diverse." And in *A Pictorial History of Television*, Irving Settel and William Laas go further: "In its golden years . . . television drama charted a course unequalled for originality and verve since the Elizabethan theatre that produced William Shakespeare." Even if the Golden Age of Television had turned out as much quality work as the Elizabethan drama, though, any advocate of the period's greatness would have to acknowledge it was guaranteed to produce an exponentially greater amount of trash by virtue of having so much airtime to fill.

Unfortunately for Coe, NBC's new leadership was more concerned with the gold in its coffers than the gold on its screens. In May of 1956, four months before Pat Weaver resigned, Coe had signed a new three-year contract with the network. The new management headed by Kintner and Robert Sarnoff (David Sarnoff's son) couldn't dislodge him, but gave him nothing to do. Except for trouble-shooting on the special *Annie Get Your Gun* on November 27, 1957, Coe produced nothing for NBC between the summer of 1956 and the winter of 1957. For Fred Coe, these were not the best of times.

"Nearly all of my people, and I considered Fred one of them, either left or were given cement shoes," Pat Weaver says. After all he had done to develop television drama as an art form and bring prestige and advertising dollars to NBC, Coe's services were no longer required. At this time, Harry Muheim, one of Coe's leading writers from *Philco-Goodyear*, visited him in his office atop the RKO Building.

"I have a clear memory of Fred with the sun streaming in in the afternoon," Muheim says. "It was not the up-time of the boy-wonder years. [I remember] his—almost bravery. Things weren't going well, and he was moving out. . . . I don't know if there were family difficulties, but there were plenty of professional difficulties. And then he had this wonderful line I've never forgotten. 'The one thing you have to remember is that nobody forced us into this business,' he said. 'We came in on our own.'"

On November 27, 1957, the *New York Times* reported Coe's resignation from NBC. "I would like to produce shows for NBC-TV, but plans and ideas that I have submitted have either been ignored or have drawn no interest," he told the *Times*. "On the other hand, I have been given no assignment. A silent telephone on your desk is a terrible thing." For remaining members of Coe's production family, it was also time to take stock. "I kept going back to the office, not believing it was all over," casting director Everett Chambers recalls. "Eventually, I realized, 'I've got to go out and find a job.'"

On December 4, *Variety* reported talks were under way with CBS executive vice president Hubbell Robinson for Coe to move to CBS. And on December 16, the *New York Times* noted these negotiations had been successfully concluded. Actually, Coe's agent, Priscilla Morgan, had held a series of clandestine dinner meetings with Robinson for months prior to Coe's departure from NBC. He refused to leave NBC without the assurance of a contract, and Robinson adhered to the unwritten rule in effect since the Paley raids of the early 1950s that the networks didn't raid each other's talent. But Morgan got Robinson to negotiate with her, and landed Coe a contract with CBS.

As Coe left NBC, many of the remaining dramatic anthologies were vanishing: *Alcoa-Goodyear Playhouse*, the successor to *Philco-Goodyear*, dropped live hour shows in September of 1957. *Kaiser Aluminum Hour* ended in June of 1957, as did *Robert Montgomery Presents*.

It wasn't just New York television that was changing, but New York itself: its postwar burst of enthusiasm was dissipating. Instead of the more individualized and elegantly crafted Moderne and Art Deco skyscrapers built before the war, towers in the International Style, large human filing cabinets of glass and steel, were appearing. In 1957, sailings of passenger liners from Manhattan reached their peak and began declining. Businesses (including the Dodgers and the Giants) were moving out; crime was moving in.

For Coe, it was a time for new directions. He had begun his first film, *The Left-Handed Gun*. Planning for *Two for the Seesaw*, his first Broadway play since 1953's *The Trip to Bountiful*, was under way. And live television drama would make one last stand, with Fred Coe right in the thick of it.

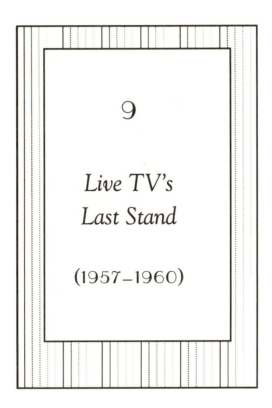

9

Live TV's
Last Stand

(1957–1960)

When Fred Coe started at NBC in 1945, television was a largely non-commercial medium in New York and four other cities. When he went to CBS in 1957, there were 496 TV stations across the country, and industry advertising revenues topped $1.3 billion. Coe rode the crest of this surge, but was starting to feel out of place. "[At the beginning], there was a tremendous vacuum," he told John Crosby of New York's *Herald-Tribune*. "If you wanted to read the Bible, it got on because there wasn't anything else. Today people come to me and say, 'How do I get on?' and I don't know what to tell them."

Along with its ad revenues, television's production costs were soaring as well—in the late forties, it cost $17,000 a week to produce *Philco Television Playhouse*; now, *Playhouse 90* cost ten times as much. "Television can't afford to have intelligent flops these days," Coe told the *New York Times*. "It astounds me sometimes what these shows cost. I'm a depression baby. I still find it hard to grasp the idea that a cup of coffee should cost more than a nickel. Television costs are just frightening."

Not that television had any interest in intelligent flops. Most New York-based anthology dramas had been cancelled or were on the way out. In the spring of 1957, *Sponsor* magazine observed, "As the TV season proceeds, more and more dramatic anthology shows are relying on straight melodrama. Behind this trend is the conviction among Madison Avenue program experts . . . that big audiences no longer are attracted by finely and soberly developed themes."

Leading broadcast historian Erik Barnouw has observed, however, that Madison Avenue program experts were usually more offended by the intelligence of these shows than the size of their audience:

> These plays [on anthology dramas] . . . held consistently high ratings. But one group hated them: the advertising profession. . . . [C]ommercials posed the same problems that [a Paddy] Chayefsky drama dealt with: people who feared failure in love and business. . . . But in the commercials, there was always a solution as clear-cut as the snap of a finger: the problem could be solved by a new pill, deodorant, toothpaste, shampoo. . . . Chayefsky and other anthology writers took these same problems and made them complicated. . . . All this was often convincing—that was the trouble. It made the commercial seem fraudulent.

This attitude was reflected by J. Edward Dean, director of advertising for DuPont. Anthology drama, he told the Federal Communications Commission, was not as "well-liked [in the advertising community] as other shows which were less stressful. The message that was taught through our commercials was not as well-learned as in those shows which were . . . lighter, happier—had more entertainment value."

Anthology drama did not always pull big audiences, though. After skewering the increasingly rampant mediocrity and commercialism of TV in the *New York Times*, Rod Serling acknowledged that his award-winning *Requiem for a Heavyweight* was one of the lowest-rated shows on *Playhouse 90* for the 1956–1957 season. Serious documentaries were also losing favor at the networks. In 1958, Edward R. Murrow's *See It Now* was cancelled by CBS president Louis G. Cowan, who had risen to prominence as a packager of quiz shows.

As the anthology drama declined, so did television production in New York. With their expansive Hollywood facilities, the networks now had the modern soundstages they lacked in New York. Coe professed to be unconcerned about Hollywood's growing role as a television production center, telling the New York *Daily News*, "I think the most deplorable thing about television is . . . more and more film, no matter where it's made. That's why I believe TV isn't exciting anymore. People are being mesmerized by an avalanche of celluloid."

But in reality, Coe was a militant New Yorker. When UPI's Vernon Scott suggested to him that New York's "downbeat, back-alley melodrama" might have been responsible for the death of live TV, he was "excited to fury," Scott wrote. "You can't blame a city for that," Coe said. "The element of conflict is the very heart of drama."

For all the convenience of TV's new West Coast sound stages, though, it was something Hollywood made outdoors that played a leading role in killing live dramatic anthologies: the western. Of the ten highest-rated shows during the 1958–1959 season, eight were westerns. Some, like *Gunsmoke*, were impressive. But most of the "oaters" were more like *The Rough Riders*, of which one critic said, "The best acting was by the Rocky Mountains." A *Variety* headline of the period concisely summarizes the role of westerns in dispatching anthology drama: "'Live' TV: It Went Thataway." Despite the worsening conditions for serious television drama, though, some superb shows would still get aired—many of them due to the efforts of Fred Coe.

Like many other talented TV professionals, however, he started to hedge his bets and began working in other media. In early 1957 he began his first feature film. Made for Warner Bros., it was, ironically, a western. Why did he make *The Left-Handed Gun*, his first film, in a genre he would later deride as the "horse-ass opera"? Westerns were popular, so it was a sensible marketing decision. And by making a western art film, Coe might have reasoned he could point up the shallowness of most Hollywood oat-mongers.

The film originated as *The Death of Billy the Kid*, a *Philco-Goodyear* episode that aired in 1955. Written by Gore Vidal, it was directed by Robert Mulligan and starred Paul Newman. The film version, again starring Newman, was directed by Arthur Penn, and written by Leslie Stevens.

Stevens found Coe a capable script editor, and a true, old-fashioned Southern gentleman. Gore Vidal, on the other hand, charges Coe with underhanded conduct on the film. Vidal says he and Paul Newman set up the film, hiring Coe as the producer, but that Coe then brought in his own people while Vidal was in New York. Vidal's memories are quite specific, even to the point of Coe's visiting him at Hollywood's Bel-Air Hotel to apologize for what he had done. Arthur Penn, on the other hand, recalls that Vidal was simply unavailable at the time.

Both Coe and Penn were television veterans at this point, but were still learning about films. Neither man learned completely on this one: for all of its spacious on-location vistas, *Gun* still has the cramped feel of a television soundstage, something several critics noted. *The Left-Handed Gun*, released in the spring of 1958, is a somewhat pretentious art-house western with a psychologically troubled antihero and a lot of philosophizing about the myth of the old West, along with the requisite amount of gunplay.

To be fair to Coe and Penn, Warners did not give them final cut, so it's hard to assign blame with any precision. The film produced mixed responses from the critics: the *Los Angeles Examiner* said it made for "very lively viewing"; New York's *Cue* magazine, on the other hand, sneered the film was just "[an] example of sniffling celluloid sentimentality dripping goo and violence in equal proportions."

• • •

A few months after filming ended on *The Left-Handed Gun*, Leslie Stevens was relaxing poolside at the Beverly Hills Hotel with a young, obscure actress named Anne Bancroft. She had been offered a role in a two-character Broadway play and wanted his opinion of the script. Bancroft started to read a scene, but the Southern California sun lulled Stevens into drowsiness, and he drifted off to sleep, waking only at the end.

"What do you think?" Bancroft asked.

"I found it kind of boring," said Stevens, who hadn't heard a word.

"Fred Coe wants me to do it," she said, "and I think I will."

"Coe's for real," Stevens said. "But if you want me to endorse the script I can't, because I didn't hear enough."

This worried Bancroft, but fortunately, not enough to dissuade her. The play was William Gibson's *Two for the Seesaw*, and it would make her a star. It would also restart Coe's career as a Broadway producer. For Fred Coe, connecting with *Seesaw* was pure serendipity.

William Gibson was a friend of Arthur Penn's. Early in 1957, he read Penn and his wife a scene from his work in progress about a brief encounter between Jerry Ryan, an emotionally buttoned-down lawyer from Nebraska going through a personal crisis and Gittel Mosca, a free-spirited young Jewish woman from the Bronx. Arthur and Peggy Penn encouraged Gibson to finish it, but when he did, his agent Leah Salisbury was unable to market it.

"She took it to all the big fancy producers in New York and got rejected by everybody," Penn recalls. "'Who wants to do a two-character play?' And her opinion was you had to get a name director, but Bill insisted on me. So there we were with this good play and nobody wanting to produce it." One weekend in the early spring of 1957, Coe spent the weekend at the Bucks County farmhouse of his agent, Priscilla Morgan. He took with him a copy of the script Penn gave him to read and, upon his return, said he wanted to produce it.

Since neither Coe, Penn, nor Gibson were household names, the play would need two stars to get financial backing. But after auditioning Bancroft at the suggestion of actor Richard Basehart, Coe felt she was perfect for the part, despite her lack of marquee value. There was now added pressure to find a bankable star for the male role. But there were no takers: Van Heflin, Paul Newman, Jack Palance, Jack Lemmon, Eli Wallach, Don Murray, and Robert Preston all rejected it.

In *The Seesaw Log*, Gibson says Leah Salisbury first suggested Henry

Fonda; Arthur Penn says it was Coe's idea. In any case, Coe did the work to reel him in. During the spring of 1957, the script was sent to Fonda, and he expressed interest, but had one concern: the man's role wasn't written as well as the woman's. Fonda then became the subject of a Fred Coe charm offensive. As reported in *Fonda: My Life* by Howard Teichmann, Coe called Fonda, telling him, "I've got a girl who'll be absolutely wonderful. Let me bring her over and have the two of you read together."

"Jesus, don't do that," Fonda said. "If she doesn't get the part, she'll think it's because I didn't like her."

"Please, let me bring her to your house," Coe pressed. "The author, Bill Gibson, will come too. You and the girl will read an act."

Fonda tried to get out of it, but Coe wouldn't be denied. A reading was held at Fonda's residence on 74th Street. He was impressed with Bancroft and the script, but repeated his concerns about the man's role and said he wouldn't decide until the play had been rewritten. He then left for a summer honeymoon on the Riviera with his third wife, Countess Afdera Franchetti.

Sometime in August, Coe sent him the first two acts of *Two for the Seesaw*, which Gibson had revised. Two weeks of silence followed. Coe sent another telegram. This apparently tipped the balance, and Fonda cabled Coe: "Start it rolling. I am yours. Fonda." Although it featured a brilliant script, one of the best directors in postwar America, a genius-caliber producer, and a great leading lady, *Two for the Seesaw* never would have jelled if Henry Fonda hadn't come aboard.

On the basis of Fonda's telegram, Coe was able to get the Booth Theater, the best small theater on Broadway, finance the show, and book out-of-town theaters in Washington, D.C., and Philadelphia. But Fonda still had concerns about the script, and Bill Gibson now had concerns about Fonda. Watching him at rehearsals in New York before the show went on the road, Gibson didn't see the self-mocking irony he intended for Jerry Ryan. When Arthur Penn passed that along to Fonda, he snapped, "Well, if *that* doesn't show, maybe I should be replaced in the part."

Even by Gibson's admission, the writing *was* better for the female character than the male. Also, Fonda's stage and screen persona was that of a decent, salt-of-the-earth American who shows uncommon grace under pressure. Jerry Ryan, for all his good qualities, is a whiner with an impressive capacity for self-deception, something he's aware of and detests, but can do little to change. There was a fundamental mismatch of actor and role, but without Fonda there was no show.

As Fonda's discontent grew in Washington, the play's first out-of-town stop, Gibson became increasingly anxious. While his anxiety ratcheted up, though, Coe stayed cool. "His manner was . . . firm and undismayed," Gibson writes in *The Seesaw Log*. "[He was] a man who could stand against me; a man who could stand against me was one I could lean upon." Gibson later noted that Coe's surprisingly broad knowledge of the theater was as important as his equanimity. "Fred was the best producer I ever worked with," Gibson says. "His conception of the role was someone who knew enough about every area of the show to challenge the experts in those areas: the set designer, the director, the author. That made him the center of operations."

But as differences hardened between Fonda on one hand and Gibson, Penn, and himself on the other, Coe's equanimity started to fray. "Fred was in control of his temper most of the time," Gibson recalls. "But once in a while, when it got loose, it was really astonishing. You would hear him yell like a banshee."

One day in Philadelphia's Forrest Theater, Coe and Fonda went at it. "Fonda was extremely nervous and rather impertinent to me," Arthur Penn recalls. "Fred, from the back of the theater, started screaming, 'Hank, if you want outta this play, you can get outta this play right now.' And he marched down the aisle." Just as Coe reached the stage, general manager Joe Harris was returning from New York in high spirits: the Shuberts had granted them the loan they needed to continue into New York. As he opened the door to the theater, there was Coe yelling at Henry Fonda, saying "*Don't* call the director *boy* anymore!" Harris looked at the check and thought, "Well, I won't be needing this anymore."

Although Fonda emerges as the heavy in *The Seesaw Log*, one participant in the show offers another point of view. "Bill did write a book, but I think everyone could have written a book," says stage manager Porter Van Zandt. "Fonda did not agree with a lot of the things he was asked to do on-stage, but he was a professional." Regardless of whose fault it was, everyone's nerves were wearing dangerously thin. "I had watched men more harrowed by daily misery, but not outside of [asylum] walls and responsibly functioning," Gibson writes in *The Seesaw Log*.

Despite all the backstage angst and numerous rewrites, New York critics loved the show. When *Seesaw* opened on January 16, 1958, Brooks Atkinson of the *New York Times* said it had "a tender style of writing and a beautiful little story to tell." Robert Coleman of the *Daily Mirror* said to "rush to the Booth box office to obtain two for 'The Seesaw.'" It was sheer inspiration on Coe's part, he added, to sign Anne Bancroft. John Chapman of the *Daily News* praised Fonda and Bancroft and gave Coe "credit for taking a big risk on a very small play."

But Fonda's concerns about Gittel Mosca having better lines than Jerry Ryan proved justified. Richard Watts Jr. of the *New York Post* said "Henry Fonda is naturally excellent," but added Anne Bancroft was "an exhilirating surprise," with Fonda hard-pressed to keep from seeming like her straight man. It was reminiscent of a scene in Philadelphia, where the show's principals gathered in a restaurant to hear the review from the local CBS radio station. "I don't mean Fonda's role is inferior," the reviewer said, to which Fonda yelled, "You just mean it's inferior."

• • •

When Coe, Penn, Gibson, and Bancroft were reunited nearly two years later on *The Miracle Worker*, they had a Broadway success under their belts and were no longer locked in combat with Henry Fonda. As a result, most of the drama in Gibson's powerful play about social worker Annie Sullivan (Bancroft) teaching blind and deaf young Helen Keller (Patty Duke) to communicate took place onstage.

Visiting the show at the Locust Theater in Philadelphia just before its Broadway opening, Maurice Zolotow of the *New York Times* noted, "In 1957 [on *Seesaw*], Mr. Gibson looked haggard and desperate. During the interview, he kept drinking straight bourbon. Now, in [October] 1959, he was a different man—calm, serene, almost imperturbable." Director Arthur Penn, he said, "was also in an urbane mood, full of bonhomie, as opposed to the mass of jangled nerves he had been."

And in her dressing room, he noted, Anne Bancroft "was cool, calm and utterly collected. Two years before, she had been in the throes of laryngitis, insomnia, and gastritis." Coe was also in lighter spirits. Joking with Judith Crist of the *Herald-Tribune* about his fear that ten-year-old Patty Duke would grow out of her role, he said, "We told her to go home and smoke cigars and cigarettes to stunt her growth."

Although not as tempest-tossed as *Two for the Seesaw*, *The Miracle Worker* would need some luck to get off the ground, and it got some from the weather. In Philadelphia, there wasn't a strong advance sale. Anne Bancroft was a star in New York from *Seesaw*, but not yet a national star. And none of the play's principals had strong marquee value.

Melvyn Douglas was starring in another play having tryouts in Philadelphia. But one hot afternoon, Douglas passed out at the matinee. The evening performance was cancelled, and management provided tickets to *The Miracle Worker*. "So now this audience came in, and they didn't know what to expect," Penn fondly recalls. "'What the hell is this *Miracle Worker*?'" Well, they sat there, and by the time it was over, they were stunned and weeping and terribly emotional. Lines formed at the telephones in the lobby, people calling their friends. And in a very short time, we sold out the entire run in Philadelphia."

One of the knottiest problems in rehearsals was the food-fight scene. A bitter test of wills in which Annie Sullivan teaches the still-wild young Helen to maintain a semblance of dining-room etiquette (it concludes with her now-famous line to Captain Keller, "The room's a wreck, but her napkin is folded"). Commenting on its realistic and roughhouse nature,

Brooks Atkinson dourly observed, "Sooner or later, Miss Bancroft or Miss Duke is going to get banged up and carted off to the hospital."

While that never happened, both actresses would earn purple hearts in the scene: Bancroft was out of commission for eight days during rehearsals because of a bone bruise on her right foot incurred after running at full speed across the stage and crashing into a fallen chair. Patty Duke suffered a chipped tooth. ("The child was all tensed up, clenching her teeth to await my slaps," Bancroft told the *New York Times*. "Since then, she has relaxed.") And mashed buns were chosen as the food eaten, spit out, and hurled around after the original entree, scrambled eggs, made the stage so slippery that Penn told the *Times*, "Patty and Annie took such spills it stopped my heart dead. The stuff is as bad as banana peels."

When it reached Broadway, *The Miracle Worker* did not slip on any critical banana peels. Richard Watts, Jr., of the *New York Post* called it "an emotional play on a painfully touching subject without going in for sentimental tear-jerking." As for the battle royal between Annie Sullivan and Helen Keller, he added, "That these strenuous brawls never seem embarrassing or tastelessly comic . . . is a tribute to the earnestness of Mr. Gibson's play and the skill of Arthur Penn's direction, but chiefly to the sincerity and truth of Anne Bancroft and 10-year-old Patty Duke."

Most reviews were in this glowing vein. Even two that weren't, however, found something to like. Brooks Atkinson of the *New York Times* said there was disarray on the stage, the result of the play's having "the loose narrative technique of a TV script," but raved over the performances of Bancroft and Patty Duke. And Robert Coleman of the *Daily Mirror* said, "We doubt that 'The Miracle Worker' has outstanding literary merit, that it will be a distinguished addition to permanent collections, but it is magnificent theatre." As he often did in television, Coe had taken two successive shows with disparate themes and moods and molded them into successes.

• • •

During this period, Coe also made his first show for CBS. *The Red Mill*, a *DuPont Show of the Month*, airing on April 19, 1958, marked an inauspicious start for his CBS career. The romantic musical was directed by Delbert Mann, and featured Donald O'Connor as a lackey to a pair of overbearing Hollywood stars (Mike Nichols and Elaine May) who breaks away from them after falling in love with a Dutch hotel keeper (Shirley Jones). The show was not a critical success. "Robert Alan Aurthur's adaptation of 'The Red Mill' will probably find a place in contemporary video history as the first major [dramatic] production done almost entirely on videotape and as Fred Coe's first effort for CBS-TV after all those years of identification with NBC," *Variety* observed. "But there its claim to fame will end."

The script was one of Aurthur's less successful efforts. And the show was a technical nightmare: the cameramen had gone on strike. "It was a mess," recalls Bo Goldman, Coe's assistant on the show. "We had Delbert Mann, an Academy Award winner for *Marty*, and Fred, the D. W. Griffith of dramatic television, and the cameramen were salesmen."

Just as Coe had made the transition from iconoscope cameras to the image orthicon in the late 1940s, he now pioneered in videotaping. Today, digital electronics allow numerous and complex edits without even touching a tape. That was not so in 1958. "We taped in long segments of ten to fifteen minutes to avoid editing to the greatest extent possible," says Delbert Mann. "Tape editing consisted of a cut with a razor blade across the tape. It would take the technician thirty minutes to do a single splice. And when the show went on the air, each splice threw the network out of sync." A technician with a long-handled screwdriver stood by. Each time a splice passed through the video tape recorder, the picture shattered on screens around the country. The technician reached in with his screwdriver and advanced the tape to bring the picture back.

Although *Variety* was unaware of it, *The Red Mill* chalked up another historical footnote, one revealing Fred Coe's remarkable fertility. If you lived in New York in the spring of 1958, you could go to the movies and watch *The Left-Handed Gun*, produced by Fred Coe. On Broadway, you could see *Two for the Seesaw*, produced by Fred Coe. Or, on April 19, you could stay home and watch the television broadcast of *The Red Mill*, produced by Fred Coe. Perhaps no other American producer has accomplished this near-simultaneous triple play.

• • •

Playhouse 90 was the last hurrah for the Golden Age of Television. It was conceived by CBS programming vice president Hubbell Robinson as a prestige vehicle for the network, and still featured live TV drama, although increasingly, shows would be taped. During its first two seasons, 1956–1958, it was single-handedly produced by Martin Manulis, who aired such stellar shows as Rod Serling's *Requiem for a Heavyweight* and the original version of William Gibson's *The Miracle Worker* before Coe took it to Broadway and the movies.

When Manulis left in 1958 to produce feature films, Hubbell Robinson brought in three producers to replace him: John Houseman, Herbert Brodkin, and Fred Coe. The show aired from Hollywood's Television City, and for the first time, Coe's TV base of operations was the west coast.

Although *Playhouse 90* was the best dramatic show in the waning years of the Golden Age, it also demonstrated how the iron triangle of sponsors, ad agencies, and networks were gaining the upper hand in television. Irritatingly, the ninety-minute show had five commercial breaks (hour dramatic shows only had two). Tacitly acknowledging sponsors' growing power, Coe told the *New York Times*, "This is not the great temple of art in which to bring up every controversial subject. I don't believe television is the place to foist issues that are tinder boxes."

For *Playhouse 90*, Coe again chose Bo Goldman as his assistant. One of the first things Goldman noted about his boss was that he did not dress for success. "Fred would buy expensive clothes sometimes. Periodically, he made these sweeps through Brooks Brothers," Goldman says. "But whether it was brand new or not, he was always rumpled, which is deeply endearing."

He also learned his boss couldn't bear solitude. In the summer of 1958, they were frequently stuck in New York while their wives were out on Long Island. "We tramped the streets on those hot summer nights and went to restaurants like Gino's," Goldman recalls. "He said, 'Can you stay at the Yale Club with me?' So he got a double room with twin beds," Goldman says, laughing. "We got into our respective twin beds and talked—it was like kids at camp, laughing."

One of the first shows Coe and Goldman prepared that summer was *The Plot to Kill Stalin*, a docudrama by David Karp starring Melvyn Douglas as Stalin; E. G. Marshall as Beria, head of the KGB; Oscar Homolka as Khrushchev; and Eli Wallach as Stalin's loyal toady Poskrobychev. It focuses on efforts in 1953 by chief lieutenants of Soviet leader Joseph Stalin (including Nikita Khrushchev, in 1958 the leader of the Soviet Union) to assassinate him because they feared he was planning a new wave of purges that might include them. Coe picked *Stalin* as *Playhouse 90*'s 1958–1959 season premiere. It would cause a sensation not only in American television, but in international politics.

To direct *Stalin*, Coe picked his old friend Delbert Mann, who made a fateful editorial suggestion. At the show's climax, Stalin calls Khrushchev, Beria, and another top Soviet official, Malenkov (Thomas Gomez), into his office to denounce them for plotting against him. During the meeting, he flies into a violent rage and suffers a stroke. Molotov (Luther Adler) tries to bring Stalin a glass of water with his medication. In early versions of the script, Khrushchev blocks Molotov's path, signing Stalin's death warrant. Mann felt this wasn't strong enough, and instead had Oscar Homolka as Khrushchev brusquely knock the glass of water out of Molotov's hand.

"The point I wanted to make was that the emerging leader was Khrushchev," Mann says. "[Until then], he had been a subsidiary figure, a figure of some fun and jest. I wanted now for him to suddenly take [center] stage. Well, Khrushchev was the premier right at that moment, and here he was being portrayed as the man most responsible for the murder of Stalin. When Fred came to rehearsal two or three days before we went into the studio, he was really quite shook up when we played the whole thing. I made a plea for it and Fred, after some debate, said, 'Okay, let's do it that way.'"

The Plot to Kill Stalin, which aired on September 25, 1958, does an effective job of re-creating the atmosphere of tension, fear, and intrigue of Stalin's rule. Critical reaction, though, was mixed: *The New Republic* praised its audacity, while *Variety* said it failed to create mounting tension, having a "johnny one-note plateau." Jack Gould of the *New York Times* praised the performances and Delbert Mann's direction, but questioned the wisdom of "showing as virtually a murderer the head of a foreign state with which this country maintains formal if very strained relations," adding, "it would seem questionable judgment for a television program to fan the flames of discord with a highly provocative hypothesis."

And one strident critic of the show had yet to weigh in: the government of the Soviet Union. Eleven days after *Stalin* aired, Mikhail Menshikov, the Soviet Union's ambassador to the United States, filed a protest with the State Department. "That was a filthy slander against the Soviet Union and the Soviet government," he told reporters. "This kind of slanderous attack is incompatible with international standards and inadvisable in normal diplomatic relations." Two days later, the Soviet government announced the expulsion of CBS's Moscow correspondent.

A *New York Times* editorial harshly criticized the Soviets for attempting to censor free-world media. Jack Gould wrote, "One stupid mistake [the show] has now been matched by a worse one [the expulsion]." The Overseas Press Club sent a note of protest to Khrushchev. He wasn't impressed: a CBS engineer scheduled to visit the Soviet Union suddenly was unable to get a visa. It was an ironic postscript to Coe's comment that television wasn't the place to foist "tinder box" issues. He had tried to conform to television's increasingly timorous nature, but his dramatic instincts had gotten the best of him.

• • •

Like many writers, David Karp would fall under Coe's spell, later writing, "Fred always seemed to carry with him a kind of promissory excitement. If he was involved, it was going to be wonderful, magical. . . . Fred Coe was the orchestra tuning up, the lights going down, the promise of something magical to come."

Surprisingly, Karp also regarded Coe with a measure of condescension: "Fred was, in some ways, a kind of gentle and sweet semi-literate." Nor was Karp alone: *Mr. Peepers* writer Everett Greenbaum noted that "even though a graduate of the Yale Drama School, [Coe] was semi-literate." These comments, by writers whose scripts Coe often improved, may reveal more about their attitude toward his Southern roots than his education.

Bill Nichols, one of Coe's chief lieutenants at NBC, grew up along Philadelphia's exclusive Main Line. "Southerners were sort of frowned on generally as being slow, sloppy, and lazy up here," he says, pointing to his head. "Fred was not up with the pace of New York City. He moved slowly, thought things through rather carefully, and would refuse to be hurried."

Although New York was Coe's adoptive home, he never lost his Southern ways. Describing those ways in a 1926 essay, Donald Davidson, a member of the Nashville-based "Fugitives" literary group of the 1920s, noted of the prototypical Southerner, "He is known to be hot-headed, intense, yet generous in a pinch. He is reputed to be lazy, but this reputation possibly comes from his comfortable personal philosophy which accepts life as something to be enjoyed. He is affirmative in what he does and says, not reticent like the traditional Yankee, and this affirmativeness of character . . . is often disturbingly pugnacious."

But even while labelling him "semi-literate," Everett Greenbaum acknowledged that Coe sprang from a rich literary soil, adding, "One felt in him the swamp ferment which had produced Tennessee Williams, Truman Capote, and Carson McCullers." Roger O. Hirson, another of Coe's writers on *Playhouse 90*, was not taken in by Coe's languorous nature. "He was deceptively brilliant," Hirson recalls. "At his house in East Hampton, he would sit by the pool. He was not physically nimble. In some ways, he was like a slug, almost. But he would sit there with his eyes half closed [while discussing a script] and sort of wander around the subject until he came up with some incredible nugget."

For Bo Goldman, Coe's Southern manner took several forms. There was Fred Coe, the wily, shrewd country boy, especially when pitted against authority. There was the Fred Coe who joined the Yale Club so he could hate the Eastern establishment from the inside. And there was the Fred Coe who couldn't abide pretense, but patiently allowed it to play itself out.

"He had probably the best bullshit detector of anyone I've ever known," Goldman says. "A lot of people have that capacity, and their immediate response is 'That's bullshit!' or 'Fuck you.' Not Fred. Fred would wait. He just loved to give you enough rope to hang yourself and you were just left there twisting in the wind, choking on your own words. And then he'd smile and walk away. That's Southern style, you know?"

Coe's style with his writers, directors, and actors, however, was more commonly one of Southern hospitality. John Frankenheimer says Coe exuded the feeling that everything was going to be okay. "He gave us a climate in which we could function creatively, and that certainly is the role of a producer," says Frankenheimer, who went on to direct such films as *Birdman of Alcatraz*, *The Manchurian Candidate*, and *Seven Days in May*. He directed four *Playhouse 90*s for Coe, the first of which was JP Miller's *The*

Days of Wine and Roses. Starring Cliff Robertson and Piper Laurie as a young couple who fall in love while struggling with alcoholism, the show owes its birth to Fred Coe.

• • •

Following the success of *The Rabbit Trap* on *Philco-Goodyear*, JP Miller went to Hollywood to write the movie version. It went badly: Miller strongly opposed the casting of Ernest Borgnine in the lead, but Hollywood producers were not as interested in his opinions as Fred Coe had been. When Miller returned to New York in the spring of 1958, he told his wife he was going to quit writing, move to Riverhead on the north fork of Long Island, and become a fisherman. Before his wife had to adjust to a lifestyle of cleaning his gill nets, though, he bumped into Coe, who encouraged him to submit ideas for *Playhouse 90*.

Soon afterwards, Miller called Coe in East Hampton. It was early in the morning, but Miller figured Coe would still be awake and probably drinking, which he was. Miller told him his idea, about two young people who like to drink. They love each other and get married, but the bottle becomes more important to each of them than they are to each other. "Pappy, I like it," Coe said. "Write it!"

When the show went into rehearsal, Miller felt things weren't going well. But unlike his recent experience in Hollywood, he now had a recourse with Coe. "Now, Piper Laurie is a great actress," Miller says. "In rehearsals, she played the drunk scene so well that Frankenheimer just let her go. She knocked you out playing a drunk lady.

"I kept saying to John, 'She's too drunk. She's playing into the drunkenness.' But John said, 'Listen, she knows what she's doing.' Well, I went to Fred. He didn't like to come into the rehearsals until toward the end, because he didn't want to stultify people. But I said, 'Fred, you'd better come in and look at a run-through, because I gotta tell you we're getting into some problems here.'

"He came in for a run-through," Miller continues. "They played it magnificently, but it was a show about alcoholics—it wasn't a love story. Fred sat there and watched the whole thing. He got up and lit a cigarette. John came over and said, 'Fred, what did you think? Did you ever see a drunk scene like that in your *life*?' And Fred said, 'Very good, John. Look—you've got the wine. Now see if you can get the roses.' And he turned around and walked away." Pausing in wonderment, Miller says, "That was all it took. It triggered a return to the love story."

The show was immensely popular with critics when it aired October 2, 1958. *The New Republic* called it "original and effective." *Variety* praised Laurie and Robertson for their "brilliant portrayals," adding: "Under John

Frankenheimer's direction, both avoided the conventionally maudlin drunk takeoffs for probing and wholly human characterizations." And, it might have further added, under Fred Coe's production.

Coe was also a great fan of the show. In a subsequent letter to a CBS executive he praised it in terms which sum up the profoundly optimistic philosophy of life that enabled him to encourage so many dramatic artists. Refuting the charge that it represented downbeat theater, Coe wrote, "*The Days of Wine and Roses* makes a strong positive statement: no matter to what depths the individual may sink, he always contains within himself the elements for survival; man is the instrument of his own salvation."

Days of Wine and Roses was not just an artistic success, but a financial one: Procter & Gamble's decision to spend $1 million for advertising on *Playhouse 90* during the fourth quarter of 1958 was a direct result of its being impressed by *The Plot to Kill Stalin* and *Days of Wine and Roses*.

It was a good thing for CBS that Procter & Gamble bought in before they saw Coe's next two efforts. *The Long March* was Roger O. Hirson's adaptation of William Styron's tale of military oppressiveness. Airing on October 16, 1958, it starred Sterling Hayden as a Prussian-style marine commander and Jack Carson as a reservist called up during the Korean War who snaps under the pressure of dealing with Hayden.

Coe and director Delbert Mann chalked up a technological first on the show: the first on-location taping for a television drama. To get realism into the forced march which is the show's climactic sequence, they took the cast and crew into the Santa Monica Mountains. "We were up on Mulholland Drive, worrying about whether there were rattlesnakes," recalls Adri Butler, the show's script supervisor. None appeared, but the show itself was snakebitten.

"In the first scene, Sterling Hayden poses a question in this Marine Corps classroom and Jack Carson's first line was, 'Sir, I'm not a student of tank tactics,'" Hirson recalls. "Well, that was a mistake. Because once he said, 'tank-tank-tac-ta . . . ,' we were off to the races." (*Variety* kindly described Carson's performance as "fuzzy.")

While none of the actors on *Word from a Sealed-Off Box* imploded, there was another problem: it was dull. The show starred Maria Schell as a Dutch resistance fighter kept in solitary confinement by the Nazis. Airing on October 30, it was adapted by Mayo Simon from the memoirs of Henriette Roosenburg, and directed by Franklin Schaffner. The problem was that a drama about a person stuck alone in a room for the better part of an hour and a half did not make for riveting television.

"Fred Coe, who ordinarily infuses his production with an electric intensity, failed to do so," *Variety* noted. Using the Roosenburg story was Goldman's idea. So was the choice of Simon as the show's writer. Yet Coe didn't berate him when the show failed. "He would never do anything like that,"

Goldman says. "He never fixed blame—he'd never do that to an under-
ling. That's what was classy about him."

Three weeks later Coe produced another show based on a supposedly
unproduceable story. Unlike *Sealed-Off Box*, though, it was a triumph. William Faulkner's *Old Man* is the story of a prison-farm convict sent out in a
rowboat to rescue a woman stranded during the Mississippi River flood of
1927. (The river, whose brooding presence dominates the show, is the Old
Man of the title.) Horton Foote's adaptation was directed by John Frankenheimer, and starred Sterling Hayden as the convict, Geraldine Page as
the woman he rescues.

Anyone seeking to turn Faulkner's story into a television drama had two
main obstacles to overcome: conveying both the action and philosophical
flavor of Faulkner's work, and realistically dramatizing in a television studio a show that takes place mostly on water. The first problem was solved
by Foote's sensitive yet unsentimental script. The second called for a lot of
elbow grease from the maintenance crew at Television City.

"We built the Mississippi River on Stage 43," CBS executive Charles
Cappleman recalls. Covering most of one soundstage was a tank just deep
enough to float the rowboat Sterling and Page spend much of the show in.
Technicians also rigged up the stage for the show's periodic rainstorms. A
second stage was used for dry-land sequences. "Everybody said that show
couldn't be done," John Frankenheimer recalls. "The whole thing was just
a nightmare. CBS thought the whole building was going to come down,
and shored it up with big beams underneath."

The show is deeply moving, and has a strongly allegorical feeling. *Variety* was ecstatic. "The gifted Fred Coe-John Frankenheimer combo, aided
by a brilliant Horton Foote adaptation, came up with a memorable 90
minutes of overwhelming drama," it said. The review also praised the performances of Hayden and Page, and Walter Scott Herndon, the show's art
director, for his "almost superrealistic sets."

Coe and Frankenheimer then tackled the work of another Nobel Prize
winner: Ernest Hemingway's *For Whom the Bell Tolls*, adapted by Hemingway biographer and confidant A. E. Hotchner. Airing in two parts on
March 12 and 19, 1959, it had an all-star cast and would prove an even
more difficult project than *The Old Man*. Jason Robards played Robert
Jordan, the American schoolteacher who fights with the rebels in the
Spanish Civil War; Maria Schell was Maria, the peasant girl he falls in
love with. The rebel troupe included Maureen Stapleton, Eli Wallach,
Nehemiah Persoff, and Steven Hill. Another of the rebels, Nicholas Cola-
santo, would later distinguish himself in a different part more typical of a
later era—as Coach, the addle-brained jock bartender on *Cheers*.

Produced in New York in order to draw on Broadway actors, the show
was originally set to air on one evening, but when Coe felt he couldn't

capture Hemingway's novel in ninety minutes minus commercials, he got CBS to do it as a two-parter. Rather than doubling the amount of work a show normally required, though, this multiplied it.

On March 11, the day before the taped version of Part One aired, John P. Shanley of the *New York Times* wrote: "By tomorrow, the world's weariest group of actors should be the 'For Whom the Bell Tolls' company." He noted the show's five weeks' rehearsal time (versus three for most *Playhouse 90's*), and that the show was being "prepared with the utmost seriousness . . . in an atmosphere of disciplined dedication." As CBS publicist John Walsh said, "In this play, all of the characters are supposed to be under the strain of war. When you see the actors at the end of their day's work, they're tired. For a troupe that's supposed to look haggard, they can't miss."

Rehearsal sessions were punishing: one stretched from 9 A.M. Sunday to 4 A.M. Monday because a set had to be rebuilt after a motorcycle mishap. The main square of Madrid was a complicated set with a lot of storefronts. In one scene, a motorcycle comes rushing up and a messenger runs in with a dispatch. Frankenheimer asked one of the extras if he could drive a motorcycle, and he said yes.

"So he gets costumed and put on a motorcycle," A. E. Hotchner recalls. "The cameras are rolling and John says 'Go!' The extra goes careening up to the front of this set, goes right through it, and brings down the whole set. The motorcycle is on its side, wheels spinning, and the extra's in a heap against the set. And John says, 'I thought you knew how to drive a motorcycle.' He said, 'I know how to drive it, I just don't know how to stop it.'"

With many stars, elaborate sets, a long rehearsal period, and the many taping retakes Frankenheimer's perfectionism required, the show did not come cheap. A typical *Playhouse 90* cost $130,000. *For Whom the Bell Tolls* was budgeted at $300,000, and final estimates of the show's cost range from $400,000 to $500,000. Coe was sensitive to cost pressures, but got into a fight with a network official when he called to complain about the overrun.

With the show running overtime and over budget, confronted by balky stars, cost-conscious executives, and marathon taping sessions, Coe turned where he usually did in times of stress: to Alice. "He started to drink, and disappeared," Frankenheimer recalls with irritation. "He ended up with his ex-wife down in Florida. In the midst of this chaos, he wasn't there. The wrath of CBS was all over me and Ed Hotchner. It was fierce!"

Hotchner has no memory of Coe disappearing. "CBS didn't turn any wrath on me," he adds. "They were furious with Frankenheimer because he was running up such a bill on them."

Critical response to the show was mixed. Part One, which leads up to the guerrillas' battle with the Spanish government forces, "brilliantly fulfilled the hopes that it would be one of the television medium's finest accomplishments," Jack Gould of the *New York Times* raved. Saying Coe and Frankenheimer's work showed integrity and artistry, he added, "thanks to performances by Maria Schell and Jason Robards Jr., the first installment of A. E. Hotchner's dramatization radiated the ecstasy and agony of love under the shadow of death." While calling it impressive, *Variety* found the 1943 movie version more compelling, saying the show was too studio-bound, a criticism it voiced of Part Two as well.

One viewer who didn't share *Variety*'s concern about production values was Ernest Hemingway. In *Variety*, he said the look of Coe's show was more authentic than that of the film, which he described as "Abercrombie and Fitch out of Helena Rubinstein."

• • •

At the house on Baiting Hollow Road in East Hampton, parties went on late into the night, and guests came and went as always. Increasingly, though, Joyce's skills as a hostess were tested by Coe's behavior. "I thought she was terrific," Roger O. Hirson says. "She was smart and attractive and very good with Fred. He could have a couple of drinks and get kinda boisterous."

Joyce apparently had other anxieties about Coe. Once she called Mab Ashforth, Bo Goldman's wife, to ask where Fred and Bo were. Ashforth said she didn't know, and there was a pause on the line. "And you don't care, do you?" Joyce asked. "You don't worry about where he might be?"

Still, the Coes and their guests passed many pleasant times together. When William Gibson and his wife and son visited the Coes in East Hampton, they went rowing in a backwater lagoon, looking for frogs. And an event Joyce must have hoped would curb Coe's boisterousness lay ahead: the birth of their first child. On May 14, 1959, Sue Ann Coe was born.

Her arrival, however, war apparently preceded by a vigorous debate. "Fred said Joyce wanted to have children and he already had his children," Alice Coe recalls. "He didn't say why he finally relented. But after Sue was born, he said to me, 'Well, now I've given her what she wants. I hope she's satisfied.'" But, Alice would later reflect, perhaps Joyce wasn't the only one who made this mistake. He was so married to his work, Alice thought, perhaps he never should have married or had children at all.

• • •

Once again, Coe made his first *Playhouse 90* of the new television season a political drama by David Karp. *The Hidden Image*, airing November 12, 1959, starred Franchot Tone and was directed by Boris Sagal. Depicting the downfall of a big-city mayor's powerful aide, it was based on the case of President Eisenhower's chief of staff, Sherman Adams.

Coe decided to do *The Hidden Image* live, not out of Luddite distaste for the new technology (increasingly, *Playhouse 90* was taped), but because he felt it would benefit from the heightened tension of a live show. CBS executives tried to talk him out of it. Technicians used to the safety net of videotape were on edge. But the show came off flawlessly, and there was rejoicing on the soundstage after the call of "Fade to black."

"The crew went nuts because they hadn't done this in a while. Everybody got excited in the control room," Bo Goldman recalls. "And Boris was sort of preening. Everybody was congratulating him. And Fred—I remember this because I was the only one who heard—said, 'Well, I've created another monster.' This was a side of Fred which I think he very carefully shielded, that he felt he had created these people like Tad Mosel and John Frankenheimer and so on. It was only in the heat of the moment that he showed it, and I never really saw it again."

On *The Tunnel*, airing December 10, 1959, Coe worked for the last time with two of his greatest "monsters," director Delbert Mann and writer David Shaw. A Civil War drama, *The Tunnel* stars Richard Boone as a cynical, world-weary Union officer and Rip Torn as the idealistic young officer who convinces him the siege of Petersburg, Virginia, can be broken by digging a tunnel to outflank Confederate lines.

Except for an irritating bout of speechifying between Boone and Torn at the show's climax, Shaw and Bo Goldman wrote an absorbing drama in which a group of Union soldiers undertake a difficult maneuver against long odds and come within reach of victory only to be undercut by bureaucratic protocol and squabbling generals. At one point, pencil-pushing officers descend upon the tunnel during its construction not to help, but to ask if it's being built in accord with a wide range of pointless and arcane army specifications. Union generals base their decisions not on military strategy, but on protecting their turf and careers.

The sands of the Golden Age had nearly run out, and the story of *The Tunnel* is in many ways the story of what happened to it. The soldiers of live television drama—producers, directors, writers, actors, technicians, and other support personnel—performed their jobs under harrowing conditions and often did so brilliantly. But the generals—network executives, sponsors, and advertising agencies—imposed so many roadblocks and restrictions that an enterprise begun with high hopes for success instead went down to defeat.

Because of all the production difficulties, Coe sent Delbert Mann his customary note of thanks before the show even aired. "I hope we will continue to work together in television, and that soon there will be a picture and/or a play on which we can amalgamate our energies," Coe wrote. But they didn't and there wasn't: they maintained a long-distance friendship after Mann moved to the west coast, but this was the fork in the road for their lives and careers.

• • •

With the era of strong television producers coming to an end, the center of gravity in television drama underwent another unwelcome shift. "When I worked for Fred, I didn't know about the network," writer Roger O. Hirson says. "Now, you have meetings with the network before you start, after the treatment, and after the first draft. At most of them, the people at the network basically tell you how to do the show. "[Producers like Coe] felt the network was the enemy. They were the artists and the network was business, and they would fight."

In the fall of 1959, faced with continued losses from *Playhouse 90*'s not being fully sponsored, CBS reduced it to every other week. In January 1960, it announced only eight more shows would appear. The last episode of *Playhouse 90* aired on May 18, 1960, ending what author Jeff Greenfield calls a brave but futile attempt to preserve anthology drama as a regular feature of commercial television.

As television slid comfortably into ossified mediocrity, Coe continued fighting a rearguard action for the medium's imaginative possibilities. In an interview with *TV Guide*, he proposed that the networks join forces and simultaneously broadcast an experimental hour devoted to finding new talent. Each network would produce it on a rotating basis from 10:30 to 11:30 P.M. The time slot was only partially programmed by the networks as late as 1958–1959, so that a non-commercial show at that hour would not have been an economic hardship. While they were intrigued, *TV Guide* noted, it was "an idea the three networks have not rushed to adopt."

Coe was a visionary in a medium which increasingly had no room for one. "Fred was a genius," says Ethel Winant, who worked with Coe as a casting executive on *Playhouse 90*. "He had a vision about television being its own art form. It wasn't meant to be theater, and it wasn't meant to be movies. It was meant to be television." Coe not only had a vision for the medium, Winant adds, but for the individual shows he produced. "He dominated his directors to a great degree. . . . Even though he wasn't in the director's chair, even though it was a collaboration, it was his vision and his image."

One by one, the artists who made 1950s television so exciting left for the movies or Broadway. When Robert Saudek, producer of *Omnibus* (which aired serious fare such as Greek drama and modern opera) said television now held the promise of a Golden Age, Frank Pierson of *The New Republic* responded wistfully, writing: "[Saudek's] words must have fallen oddly on the generation of bright young men contemplating from their refuge in movies or Broadway the wreckage of their television careers."

There were no new live shows scheduled for the 1960–1961 season. Signs of the end of the Golden Age did not come in drama alone. On April 1, 1960, Lucille Ball and Desi Arnaz made their final appearance together in "Lucy Meets the Mustache," an episode of *I Love Lucy* with guest star Ernie Kovacs. One month later, Ball and Arnaz divorced.

"To have a solid place in the community," *New York Times* theater critic Brooks Atkinson has written, "the theater has to be a criticism of life by writers with ideas and passion." Television had been a national electronic theater, but was so no more. Having mourned the departure of so many talents from television, *New York Herald Tribune* writer John Crosby joined the parade himself, announcing in his column of November 1, 1960, that he would no longer write television criticism:

> Television no longer deserves daily criticism on a serious level. . . . Silence is the only sensible greeting for "Pete and Gladys," "Hong Kong," "Argonauts" and the rest of the dreary new shows. . . . Television isn't awful. Awful things are fun to write about. If it were bad enough, we critics could denounce it. But "Rawhide" isn't really that awful. It's a bore.

When Coe started in television in 1945, it had been nothing. Now it was nothing again, only a much bigger nothing. The Golden Age was over, and Fred Coe would have to make his way in the world outside the framework of live television drama. With two Broadway hits in a row to his credit, it didn't seem as if that would be a problem.

ACT III

Blackberry Winter

[For] the contemporary Southern writer
. . . the literary spring is indeed an
uncertain weather, a kind of
"blackberry winter" that blows frost
upon the early blooms.

—Donald Davidson
"The Artist as Southerner" (1926)

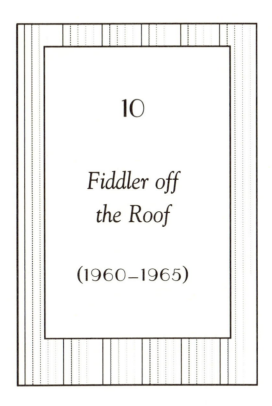

10

*Fiddler off
the Roof*

(1960–1965)

Normally, Tad Mosel looked forward to lunch with Fred Coe, but this time was different. Mosel knew Coe had bought the rights to James Agee's *A Death in the Family* and that Coe was still producing for CBS. He correctly assumed Coe wanted him to adapt it for *Playhouse 90*, and there was no way he was going to do it.

Playhouse 90, with its five commercial breaks, would be the ruin of *A Death in the Family*, Mosel thought. Agee's book was lyrical, impressionistic, and lacked a driving story line to preserve its coherence through all those commercials. But he knew how charming and persuasive Coe could be, so before they met at a midtown restaurant for lunch in the spring of 1960, Mosel rehearsed his arguments.

At lunch, Coe and Mosel had their usual few drinks, and the conversation rambled. Then Coe leaned across the table and said, "Pappy, how would you like to dramatize *A Death in the Family*—for the stage?" This was neither what Mosel expected, nor what Coe intended to ask. But, Mosel would later reflect, it was as if the idea popped into their heads simultaneously.

Coe bought back the rights to Agee's story from CBS, and the tale of how a father's death simultaneously shatters a family and pulls it together was headed for Broadway. Although Coe apparently never told anyone he did it as a tribute to the father he never met, it's a virtual certainty this was the case: Jay Follet, the play's protagonist, is a good-natured young Tennessee lawyer who dies prematurely in the summer of 1915, leaving behind a pregnant widow. Coe's father, Frederick Hayden Hughs Coe, was a good-natured young Tennessee lawyer who died prematurely in the summer of 1914, leaving behind a pregnant widow.

Coe recruited Arthur Penn as the show's director, making it, in Mosel's words, "a *Philco-Goodyear* package." Coe would later deride CBS for having changed the title from *A Death in the Family* to *All the Way Home* while it was a *Playhouse 90* property. But when Coe had the chance, he didn't change it back, either. With all the travails the show would face even without the word "death" in the title, it's probably just as well.

Arthur Cantor, who became Coe's partner on several Broadway shows, says although he bordered on genius in his ability to discern artistic brilliance, he was no genius at fund-raising. *All the Way Home* went into rehearsal still short half the money it would need; Coe called in Cantor, who raised it in about a week. Coe's approach to soliciting investors, Cantor recalls, was to send out a form letter and wait for money to roll in.

Coe and Cantor were a strong team, producing *All the Way Home, Gideon,* and *A Thousand Clowns.* Coe supervised literary and artistic matters, Cantor handled business, publicity, and fund-raising. Later a major Broadway producer in his own right, Cantor gives much of the credit to Coe. "He was very good with scripts," Cantor says. "If I have any taste at all in the theater . . . it's due to my association with Fred Coe."

Coe and Cantor took the show on the road in November of 1960. The cast included Arthur Hill as Jay Follet, Colleen Dewhurst as his wife, Mary, and Lillian Gish as Mary's mother, Catherine. *All the Way Home* was set to open in New Haven, the day after election day. When Coe and Mosel arrived in New Haven on election day, the bars were closed to promote sober voting. "That was a tragedy to Fred and me," Mosel says. But not as oppressive as the extensive rewriting the show required.

In New Haven, the third act was too long—"a parade of people going back and forth in black clothes," Mosel says. On a bleak, rainy November day, Mosel had to write a new third act in his room at the Taft Hotel. Several months earlier, the actress Margaret Sullavan had committed suicide in a New Haven hotel room, and Mosel gloomily wondered if he had the room she had done it in. But he turned out a tighter third act, and the company headed to Boston.

Here, the focus fell on the second act, in which benevolent father figure Jay Follet dies unexpectedly and family members struggle to cope. In one scene, Mary's pious, never-married Aunt Hannah leads her in an almost bullying manner through the prayer "Our Lord on the Cross." As Mosel and Penn watched a rehearsal in the Wilbur Theater, Mosel felt the scene was starchy and pompous.

"If I were Mary," Mosel said, "I'd hit her."

Penn turned to Mosel in the darkened theater. "You go back to the hotel and write that."

Knowing Penn did not mean for Mary to deck Aunt Hannah with a right cross, Mosel added a line strong enough to make the audience feel she had: "You've never had anything *but* God, Aunt Hannah. I was married to a *man*. I won't *have* God in his place." In a later scene, family members break into a laughing jag, their nerves frayed by tension. Mosel was stuck for a line that would trigger this outburst until serendipity, in the form of Arthur Cantor, came to the rescue.

During an anxious discussion of script and production problems at the hotel Coe ordered room service and Cantor asked for buttermilk: "My mother always said that in times of stress, the best thing to drink is buttermilk." "My God, that's the line," Mosel thought. It went in the play the next night.

The changes Tad Mosel made to the script in Boston paid off: leading Boston theater critic Elliot Norton, who had given the show a mediocre review when it opened, returned to praise it at the end of its Boston run and wish it well in New York. Heartened, Coe offhandedly told Herbert Mitgang of the *New York Times*, "In New Haven, we were one-third of the way home, in Boston we're about halfway home, and in New York next week, I hope we'll be 'All the Way Home.'"

But getting home isn't always so easy. The play opened in New York on Wednesday, November 30, 1960, at the Belasco Theater on 44th Street. Although appreciative, the critics were dutiful and lukewarm. Most reviews praised Mosel's writing and Penn's direction but were ambivalent. Howard Taubman of the *New York Times* noted, "Tad Mosel has . . . had the taste and wisdom to let Agee's vision shine through lucidly and purely." He also noted a lack of action in the second act. Robert Coleman of the *New York Mirror* called Mosel "a fine, sensitive new playwright" but said he had fashioned a grim play from a grim novel. "Imagine Grant Wood characters in a Chekhov mood piece," he wrote.

There was little advance sale, and the box office was dismal. By Thursday, only $3,500 worth of tickets had been sold for the next week against weekly operating expenses of $23,000. Cantor urged Coe to close the play. "Most people believe the Warner Bros. movies about the theater," Cantor says, "but except in very rare instances, a dead duck is a dead duck. And this seemed dead to me. A lovely play, but no box office."

Coe agreed, and after Thursday's show, they posted a notice that it would close Saturday night, setting in motion a chain of events that would pass into Broadway lore as the Miracle on 44th Street. Unaware any miracle was afoot, Arthur Penn desperately tried to get Coe to change his mind.

The decision to close stood, however. The show's advertising was cancelled and moving trucks were rented to return the play's scenery to the warehouse. After Thursday night's performance, Cantor picked up an early edition of Friday's *Daily News*. It featured a column by Ed Sullivan raving about *All the Way Home*.

In a Warner Bros. movie, Cantor would be elated, but instead he felt a sense of foreboding. The *Daily News* didn't have the influence on theatergoers that the *New York Times* did, and Sullivan, who also hosted one of the most popular shows on TV, wasn't even its theater critic. Cantor read Sullivan's column and thought, "Oh, for Chrissakes. We're in trouble now." He knew there would be pressure to continue, and felt there was no point in continuing. Sure enough, Coe called Cantor the next morning. "Do you think that review means anything?" he asked.

Cantor didn't. Nonetheless, he called Sullivan and thanked him for the column, but said they had already posted the closing notice.

"My God, you can't close the show," Sullivan said.

"We're not doing any business," Cantor responded, adding hopefully, "Do you think you could say something on television?"

"I will, but you've got to agree to keep it open for another week," Sullivan said. "And bring the cast down so I can introduce them on the show."

On Thursday night, ticket sales were only $881. The next day, there was an article in Friday's *New York Times* announcing the play's closing Saturday night. In the article, a spokesman for the play—unidentified, but probably Cantor—said it would continue if there were a sudden upturn in business.

The public responded. Friday night's ticket sales were $2,600, and there were capacity audiences for the matinee and evening show on Saturday. Now Cantor had to get some ads back in the newspapers. On Sunday morning, he called Ingram Ash, in charge of the show's advertising. Ash called several newspapers to find only skeleton staffs on duty in advertising departments. Setting up a large typeset ad would be impossible on such short notice.

Ash called Max Ginsberg, the head of entertainment advertising for the *New York Times*, and got him to come into the office and work with him. An ad, an open letter from Coe and Cantor to the theater public, was typed on a manual typewriter. Its rough-and-ready look made it stand out from the elegantly typeset ads around it. That evening the cast of *All the Way Home* appeared on *The Ed Sullivan Show*.

Now business was booming. "It's a Broadway miracle," Cantor told the *New York Times* on Monday. "We've now set the closing date for next Saturday night," he said, hastening to add, "Of course, if business is good, there'll be another extension." *All the Way Home*, slated for extinction after two performances, ran for 334, was named the best American play of 1961 by the New York Drama Critics' Circle, and won the Pulitzer Prize for drama.

• • •

Although Coe and Mosel had regarded it as a tragedy to find the bars closed in New Haven on election day, the 1960 election was also a triumph for Coe. Along with Arthur Penn, he served as an adviser to the presidential campaign of John Kennedy as the Democratic senator from Massachusetts prepared for his televised debates with Vice President Richard Nixon.

These were the first televised debates in the history of American presidential politics, and the stakes were high. In the first debate, closeups revealed Nixon's sweaty nervousness and five o'clock shadow, while Kennedy looked calm and composed. Although he didn't know it, Nixon had Fred Coe and Arthur Penn to thank for those closeups. "Fred and I decided that a closeup would benefit our candidate and do no good for Richard Nixon," Penn recalls. "That's what we advised, and that's the advice that was taken."

Closeups, a staple of dramatic anthologies in the 1950s, also may have played a crucial role in America's leading political drama of 1960. Authors Irving Settel and William Laas note that more than 115 million Americans watched the debates, adding: "How many voters made their choice between the candidates on the basis of what they saw on TV, no one knows, but the election was so close that the debates might well have been decisive."

• • •

Coe's next Broadway show reunited him with his most famous writing protégé from *Philco-Goodyear Playhouse*: Paddy Chayefsky. *Gideon*, directed by Tyrone Guthrie, was a dramatization of the Biblical legend of an unassuming shepherd who, with God's help, rises to heroic stature and successfully leads the tribes of Israel into battle against the Midianites. Fredric March starred as an angel, Douglas Campbell as Gideon, and George Segal as an Israelite tribesman.

Gideon opened on November 9, 1961, at the Plymouth Theater. It was the first year of the Kennedy administration, a time when romantic ballads like "Moon River" and "Where the Boys Are" were popular and America's optimism and sense of potential were at their zenith. In retrospect, what seems even more remarkable is that a play like *Gideon* could expect reviews from seven different New York City daily newspapers.

Reviews were mixed, but mostly favorable. Howard Taubman of the *New York Times* said *Gideon* had "the modesty and sweetness of legend." John McClain of the *Journal-American* called it a play of enormous power, humor, and persuasion. There were dissenters, though: Walter Kerr of the *Herald-Tribune* said "What is missing this morning is a miracle" and Norman Nadel of the *World-Telegram and Sun* derided Gideon's aggrieved line ("I've tried to love You, God, but it's too much for me. You are too vast a concept") as "cocktail-party psychiatry." Nonetheless, *Gideon* ran for 236 performances, a decline from *Two for the Seesaw* (750 performances, or nearly two years), *The Miracle Worker* (719), and *All the Way Home* (334). But it was still an impressive run for a somewhat talky, philosophical play.

• • •

Cartoonist Herb Gardner was about to abandon his dream of becoming a playwright. The author of the comic strip "The Nebbishes" had written a bittersweet play about a non-conforming, unemployed television writer. Several Broadway producers had relinquished options on the work, tentatively titled *Thousands of Clowns*. Running out of money and confidence, Gardner showed the script to Mel Brooks. Brooks gave it to his wife-to-be Anne Bancroft, who passed it along to Coe, who called Gardner.

"Hello, Pappy?" Coe began in his soft Southern drawl. "Just read your play. This really made me laugh and made me think about things. So I think I'll put this one on. What do you say?" In an instant, Gardner's life changed. "If Annie hadn't given Fred that play, I'd be doin' my comic strip this minute," says the author of *I'm Not Rappaport*, *The Goodbye People*, and *Conversations with My Father*. "I had been through five producers in two and a half years and was nearly broke. It was time to go back to work. I couldn't keep it up."

A Thousand Clowns went into rehearsal in early 1962. It starred Jason Robards as Murray Burns, who quits his job as a writer on the mediocre *Chuckles the Chipmunk Show*, only to return when threatened with losing custody of his nephew, played by Barry Gordon. Also featured were Sandy Dennis and William Daniels as social workers who determine whether Robards can maintain custody of his nephew; Gene Saks as the loud, oppressive "Chuckles the Chipmunk"; and A. Larry Haines as Arnold Burns, Robards's sensible, conformist brother.

Until now, Coe had produced but not directed his Broadway shows, and that was the plan for *A Thousand Clowns*. But when Coe felt the director wasn't getting the job done, he fired him and stepped in to direct. This was why he came to New York nearly twenty years ago: to direct on Broadway.

It was such a heady experience that he directed his next three shows as well.

Arthur Cantor says that of all his plays, *Clowns* was probably Coe's favorite. He must have strongly identified with both brothers: Coe had started out as a talented, anarchic TV rebel like the disenchanted Murray Burns, but now he had two homes, two families, and would soon have a fourth child. His expenses were mounting, and he would end up like Arnold Burns, who replaces his boyhood dreams with the goal of being a good provider.

Coe the director was as popular with actors as Coe the producer was with writers. Sitting in the back of the theater watching rehearsals, he bellowed with laughter, a gleeful, exuberant laugh that tapered off into wheezing and gasping, the result of his constant smoking. "You know why it works so well with him?" Sandy Dennis once said to Herb Gardner. "He's the best audience you're ever going to find."

Finding Jason Robards was not always such an easy matter, though. He was drinking, and disappeared during out-of-town tryouts in Boston. The scavenger hunt ended when someone spotted Robards leaving a Boston bar. Coe also had to convince Gardner to pare down his script. Curtain-down time was usually around 10:45, but *Clowns* ran until 11:30 in Boston. People left early in droves.

"Pappy, don't you think we could make this one a little bit shorter?" Coe asked.

"I guess I'd better," Gardner said.

"You don't," Coe replied, "we'll have to start putting machine guns in the lobby." Gardner shortened it, but not enough to satisfy Arthur Cantor. "You had to pack a dinner basket in order to sit through that play," he dourly observes.

A Thousand Clowns opened to largely enthusiastic reviews at the Eugene O'Neill Theater on April 5, 1962, and ran for a year. In addition to praising Gardner's script and the performances (Robards and Sandy Dennis in particular), the reviews were consistent in their praise for Coe's direction. Some reviewers called *Clowns* the best comedy of the season, but several felt the play was still too long. And reviewers did not always find the free-spirited, unemployed Murray Burns morally superior to his working brother Arnold. Walter Kerr asked, "Isn't Mr. Robards as guilty of guff as his arch-enemy Chuckles the Chipmunk? . . . Is Mr. Robards right or wrong, a free soul or a selfish one? The question is complicated and perhaps subtle. But it isn't answered."

That unanswered question may help to explain the play's enduring popularity. By the fall of 1962, *Clowns* already had twenty-six road companies. More than thirty summers later, there were still twenty road companies.

That popularity is due not only to Gardner's wit, but his ambivalent arche-type. Theatergoers admire Murray Burns for his free spirit, but can't escape the nagging feeling that he's selfish and immature. He makes them laugh, and he makes them think about things.

A *Thousand Clowns* would also have an enduring personal legacy for Coe. On April 5, 1962, the night it opened on Broadway, Joyce gave birth to their second child. After the show, Coe rushed to the hospital to be with Joyce and his new son, Samuel Hughes Coe.

•   •   •

With the success of *A Thousand Clowns*, Coe had had five Broadway hits in a row, and in the fall of 1962, he added a pool to the house on Baiting Hollow Road in East Hampton. In quiet moments, he and Joyce sat at the piano singing "Down by the Old Mill Stream." And when it was time for company, Joyce was an excellent hostess. John and Laurie were frequent guests in East Hampton, and both recall Joyce as an affectionate and atten-tive stepmother. (Joyce's artificial elegance of speech amused Laurie, though: instead of "half-and-half," she called the dairy creamer "hahf-and-hahf," a Gatsbyesque affectation.)

Despite the pleasant times, strains were developing between Coe and Joyce. "I'm sure Fred got a little tyrannical with Joyce," JP Miller adds. "She was sort of a docile person, at least in public. If you weren't properly subservient, under certain circumstances, he got explosive. I'm sure that in the last few years with his drinking, it became difficult." Arthur Penn agrees. "Fred would get drinking," he says, "and it would get a little wild out there."

Coe's next show, one of the worst flops of his theatrical career, would aggravate that drinking. *A Matter of Position* was Elaine May's bloated three-hour-plus epic about an office worker who wilts under the stress of modern life and regresses to childhood. May's partner, Mike Nichols, starred as Howard Miller, the man who can't cope.

When *A Matter of Position* opened in Philadelphia's Walnut Theater on September 30, 1962, the critics made short work of it. Henry T. Murdock of the *Philadelphia Inquirer* noted that May was attempting a form of impro-visation, adding, "You cannot improvise a play for three and a quarter hours. At least Miss May can't." Ernest Schier of the *Evening Bulletin* put it more succinctly: "For a while there, Saturday night at the Walnut, I thought they'd never shut up."

Nominally the show's director, Coe in effect yielded this role to May because he couldn't cope with her any more than Howard Miller could with modern life. May wouldn't agree to shorten the play, so Coe and Arthur Cantor cut it themselves. May appealed to the Dramatists' Guild and the cuts had to be restored. Instead, Coe and Cantor closed this theatrical *Ishtar*, the only time Coe ever closed a show out of town.

Despite the brevity of its run, *A Matter of Position* had several lasting—and damaging—effects on Coe. First, it aggravated his drinking. And it started to open a breach between him and Cantor. Unlike Coe, he never thought the play was funny, and he bridled at Coe's verbal abuse when they disagreed. They would go their separate ways professionally, a course of action which would return to haunt Coe a year and a half later.

Coe's next foray into theater can be filed under "the one that got away." Groucho Marx was planning a musical, based on the early years of the Marx Brothers, for the spacious Winter Garden Theater on Broadway. He asked Coe to produce it, and in November 1962, Coe and Harry Muheim, one of his top *Philco-Goodyear* comedy writers, met with Marx.

During a long evening which included meetings at Marx's Beverly Hills home and dinner at Chasen's, Marx discussed his plans for the show. At one point, during a phone conversation with disaster-film producer Irwin Allen, Marx said: "Coe's been doing these small-screen kitchen dramas for too long, Irwin. We're going to break him out of the kitchen with something big. The Marx Brothers story! With *music*! Next year at the Winter Garden!"

But as is often the case with the Passover invocation "Next year in Jerusalem," it was not to be—at least not for Coe. *Minnie's Boys* became a Broadway success, but instead of working with Coe and Muheim, Groucho turned to his own son, Arthur Marx, an accomplished playwright. This would not be the last big-fish musical to get away from Coe.

Setbacks like these took a toll. Shortly after the success of JP Miller's *Days of Wine and Roses* on *Playhouse 90*, Coe took an option to produce *Madonna With Child*, Miller's play about an unhappy marriage. But nothing happened. At script conferences, Coe would have three or four whiskey sours, and little discussion of the script took place.

Miller would turn the talk to the film version of *Days of Wine and Roses*, which Coe had said he wanted to produce. Miller had other offers, but he and Coe had shaken hands on it. "He would say, 'We're gonna do it, Pappy,'" Miller recalls. "I says, 'When?' And he says, 'Pappy, trust me. We're gonna do it.'"

Finally, Miller's agent Ingo Preminger got a good offer from Martin Manulis, and Miller told him to take it. "You son of a bitch," Coe drunkenly shrieked at Miller when he learned of the deal, "we were gonna make that movie!" "I waited two years for you, Fred," Miller said. "That's a long time when people are making offers."

A few years earlier, Robert Alan Aurthur had written, "We were a family in a certain time and place." At NBC, Coe created and presided over a family in many ways more real to him than his own. He had a hard time accepting the dissolution of his NBC family, and with his option money and well-intended promises to Miller, may have been trying to hold it together after it had ceased to exist.

• • •

John and Laurie Coe would recall their youth in Fort Lauderdale as almost idyllic. Alice rarely if ever spoke ill of their father, and the house was surprisingly free of post-divorce bitterness. They lived a block from the ocean, with seagrass stretching endlessly northward, and sea turtles swimming ashore.

John's relationship with his father, however, was less than idyllic. In his senior year at Fort Lauderdale's Pinecrest School, the tall, skinny John, now a star swimmer, decided to go out for football. In the fall of 1962, Pinecrest won its first nine games. Their last game held the promise of an undefeated season. For John, this was a chance to prove himself. "I got on the phone and *begged* my father to come," he recalls, his voice becoming subdued. "And he wouldn't."

Alice called Coe, who relented and came. He had just been through the *Matter of Position* fiasco and had lost the Marx Brothers musical. Still, he wanted to be a Pappy to his older son. But even when Coe tried to do right by John, it didn't work. He and Alice were late for the game. John was injured in the first half, and out of the game by the time they arrived. Pinecrest lost 33–6, although John was so traumatized by the episode he would remember the score as 64–0.

Despite his good intentions, Coe was a better father to his writers than his own children. "His sense of justice was keen, a powerful morality that formed every fiber of his body," Bo Goldman recalls. "He never did anything dishonest in a legal or moral sense, but I think sometimes he was dishonest with himself and people very close to him, like Joyce and the children. We didn't live with him, but we got all the best of his fatherhood."

Despite the obvious affection Coe's letters to Alice show for John and Laurie, John would agree. "My father held court," John says. "He paid all the bills. He was Big Pappy." But, John adds ruefully, not for him. Not when he needed it. "He was a giant to me. He was a persona to me. He was someone I was very proud of." In a sad, reflective tone, John pronounces his indictment. "He wasn't my father. He didn't father me. He taught me nothing that a father would teach a son. Absolutely nothing."

• • •

Feature films are the shortest part of Fred Coe's resume. When live television drama died, many of Coe's colleagues moved to Hollywood to make films. But Coe didn't like Hollywood's deal-oriented culture, couldn't stand film's lack of procedural and financial accountability, and had no patience for film editing or post-production in general.

He was on location in Red Bank, New Jersey, for the *The Miracle Worker* when David Hays, the stage designer for several of his plays, visited the set. "I hate this film business," Coe told Hays. "It's just like standing next to a cash register. Anyone can come up, make you hit the button and ring the bell, dip in their hand for as much as they want and walk away."

Television and the stage were indoor media. But if the weather wasn't right on a location shoot, Coe had to wait and keep the meter running. Coe was no happier working indoors. Movies rise or fall on the quality of their editing, and editing rooms gave him claustrophobia.

For William Gibson, it was still an easy decision to have Coe produce the film version of *The Miracle Worker* and have Arthur Penn direct it. Gibson knew that if he sold the film rights to Hollywood, the studio could rework his play as it saw fit. He was haunted by visions of a Hollywood-style happy ending in which social worker Annie Sullivan not only teaches Helen Keller to communicate, but marries her brother James and moves into the Keller home to trade Yankee versus Confederate barbs with Captain Keller.

Once again starring Anne Bancroft as Annie Sullivan and Patty Duke as young Helen Keller, the film featured Victor Jory as Captain Keller, Inga Swenson as his wife, and Andrew Prine as James Keller. *The Miracle Worker* received critical acclaim and several major awards: Anne Bancroft won the Academy Award for best actress, and Patty Duke for best supporting actress. Penn was nominated for best director, Gibson for best screenplay based on a work from another medium. The film earned $2 million at movie theaters in the United States and Canada, although Gibson, slyly noting Hollywood's Byzantine accounting practices, points out that was after the studio did the bookkeeping.

Coe's next film was *This Property Is Condemned*, a Ray Stark presentation produced by John Houseman and directed by Sydney Pollack from a one-act play by Tennessee Williams about a depression-era young woman (Natalie Wood) who feels trapped in a small Mississippi town and tries to break out of it. Robert Redford co-stars as the man she falls in love with.

Although originally slated to serve as the film's producer, Coe received joint screenwriting credit with the young Francis Ford Coppola and Edith Sommer. Coppola regarded Coe as someone of great substance, experience, and humanity. "He was a drinker, a fine Southern gentleman, and a very savvy person," Coppola recalls. "I remember him loosening up at different times, and thinking it was a little bit like Budd Schulberg's *The Disenchanted*."

One of Coe's greatest *Philco-Goodyear* writers, however, says he was less than a gentleman on this film. Coe originally hired Horton Foote to write the script. But when a production company executive told Coe that Foote had written an art-house movie which wouldn't make a nickel, Coe neither defended Foote, nor asked him to revise his script. He fired him.

"Fred behaved very badly and almost ruined our friendship," Foote says. "I was busy with other things, so it really didn't matter. But this is often how it would happen with Fred. He would get enormous crushes on people, and then turn [against them]." When Foote and his wife were in East Hampton visiting Vincent Donehue shortly afterward, Coe avoided them.

Most of the people who worked with Coe praise his personal and professional integrity ("He always kept his word," Herb Gardner says. "Which is almost bizarre these days.") Coe's refusal to see Foote in East Hampton may be explained by a line David Karp attributes to David Shaw: "'The worst that can happen when you deal with Fred is that when he does you dirt, he never forgives you,'" Karp says, adding, "The sense of shame overcomes him and he gets mad at you." In avoiding Foote, Coe may have tacitly acknowledged that he did him dirt on *Condemned*, just as he felt awkward about the incident involving Gore Vidal and *The Left-Handed Gun*. In both cases, it almost seems as if he was anxiously trying to assert control at a time when events in the entertainment industry were changing in ways beyond his control.

Because Coe strongly identified with *A Thousand Clowns*, he was eager to produce the film—perhaps, as it later turned out, too eager. His debut as a movie director, *Clowns* featured the Broadway cast with two exceptions: Barbara Harris played the social worker who falls in love with Jason Robards and Martin Balsam was now Robards's shoulder-to-the-grindstone brother. Unlike the play, the movie could go outside, making New York City a featured player. Scenes at Grant's Tomb, Battery Park, Ellis Island, and other sites make the film a visual tapestry of New York, especially when combined in montage sequences that give the film a still-contemporary feel.

Coe had some involvement with this artistically important location shooting, but little with the film's post-production. Principal photography, mainly indoors, was shot between mid-May and mid-August of 1964. When writer Herb Gardner reviewed the footage, he decided his script lacked the filmic quality New York backgrounds could provide. Ralph Rosenblum, the film's editor, later wrote, "Herb revealed his dissatisfaction to Fred. . . . Fred, who was enormously fond of Herb, never very possessive about the picture and not much inclined toward spending painstaking months in the cutting room, agreed to hand over the entire project to the younger man. And that was the last we saw of Fred Coe."

The outdoor montage sequences were shot in September by cameraman

Joe Coffee. Gardner recorded Robards strumming a ukelele and singing, "Yes Sir, That's My Baby," the film's signature song. Gardner generously attributes the film's success to Coe, saying, "Most of the film you see, that's Fred." But Rosenblum recalls otherwise. When he talks about top New York directors he's worked with, he names Woody Allen, Sidney Lumet, Larry Peerce—and Herb Gardner. With his typical selflessness, Coe acknowledged as much. "At the very end, he asked if I wanted a co-director credit," Gardner recalls. "I said, 'If the credits list two directors, [the critics] will kill us.'"

Like *The Miracle Worker*, *A Thousand Clowns* won an Academy Award (for Martin Balsam as best supporting actor), and received several nominations: for Coe as producer, for Gardner for best writing based on material from another medium, and for Don Walker's musical score. It also earned over $2 million at theaters in the United States and Canada (after the studio did the bookkeeping).

• • •

Fred Coe's dramatic television work during this period is the least distinguished of his life. With live TV a thing of the past, videotape made television drama seem more like movies, and Coe struggled to adjust. "Fred rose so high so quickly and was riding so firmly in the saddle," Delbert Mann says. "But when the world of live television drama began to drift away, it deprived Fred of his footing in a strange kind of way. The business in which he had triumphed left him, and it became a different world."

When *Playhouse 90* ended, Coe proposed a series to CBS called *Biography*. It fell through. Along with Arthur Penn and Tad Mosel, he made *Three Roads to Rome*, a group of one-act plays starring Deborah Kerr, for English television in the fall of 1961. And Coe did get a dramatic series on the air—*Theatre '62*, which consisted of boiled-down rehashes of David O. Selznick movies; it aired on NBC in the 1961–1962 season.

Theatre '62's most important role may have been to expedite Bo Goldman's transition from executive assistant to Academy Award–winning screenwriter. "Fred gave me two of them [*The Spiral Staircase* and *The Paradine Case*]," Goldman recalls. "That's really what gave me the boost. He said, 'You're a writer, Pappy. I've never seen you write a bad sentence in your life.'" But Coe showed little interest in the project, and Goldman often had to explain to ad agency representative Max Wiley why Coe was never there. "He kept asking me, 'Where's Fred? There are going to be big production values, aren't there?' And I said, 'Oh yeah, Max. Big!' I was longing for Fred to be around. I think he'd sort of begun to lose interest."

Critics disdained the series. Reviewing *Notorious*, *Variety* said "'Film '46 [the year of the film] stayed way ahead of 'Theatre '62'." Regarding *Spellbound*, it asked, "How wise is it to produce . . . a whodunit to which a goodly portion of the audience must already know the answer? And of what value is it to have done it badly?" *Variety's* highest praise was for *The Paradine Case*, noting that "Goldman did an okay job of pruning David O. Selznick's original script."

Oddly, Coe's response to these bad reviews was to make an ambiguous reference to his television work of the 1950s. "I'm not claiming pretensions with this series, and I mean that in the best sense of the word," he told *Show* magazine. "When I try to do shows like Faulkner's *The Old Man* or *Days of Wine and Roses*, there is an element of pretension. With this series, I'm working purely for the entertainment values." But in a 1973 interview, he spoke more honestly. "The lowest I ever stooped was doing a year adapting David Selznick movies," he said. "The money was good, but those shows were awful. *Jesus!*"

Like *Theatre '62*, Coe's next television project had more to do with commerce than art. *The Reporter* was conceived and ordered by CBS in the spring of 1964. Coe called David Karp, who had written several *Playhouse 90*'s for him. "They want to do a series," Coe told him. "It's sold! All you have to do is come up with a story. We're going to make a fortune."

But after several meetings with Karp on a pilot script bogged down, Coe bowed out before the show went into production. Coe was torn by two instincts, Karp thought. The first was artistic, and was purposeful and important. Increasingly, though, it was counterbalanced by the need to make money to meet his high expenses.

Theatre '62 and *The Reporter* are low points in Coe's television career, but the lowest may have come earlier. In the spring of 1961, the FCC held hearings in New York on sponsor interference in network television programming. Coe, a legendary adversary of sponsors and ad agencies, had testified vigorously—in defense of sponsors and ad agencies. "The sponsor, if he buys a program, has the right to control it," Coe said. "The sponsor has the right to have a program on or not have it on." And Coe had agreed with the American Gas Association when it had ordered the deletion of the phrase "gas chamber" from the *Playhouse 90* dramatization of the Nazi war-crime trials, *Judgment at Nuremberg*. "I would have found myself on the side of the network or sponsor," Coe had said. It was a long way down from telling Harry Muheim, "The sponsor *pays* for this show, but *I* run it."

Coe's testimony was greeted with astonishment. Hal Humphrey, the television and radio editor of the Los Angeles *Mirror*, sardonically noted that Coe always chided Hollywood for its lack of integrity. "It's supposed to be only in Hollywood that money corrupts the artist. That's why it's such a surprise to see Madison Avenue do it to a nice young fellow from Alligator, Miss."

Coe was floundering in the new world of television. While working on *The Reporter*, he called David Shaw, his most prolific writer on *Philco-*

Goodyear Playhouse, now a story editor on *The Defenders*, asking him how to get quality scripts on a weekly basis. "He was asking me stuff he had been an expert at," Shaw says with a surprised laugh. "But the weekly series seemed to frighten him."

Just as D. W. Griffith failed to adjust to the Jazz Age and the Depression, Coe could not make the adjustment from the live drama of New York in the 1950s to the filmed and taped drama of Los Angeles in the 1960s. "The next few years should see a renaissance in television spearheaded by a 'retreat' to New York," Coe told *Show* magazine in a hopeful but futile spirit. "What we now need is the creative element, which can only be found in New York."

• • •

A good example of that creative element is *Fiddler on the Roof*, which would become a cultural landmark and a financial goldmine. The musical about oppressed but resilient Jews in Czarist Russia was written by Joseph Stein, Sheldon Harnick, and Jerry Bock, based on the stories of Sholom Aleichem. *Fiddler* starred Zero Mostel as Tevye, a philosophical, wise-cracking milkman, and was directed by Jerome Robbins and produced by Harold Prince. But Prince was not the show's original producer. Fred Coe was, and losing *Fiddler* would be a watershed in his life.

Stein, Harnick, and Bock first took their show to Prince, who turned them down. Joseph Stein says Prince was hesitant; according to Sheldon Harnick, Prince said, "It's not my cup of tea." By the summer of 1962, they approached Coe, who enthusiastically agreed to do it. "The boys were surprised, a gentile from Mississippi wanting to produce their show," Coe later told Robert Alan Aurthur. "But to me it was pure folk material, and I could relate a lot of it to things I knew and cared about."

Coe gave the project a much-needed lift. "Fred was really important, because he was the first person who said, 'I want to produce this show,'" Stein says. "He made efforts to raise the money, but it was very difficult—no one believed in it at the time."

Fund-raising, never his strong point, was not Coe's only problem. The writers wanted Zero Mostel to star as Tevye, but for eight months, from late 1962 through mid-1963, Mostel played hard-to-get. In early 1963, Coe frequently called Mostel's agent Toby Cole. Mostel, who was also considering another play, wouldn't authorize a yes or a no. Cole told him to tell Coe he wasn't interested, but Mostel enjoyed the game of cat and mouse. "Don't be so fast in refusing," he told Cole. "Let him hang on a bit. Don't be so eager. He'll wait."

Coe didn't have a theater to put Mostel in, anyway: on November 6, 1963, the *Herald-Tribune* reported fourteen musicals were scheduled for the second half of the Broadway season, noting that because there weren't enough large theaters for them, *Fiddler* was being postponed until next season. Coe would now have to co-produce *Fiddler* and direct the film version of *A Thousand Clowns* at the same time.

Coe got a major fund-raising break when he wrote to William Paley at CBS, hoping the network would back the show completely, as it had *My Fair Lady*. Paley sent Michael Burke to an audition. Burke was enthusiastic, and a few days later CBS became the sole backer.

But this triumph was short-lived. One day, Coe came to his office and was told Paley had asked to see a script. He sent one to CBS, and a few days later, his lawyer Edward Colton got a wire that CBS was breaking off negotiations. As David Halberstam writes in *The Powers That Be*, CBS participation in *Fiddler* ran aground on the shoals of Paley's mixed feelings about his own Jewishness.

> Paley never ceased to be a little ambivalent about his origins, both about being Jewish and about being a Russian Jew. . . . As he tried to put it aside, hang around not just with WASPs but super-WASPs, it somehow always lurked in the background. It worked on him so powerfully that it could even warp his normally keen sense of popular entertainment. His aides secured an early option on *Fiddler on the Roof*, which they were sure would be a smash hit. They were surprised when Paley, after reading the script and listening to the music, turned it down. To Mike Burke, one of those who suggested he buy it, Paley said, "It's good, but don't you think it's too Jewish?" Burke, startled by the comment, answered that no, as a non-Jew, he did not.

Coe was in trouble. "Suddenly, no one was interested," he later told Robert Alan Aurthur. "Everywhere I turned, to backers, to theater-party people, I heard the same thing: *Fiddler on the Roof* was too special, too Jewish; no one would come to see the show." Coe had one more chance to raise the money, but he blew it.

One day after CBS dropped its backing, Arthur Cantor, who had put together the financing for *All the Way Home*, called Coe and offered to help out. Cantor's fund-raising skills might have kept Coe afloat on *Fiddler*, but Coe turned him down. "He said, 'I can cope with it myself,'" Cantor recalls. "But he couldn't."

Events started slipping out of Coe's control. In *The Making of a Musical*, Robbins's assistant Richard Altman and Mervyn Kaufman write that when Robbins (whom Coe hired) entered the picture, the situation became critical: contracts were not getting sent out and other key procedural details were left unattended. They quote Sheldon Harnick, who recalls Robbins saying, "I don't know what's happening with Fred Coe, but nothing's getting done. We're going to need a producer. Let's get Hal."

By the fall of 1963, Prince was Coe's co-producer. Coe later recalled he and Prince agreed that Prince would raise most of the money, because Coe had brought the project so far. This apparently was not Prince's understanding. Bo Goldman remembers it, "Harold Prince said 'If you wanna be a producer, you do your share of raising the money.'" Nor was Prince happy with Coe's frequent absences. By the spring of 1964, A *Thousand Clowns* was filming, and Coe was overextended.

"Fred would rarely show up for meetings," Sheldon Harnick says. "I later compared notes with Herb Gardner. Fred would tell him he couldn't meet because of *Fiddler* and he was telling us he couldn't meet because he had a meeting with Herb. He was undergoing some crisis in his own life, so I never really got to know him."

Prince was exasperated, and in late June or early July of 1964, about a month before *Fiddler* opened on the road in Detroit, he bought out Coe and became the show's sole producer, with Coe retaining a small percentage of the show. Coe had fiddled while the show's creators burned. His participation in *Fiddler* fell victim to events beyond his control, but also to the lassitude which becalmed his production of JP Miller's play and his participation in the film version of *Days of Wine and Roses*.

Fiddler on the Roof opened at the Imperial Theater on September 22, 1964, and was an overnight critical and financial success. In 1973, it became the longest-running show in Broadway history to that point. By the early 1970s, it had grossed $7.2 million, and by 1989, *Fiddler's* worldwide box-office grosses had hit $20 million. Coe used to tell his son John it was important to keep a lot of irons in the fire. But, he added, you didn't want too many to heat up at the same time. This is what happened, and Coe got burned. Badly.

On the strength of *Fiddler*, Hal Prince's star waxed. For the next dozen years, his biographer Carol Ilson has written, backers supported anything he chose to do. Musing in 1973 about his withdrawal from *Fiddler*, Coe told Robert Alan Aurthur: "I'm sorry I had to do that." He paused. "No, I'm not really," he added. "I saw *Clowns* again the other day, and I directed a pretty good picture." Of course, Coe had dropped out of that at the end as well.

• • •

Coe had produced *Journey to the Day*, Roger O. Hirson's play about therapy for a group of instutionalized psychotics, for television on *Playhouse 90*, and on the stage in Westport, Connecticut. Then, in November 1963, the two men brought the play to the Theater de Lys in Greenwich Village, with Coe now directing as well as producing. Lewis Funke of the *New York Times* wrote that Hirson had lavished great skill on the play, and that it was supported by Coe's painstaking direction and a superb cast. But he nonetheless gave it a mixed review.

Journey to the Day had a short run, less the result of ambivalent reviews than its being swamped by history. It opened on November 12, ten days before the assassination of President Kennedy. In the wake of the assassination, the show closed for several days. The day it re-opened, Hirson was watching TV in his Westchester County home while he dressed for the theater. As he watched, Jack Ruby murdered Lee Harvey Oswald, Kennedy's assassin.

"I said to my kids, 'You gotta come in and see this!'" Hirson recalls. "And then I said to myself, 'Why would anybody go the theater when the greatest drama in our lifetime is being played out on this damn television set right now?'" They tried one more week, with Coe and Hirson each putting a thousand dollars into the play, but it was to no avail. One night there were only eight or ten people in the audience.

Coe's next Broadway show could not blame circumstances beyond its control. *Xmas in Las Vegas*, Jack Richardson's play about a compulsive gambler starring Tom Ewell, was hooted off the boards by critics soon after it opened on November 4, 1965, at the Ethel Barrymore Theater. Whitney Bolton, writing in the *Morning Telegraph*, gibed, "Mr. Richardson has symbols strewn throughout the play like gravel on a suburban driveway." And John McClain of the *Journal-American* wrote, "It seems incredible that people like Fred Coe and Tom Ewell should have taken this play beyond the reading stage."

How could Coe produce and direct such a bomb? We don't know if the theme of compulsive, self-destructive behavior was so close to him that it short-circuited his normally infallible script sense, or if other causes were to blame. And there was more bad news: Coe's mother, now in her eighties, had suffered a stroke in Nashville. She never fully recovered, and was institutionalized for the rest of her life.

By now, it was obvious what Coe had given up with *Fiddler*. While Hal Prince was basking in acclaim and printing money at the Imperial Theater, Coe had thrown snake eyes at the Barrymore. His best days in television were behind him, he had never cared much for films, and his main chance on Broadway had slipped away. Just as this must have started to sink in, the bottom fell out of his personal life.

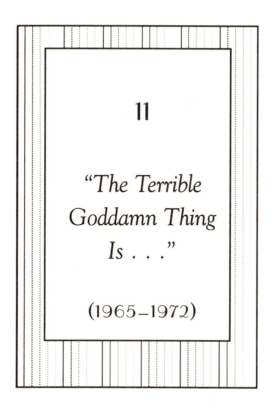

11

"The Terrible Goddamn Thing Is . . ."

(1965–1972)

*P*hilco script girl Adrienne Luraschi lost touch with Fred Coe when live television ended, and as far as she knew, Coe and Joyce Beeler married, had children, and lived happily ever after. Even many of those who stayed in touch with them thought theirs was a brilliant match. "They were the perfect couple," says Jane Aurthur. "She was pretty, bright, alive. He was like a father figure to everyone. And the kids were adorable."

It appeared the marriage was on a rising curve. By 1965, they had moved into a townhouse at 718 Madison Avenue, near East 63rd Street. It was their largest and most expensive New York residence, with a white color scheme whose style and grace reflected Joyce's own understated elegance. They maintained the house on Baiting Hollow Road in East Hampton and, like their family, it continued to grow: in 1967, they added a large living room with a cathedral ceiling and hand-laid tile floor.

Coe's income, however, was not keeping pace with his obligations. He still sent support payments to Alice. John and Laurie were ready for college. Sue and Sam, as they grew, would attend the best private schools. His mother was in a Nashville nursing home. He rarely called or wrote her, but paid her bills. As his career declined, his expenses rose. He was in a financial vise.

Coe's relationship with Joyce soured as his difficulties increased. "I think she envisioned a tremendously glamorous life with him," says Rhoda Herrick, who worked as a secretary to Coe when Joyce was his assistant at NBC. "And when it didn't happen, she probably became embittered." Coe, increasingly embittered as well, started drinking more heavily. "Fred Coe was a great drinking partner of mine—and of everyone's," says Tad Mosel.

A character in Sumner Locke Elliott's 1966 novel *Some Doves and Pythons*, apparently based on Coe, views him through a shot glass darkly. In the book, a cast of characters from the New York entertainment scene pivots around Tabitha Wane, a charismatic, high-powered female agent strikingly similar to Coe's agent, Priscilla Morgan. One of her clients is novelist-in-decline Castle Caldwell, or "Cass" (like "Coe," a one-syllable name beginning with C).

Capturing Coe's still-youthful but increasingly troubled appearance, Elliott writes of Caldwell: "He looked like an aging choir boy with an innocent, questing face, across which bewilderment and alcohol had begun to paint bags and blotches." While Coe's face had not yet assumed the sallow pallor of later years, both factors had begun to work upon him.

Caldwell also has a tendency, as Elliott writes, "to pass from daylight sweetness to evening malice," a transition marked by "the tone, the look of indecision which meant Cass had reached the dividing line between sweetness and the setting alight to people." Similarly, JP Miller says that at parties, Coe could begin the evening as an urbane Southern gentleman, but end it as a ferocious critic of everything you stood for.

However, Coe's drinking was not a problem on *Wait Until Dark*, the thriller he was bringing to Broadway about a blind woman menaced by a sociopathic drug dealer. Written by Frederick Knott, it starred Lee Remick and Robert Duvall, and teamed Coe for the last time with director Arthur Penn. From Penn's viewpoint, things were going well: Coe wasn't drinking any more than usual, was always in control, and was there when needed.

But a few weeks before the show's February 3, 1966, opening, Kate Wells called Coe to tell him that his mother had suffered a serious intestinal blockage and was going to have an operation. Although Coe had largely been a stranger for the year and a half his mother was in a convalescent hospital, he was distraught. "He called in tears almost, for me to tell her he was coming," Kate Wells recalls. I said, 'Fred, I can't tell her. She's already gone up to surgery.'"

Annette Harrell Coe died while her son was en route to her side. She had stoically endured a difficult life: putting her husband through law school only to have him die soon afterwards, then raising her only son against great odds to be a success, only to become estranged from him.

When Alice called Coe from Fort Lauderdale with her condolences, he asked her to fly to Nashville and be with him for the funeral. Coe, Alice, Dr. Sam Wells (who helped raise Coe as a child), and his daughter Kate then drove to Memphis, where, on a cold and drizzly day, Coe's mother was laid to rest beside the husband she had outlived by fifty-two years.

Back in Nashville, Coe, Alice, and Kate Wells opened a trunk containing his mother's effects. Among them: love letters from Coe's father and information revealing that they, like Coe and Alice, had been secretly married. "I found the father I never knew I had," Coe said angrily. "Why wasn't I told about this?'"

Back in New York, *Wait Until Dark* was a hit for Coe. It ran for a year and became a successful film starring Audrey Hepburn and Alan Arkin. It was, however, Coe's last success on Broadway for some time to come.

• • •

Television produced several good dramatic series in the 1960s, such as *The Defenders*, *The Twilight Zone*, and the short-lived *East Side, West Side* (all created or produced by veterans of 1950s live television). It also gave birth to the made-for-TV movie, which would flourish in the 1970s with films such as *My Sweet Charlie* (1970) and *Brian's Song* (1971). But most dramatic shows of the 1960s easily fit into Newton Minow's "vast wasteland." John Houseman has described the television drama of this period as the province of artificial heroes struggling against, and always conquering, artificial dilemmas of no real relevance.

Mike Dann, now vice president of programming at CBS, decided to buck this trend. In June 1966, CBS announced the creation of CBS *Playhouse*, an occasional series of original dramas showcasing leading television producers and writers from the 1950s, as well as new talent. Throughout the 1960s, veterans of live television had decried the sterility of television drama. Now, as Tad Mosel succinctly told New York's *Daily News*, "They're calling our bluff."

Dann named Barbara Schultz as executive producer for the series, and both agreed Fred Coe should produce the premiere, *The Final War of Olly Winter*, by Ronald Ribman, author of the off-Broadway plays *Harry, Noon and Night* and *Journey of the Fifth Horse*.

The Final War of Olly Winter is a landmark in American cinema and television. Not until the mid- and late 1970s, with the end of the Vietnam War, did American films or television drama begin to deal with it. But in the fall of 1966, barely twenty-four months after the Gulf of Tonkin Resolution expanded America's military role in Vietnam, Fred Coe began producing a show which predicted disaster for America in Vietnam.

Directed by Paul Bogart, *Olly Winter* stars Ivan Dixon as a black GI in Vietnam in 1963. An atheist, he is a tough but humane veteran of World War II and Korea, and the poverty of the American inner city. Wandering alone in the jungle after the South Vietnamese army unit he advises is wiped out in a firefight with the Vietcong, he meets a Vietnamese woman (Tina Chen). Despite their inability to speak each other's languages, Dixon and Tina Chen fall in love, only to eventually die in a hail of bullets from a Vietcong ambush.

"It was a very tough show, and it required an enormous amount of courage for CBS to do it," Ronald Ribman says. Barbara Schultz recalls no pressure from the network, but says there was anxiety, with CBS President Thomas Dawson worried about possible adverse reaction from soldiers' parents.

Olly Winter was not only avante-garde politically, but linguistically as well. Patrick Adiarte plays a Vietcong guerrilla Dixon captures, an opponent with whom he gradually develops a mutual respect. Just after Dixon captures Adiarte, the Vietcong guerrilla has several arguments with Chen, who sides with the American soldier. These arguments are conducted in Vietnamese, without benefit of subtitles.

It was hard to find sponsors for the show, and CBS had to offer slots at discount rates. It still didn't find many takers. When the show aired on January 29, 1967, Kellogg's Cornflakes was the only advertiser. CBS ran promotional spots for its own programs, and took a $300,000 loss on its $500,000 investment. Despite the script's controversial nature, though, Coe would brook no changes to it. "Thanks to Fred, this show was shot as it was written," Ribman says. "This itself is startling. At the time I thought, 'Well, you write the script, they shoot the script.' I have been disabused of that notion a dozen times since."

Neither Bogart nor Ribman recalls Coe having drinking problems during the show. Barbara Schultz, however, remembers him drinking heavily and, on several occasions, not being completely sober in the control room. Nonetheless, Coe oversaw a superb show. "The Golden Age of Television Drama returned for 90 minutes last night," proclaimed the *Detroit News*, while the *Baltimore Sun* added: "Ronald Ribman's first television script would have stood out in the palmiest season of the middle Fifties." The show was a ratings success as well, with more than thirty million viewers.

Most episodes of *CBS Playhouse* were sponsored by General Telephone and Electronics and ran on an intermittent basis through 1970, featuring the work of such leading producers as Herbert Brodkin, George Schaefer, Martin Manulis, and director-turned-producer Delbert Mann, and writers like JP Miller, Tad Mosel, Reginald Rose, and Ellen Violett. The show was a class act, but when GTE bowed out as its sole sponsor, no replacement could be found. *CBS Playhouse* was a heroic rearguard effort to revive the great dramatic anthologies of the 1950s on commercial television. But with no new sponsor, it died.

• • •

In 1967, Coe was named to direct the film *A Dream of Kings*, based on the novel by Harry Mark Petrakis. Although both Coe and Petrakis later left the film, they flew to Italy that summer or fall in a successful effort to convince Anthony Quinn to star in it. With them were Joyce, John Coe, and Sue and Sam, Coe and Joyce's two young children. It was the first time Petrakis had met Joyce, and he was impressed. When she wasn't present, however, Coe remarked upon some erratic behavior of hers, and the two of them were sleeping apart. Joyce must have known she was feeling troubled, since she apparently sought help from a therapist about this time. One thing apparently preying on her mind was whether Coe was still faithful to her. Although the only extramarital affair we are certain Coe had is the one he had with Joyce while married to Alice, it remained a preoccupation of Joyce's.

To a friend of theirs, Coe's goals and Joyce's were hopelessly in conflict: he wanted to create great art; she wanted to live well and rise socially. "He never understood what her needs were when he married her," says Mab Ashforth. "Their needs ran completely counter to each other. She drove him crazy with her choices."

Reports started to filter out that Coe was violent with Joyce. Barbara Schultz heard that Joyce felt Coe was abusing her, that he would come to the house in East Hampton, and she would sneak out, afraid that he might hurt her. "I did hear one time that Fred had gotten very angry and slapped her or something," says JP Miller. "But I would not classify Fred as a wife-beater." Once, his son John was at the house on Baiting Hollow Road when Coe was in a drunken rage. Joyce locked herself into the ground-floor bathroom. Coe started kicking on the door, and would have kicked it down, but John got between him and the door.

Another time when Joyce didn't want to be alone with Coe and the children, she asked Barbara Bolton (who lived in nearby Amagansett with husband Bob Costello) to come over. Joyce seemed frightened, but Bolton saw no signs of violence, only that Coe had been drinking too much. Neither did she see much communication. "I never felt it was totally Fred's fault, I really didn't," she says. "Joyce would remain totally silent when he was trying to talk or argue. I think her very removal annoyed him, and I think she knew it did. She would absolutely sit quietly and let him rave on. It was almost like she was saying to me, 'You see? You see how violent he is?'"

By the end of 1967, Coe and Joyce had separated. For about a year and a half, Joyce and the children lived in the house on Baiting Hollow Road, with Sue and Sam attending the Hampton Day School. The loss of live television deprived Coe of a unique and powerful niche and aggravated his drinking. But his marital problems were also an increasing source of distraction to him.

Between the fall of 1961 and the spring of 1966, with live television a thing of the past, Coe produced seven plays, two feature films (co-scripting a third), a show on British television, and *Theatre '62* on NBC. Between the fall of 1966 and the spring of 1971, he produced only one television show, directed one feature film, and produced one musical play. His drinking made the marriage worse, but the marriage made his drinking worse as well.

· · ·

Wait Until Dark and *The Final War of Olly Winter* were trademark Coe quality original dramas. His next two projects, however, were unsuccessful forays into America's burgeoning youth culture. His assistant at the time, Jan Monkhouse, worked with him in an improvised first-floor office in his Madison Avenue townhouse from January 1968 through the spring of 1969.

Monkhouse found Coe slow and understated, and wasn't sure if this was because he was Southern or because he wasn't well. She knew he had heart problems, but that he continued to smoke. Some days he came downstairs in his pajamas, shuffling along in what Robert Alan Aurthur called "his familiar duck-footed amble." He would lie down on the couch, smoke, read the newspaper, and make phone calls while Monkhouse made his coffee. Without Joyce and the children there, though, the house felt deserted and empty.

In May 1968, he became director of the film *Me, Natalie*. It reunited him with Patty Duke, who would benefit from having him as a father figure at a time when her life was unraveling. Coe had his own problems, however, and despite his fatherly affection for her, the two would clash.

Produced by Stanley Shapiro and written by A. Martin Zweiback, *Me, Natalie* is the story of an unattractive Jewish girl in Brooklyn (Duke, outfitted with a Cyrano-like nose) who feels like a social outcast. Her parents, Phil Sterling and Nancy Marchand, can't assuage her fears of being undesirable. Neither can her lovably eccentric Uncle Harold (Martin Balsam). She becomes a radical, moves to the East Village, and falls in love with a handsome artist (James Farentino) who, to her surprise, returns her love.

In its review of *Me, Natalie*, New York's *Cue* magazine recalled Duke's performance in *The Miracle Worker*, saying she was an expert at showing raw nerves. At this point in her life, however, she was nothing but raw nerves. Her own marriage was falling apart. She campaigned for Senator Robert Kennedy in the 1968 Democratic primaries, only to see him assassinated live on television just after rehearsals for *Me, Natalie* began. The twenty-one-year-old Duke was abusing drugs and teetering on the edge of a nervous breakdown.

Alone in the studio one night, she took a full bottle of sleeping pills, which she later estimated as thirty Seconals. A car was sent for her because it was felt an ambulance would attract too much publicity. Coe went to the hospital where Duke was taken and with his Southern charm, convinced them not to formally admit her in order to avoid publicity. For a few weeks, he took her to live at his townhouse on Madison Avenue.

Coe's son John was now living in the townhouse as well. "Patty was drinking and doing tranquilizers," he says. "She was late every day. It was the three of us [Coe, John, Patty Duke]. That's what got her to work." John's moral support during this film also bolstered his father. "We went through crisis here, daily crisis," John grimly recalls. "He needed help just to get through the day. I happened to be there, and was able to provide help in a fatherly way." In spite of two major blow-ups, Coe displayed great diplomatic skills in coaxing Duke through the film. "Fred saved the picture," says art director George Jenkins. "I never would have figured out how to do it."

Another long-term associate of Coe's on the picture was Dick Smith, now one of the leading makeup artists in the film industry. This was the first time he had worked with Coe since *Philco-Goodyear*. Coe was a different person, Smith felt, and a better one. "Fred, you were a son of a bitch to work for back at NBC," Smith told him one day. "You now seem to have reached a point in your life where you've found a serenity and patience I couldn't have believed you would ever attain." It was another example of Coe's remarkable ability to hide his own pain and project an air of confidence on the set.

For Coe, there was also turmoil on the parental front. Like Patty Duke's Natalie, Laurie had become a college radical. A freshman at Georgetown University, Laurie dropped out of school, joined the radical Students for a Democratic Society (SDS), and moved in with her boyfriend. Although Coe was concerned, he also admired a radical career that led Laurie to cut sugar cane in Cuba with the Venceremos Brigade. Years later, when John was a successful manager with McDonald's, Laurie and her husband were engaged in the improbable task of trying to radicalize steelworkers in Birmingham, Alabama. "At least you're trying to change the world," Coe told Laurie. "What can you change about a hamburger?"

During the filming of *Me, Natalie*, Coe's relations with Joyce were a continuing source of anxiety. On her visits to the townhouse on Madison Avenue, Jan Monkhouse found Joyce a bit like Jackie Kennedy: beautiful and elegant, but cool and somewhat aloof. "I thought she was cold," Monkhouse says. "There were times when things were falling apart and he was pleading for her to come back." When Joyce did come into town, Coe made a big fuss getting the house perfect. He'd spend $100 or more on flowers and the house was filled with them.

. . .

Although produced, directed, and written by men, *Me, Natalie* is an early example of the vengeance feminism that would make offering to hold a door for a woman or pay for her dinner such a risky proposition in the early 1970s, and that would lead to "mow 'em all down" films such as *Old Boy-friends*. Natalie exacts reprisals against practically every male character in the film for slights real or imagined, most notably James Farentino. When he decides to leave his wife for her, she encourages him to do so, then abandons him. Natalie is an unappealing figure, and it's a tribute to Coe's skill as a director and Patty Duke's as an actress that they make her sympathetic and engaging for stretches.

Critical reaction to the film was mixed. New York's *Cue* magazine said "What [Patty Duke] ultimately does to [Farentino] in the name of finding herself should be a warning for men to stay away from ugly ducklings who aren't over their inferiority complexes—and in some cases, from movies made about them." On the other hand, the Los Angeles *Herald-Examiner* said, "'Me, Natalie' has just the unaffected, girlish, charming candid self-revelation its title suggests." It did not do well commercially, however.

Opinions were also divided on Coe's direction. "When raw nerves are exposed, the smart director will opt for understatement," *Cue* magazine said, adding Coe had done the opposite. But the *Los Angeles Times* called Coe's direction "expert." *Me, Natalie* feels less stage-bound than the portions of *A Thousand Clowns* Coe directed, suggesting he was becoming more comfortable with films. However, Bo Goldman, says, "It was a nice movie, but it wasn't Fred. There were flashes of him, but I could see he wasn't at home with this medium."

. . .

When *Me, Natalie* was released in the fall of 1969, Coe was on the road in Boston with his first musical since *Fiddler on the Roof*. *Georgy* was based on the 1966 film *Georgy Girl*, starring Lynn Redgrave. The story of a young English woman in swinging London who feels unattractive and unloved, she is a kind of British *Me, Natalie*, although less of an avenger. Coe produced and Peter Hunt directed, with Dilys Watling starring in the Lynn Redgrave role. The book was written by Tom Mankiewicz, with music by George Fischoff and lyrics by Carole Bayer (later famous as pop songwriter Carole Bayer Sager).

Coe liked the show's youthful spirit and its heroine. "Something about the movie obviously moved him," Peter Hunt says. "And he cared deeply for the character of the girl." But that youthful spirit may have eluded Coe. "I think he admired the youth of it. He wanted to tap in to what was going on," Hunt adds. "Whether he succeeded is another question. There was a big generational gap. He came from William Gibson and those kind of writers, and these kids were basically trying to bring rock into the theater. So I think there were some confusions, generationally speaking."

As times changed, Coe tried to change with them, in appearance as well as choice of material. No longer sporting a crew cut, he grew his hair, swapped his horn-rimmed glasses for steel frames, and now wore cowboy boots. One day he ran into Milt Myers, who had been *Philco-Goodyear's* production supervisor. Myers walked right past him: Coe's 1950s look was so firmly etched in Myers's mind he couldn't see him any other way.

In rehearsals, Coe was frustrated. He knew the show had problems, but couldn't figure out how to attack them. Several critics later said the show's songs were its weak link. Fred Coe was a theatrical genius, but he didn't know how to rock and roll. To his director, Coe was an admirable figure, but one in decline. "He was a very sweet man, a gentleman, certainly knowledgeable," Hunt says. "I had a feeling, however, that I was dealing with somebody in a twilight zone. That he'd done it all and wasn't quite the man he had been."

Coe's personal problems were also apparent. Was Coe drinking much? "Yes," Hunt says tersely. "The answer is yes." However, Coe was always functional as the show's producer. His separation from Joyce also weighed heavily on him, Hunt adds. "It was very painful, and I think it was part of the reason for his being slightly unfocused when he was unfocused."

An incident on *Georgy* suggests Dick Smith may have spoken too soon in saying Coe had mellowed out, though. In an effort to fix the show in Boston, several minutes were added to one act. The woman who sold orange drinks in the lobby didn't realize this, and began to set up her stand at the usual time. The sound of orange drink bottles clinking during the show unleashed the old Fred Coe, who stormed into the lobby and swept all the orange drinks off the counter, sending them crashing to the floor.

Coe became fearful for the show's prospects. Following its unsuccessful opening night in Boston, Hunt told Coe he wasn't going to wait up for reviews. But at two-thirty in the morning, Hunt's phone rang. It was Coe, summoning him to his hotel suite, where he and a man from the William Morris agency were bewailing the reviews.

One of those blasts came from Elliot Norton, drama critic of the Boston *Herald*. Norton also had a local TV show, on which Coe and Hunt subsequently appeared. As they were leaving the studio afterwards, Hunt was walking down the hall with Norton, who told Hunt he thought the show would turn out fine. "Gee, I wish you'd put that in your review, because you scared my producer to death," Hunt said. Norton replied that he would be more upbeat in his follow-up review, and he was. "But the damage had been done," Hunt says. "The fear factor had set in, and it's very hard to deal with that."

Coe's fears were justified: New York critics took the tone of Norton's first review. *Georgy* opened in Broadway's Winter Garden Theater on February 26, 1970. It closed after four performances on February 28.

When the show was in Boston, Coe had called William Gibson, asking him to view a rehearsal and critique it. They went up to Coe's room afterwards. The show was obviously going to be a flop, and Coe seemed very lonely. "Oh, isn't it wonderful about Arthur?" he said to Gibson. (Arthur Penn's film *Bonnie and Clyde* had just vaulted him into the front ranks of American directors.) "It was very sad," Gibson recalls, "because underneath there must have been a great feeling of his own failure."

On his way down, Coe showed a remarkable lack of bitterness toward his many successful acolytes. "Fred never resented it when the writers and directors who had worked for him became famous," says Dominick Dunne. "He was never saying, 'I started that guy.' He was that kind of man. If you've lived in Hollywood, you know that attitude is *unheard-of*."

That spring, Coe and Harry Muheim walked past the Winter Garden's huge *Georgy* sign. "The terrible goddamn thing about producing a failure at the Winter Garden," Coe said, "is that that damn sign sits there and hollers at you for a year until somebody paints it over." Coe had heeded Groucho Marx's call, "Next year at the Winter Garden," but he had come in with the wrong show.

• • •

A few months later, Coe got better news: Joyce agreed to a reconciliation and moved back into the Madison Avenue townhouse with Sue and Sam. As part of that reconciliation, they went through counseling. John recalls that Joyce did have a positive influence on Coe during this period, getting him not only to go into counseling, but to give up alcohol. Coe's giving up alcohol, however, was fitful, and the reconciliation would be as well.

One day in the summer of 1970, Coe returned to the Madison Avenue townhouse from a meeting with Jerome Robbins, and it was obvious something was wrong. He sat in the living room and complained of pain in his chest. Coe's new assistant Ann Levack called Edward Colton, his lawyer, and Coe called his doctor. It didn't seem like a heart attack, but he was very uncomfortable and frightened.

His doctor sent an ambulance and went to meet him at the hospital. When the ambulance came, Coe was embarrassed, because they insisted on carrying him out on a stretcher. It was not a heart attack, but angina, and Coe was in the hospital for a few days.

• • •

In August of 1970, Tad Mosel joined Alcoholics Anonymous. That fall, he kept calling Coe to tell him how helpful it was. Both were busy men, though, and Mosel never got through. In January of 1971, Mosel was set to make his first speech at an AA meeting, in the cavernous Church of the Heavenly Rest at 90th Street and Fifth Avenue on Central Park. Mosel was nervous, accustomed to writing for large audiences, but not to appearing in front of them.

When it was time for him to speak, he climbed onto the stage and walked to the microphone. As his stage fright subsided and he could focus on the crowd, he saw a familiar face in the middle of the front row: Fred Coe, beaming at him. "That day he had called of his own volition," Mosel recalls in a tone of wonder. "And there he was. It was a magnificent moment. We went out afterwards, to a coffee shop down on 42nd Street, and sat there talking about everything until three o'clock in the morning."

Coe played a more direct role in getting Bob Costello into AA, encouraging him to join. Fortunately for Coe, his AA group was like "Old Home Week." Not only were Mosel and Costello in it, but Ellen Violett, who had written several shows for him, and agent Yvette Schumer.

Although Coe joined AA to win Joyce back, it was Alice, visiting New York, who attended an AA meeting with him. She brushes aside any suggestion that it was unusual for her to still be supportive of him. "There was never anything but closeness between us," she says. "He was the best friend I ever had. In spite of everything that happened."

Initially, Coe displayed unqualified enthusiasm for AA. Yvette Schumer felt it was making an impact. "He seemed to be all right, to sort of have it under control," she says. Bob Costello wasn't so sure, though. "Fred didn't talk a lot," he says. "Tad talked a lot—Tad you had to sit on. Fred never got into it."

• • •

With Sue and Sam starting to grow, Coe encouraged them to get to know John and Laurie, and there was a surprising amount of mingling between his first and second families, both in East Hampton and New York. "He raised us all to think of ourselves as brothers and sisters," Laurie says. "There was no step-this or half-that." John fell easily into the role of Sam's big brother. Although Coe had not been keen about having children with Joyce, he became intensely fond of Sue and Sam, and was able to express his affections for them openly, a knack he apparently never developed with John and Laurie.

• • •

Coe directed the television version of *All the Way Home* for *Hallmark Hall of Fame* on December 1, 1971. The producer was his old nemesis David Susskind, but as far as Tad Mosel could see, they got along. Now in AA, Coe seemed calm. "Fred was in a very benign period of his life," says Mosel, who reworked his Pulitzer Prize–winning play for the small screen. "I don't think it was benign as far as Joyce went, but as far as himself and his work, he was in good shape."

The show starred Joanne Woodward as Mary Follet, Richard Kiley as Jay Follet, the husband she loses in an auto accident, Eileen Heckart as Mary's pious Aunt Hannah, and Pat Hingle as Ralph Follet, Jay's constantly intoxicated brother. In another example of Coe's ability to spot talent, Mary's younger brother Andrew is played by James Woods, in one of his earliest film or television appearances.

While Coe was a stellar producer, watching *All the Way Home* reminds us again that he was also a first-rate director. In the scene where Jay drives the family to see 103-year-old Grandma, the camera moves in for a closeup of Jay's father while he speaks, then pulls back smoothly. The viewer may not even realize a closeup has occurred, only that somehow the impact of the father's remarks has been magnified. And when Grandma is wheeled out onto the lawn of her home at night, it's a beautiful scene with an almost abstract composition. She and her assistant are shown on a hillock above the family members, who gather around them. The background is darkness, but Grandma is bathed in a kind of celestial light, as if soon destined for heaven.

The show resonates with echoes from Coe's own life. Because he was now in AA, he could identify with Jay, the noble brother who gives up alcohol, rather than Ralph, the loud, crude brother unable to wean himself from liquor. And when the family learns of Jay's sudden death, his portrait, recently painted, looms as a silent witness, much as the image of Coe's absent father loomed over his life.

Along with favorable critical reaction and a coveted Peabody Award, Coe had more good news. Just before the show aired, on November 23, 1971, his son John married Ann Hoffheimer in Cincinnati. And on March 8, 1972, Laurie married Haynes Dyches in Havana, a small town north of Tallahassee, Florida. But Coe's problem drinking resumed.

As at Peabody College and Yale Drama, he would drift away from AA without completing his course of study. Tad Mosel would make it. Bob Costello would make it. Fred Coe, who had encouraged them both, would not make it. But he had performed a kind of cardiopulmonary resuscitation on the lives as well as the careers of his protégés. And as any CPR teacher will tell you, the nobility in learning it lies in the fact that you can use it to save others, but not to save yourself.

His marriage with Joyce was beyond repair, and for Ann Levack, it was painful to watch her boss. "The whole time I worked for him, he desperately wanted a reconciliation," she says. "He was very broken up about the fact that this marriage was going to end. And losing his kids was probably the thing he was dealing with the most."

Coe moved into the Yale Club. From his room high above Grand Central Station, he could look through the windows of an adjoining building and watch the office workers, most of whom had a home and family to return to that evening. There were few things Coe could bear less than solitude, and few he was now more afflicted with. On July 1, 1972, he and Joyce signed a formal separation agreement, and would never live together again. Coe would now have his most productive year in nearly a decade.

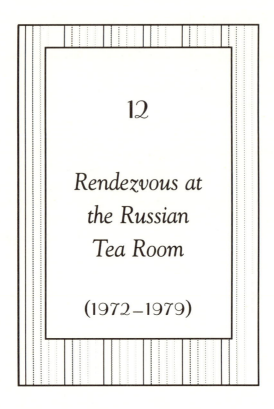

12

Rendezvous at the Russian Tea Room

(1972–1979)

One spring in the early 1970s, Robert Alan Aurthur visited Fred Coe at the house on Baiting Hollow Road in East Hampton to write a profile of him for *Esquire*. Aurthur praised Coe's still-youthful appearance, noting that his face was still unlined and his curly brown hair longer and curlier. Aurthur enthused that Coe, who was in his late fifties, looked like a man in his mid-forties. But a careful reading of the article shows that physically, Coe was beginning to fall apart.

Although it was 11:30 in the morning, Coe instantly sagged onto a couch and fell asleep, causing Aurthur to muse that he would have to wake Coe up if he were going to interview him. Aurthur diplomatically noted "a few more pounds" on him, and that he started to wheeze when he laughed. The wheeze intensified during the course of the interview, but he just continued to smoke.

In 1972 Coe returned to the theater with his first non-musical play since 1966's *Wait Until Dark*. Broadway was changing in several ways, however, and most of those changes were uncongenial to him. As Brooks Atkinson noted, the physical environment of Broadway was deteriorating:

In the 1970's a veneer of seediness began to cover the surface of Broadway. The shops looked crummy. Many of them were in the pornography business. Although one thousand police patrolled the area every day, prostitutes, drug peddlers, thieves, muggers and their customers or victims assembled there instinctively, as if it were their turf. The Great White Way had become both shabby and fidgety.

The intellectual environment was less than hospitable as well, but Coe would adapt to it as best he could. His three remaining Broadway plays would be a formula thriller, a light comedy, and a tearjerker, a far cry from such innovative plays as *The Miracle Worker* and *A Thousand Clowns*.

The thriller was *Night Watch*, which Coe directed for producers Barnard Straus and George W. George. Written by Lucille Fletcher, it starred Joan Hackett as a woman who appears half-mad with fear, convinced that her husband and his lover plan to kill her. But she plans to kill them and does.

Critics liked the show, which opened on February 28, 1972. Richard Watts of the *New York Post* wrote, "The call for a good American mystery melodrama was answered last night at the Morosco Theater." Betty Rollin of WNBC-TV called it "superb" and Douglas Watt of the *Daily News* said "the twists and turns of this headlong thriller are fun." All three praised Coe's direction. The play had its critical detractors as well (notably Martin Gottfried of *Women's Wear Daily*, who called it a shameless imitation of *Sleuth*, the previous season's hit thriller). But the play was popular, and audiences came to the Morosco for a year and a half.

Coe appeared to be in good spirits, and Margaret Sheffield, who dated him during this period, found him witty and delightful. One weekend, they were part of a larger party at a friend's house in the Hamptons. In rare form, Coe flirted with the hosts' eighty-year-old Irish maid. "Ah, he gave me a kiss!" the maid complained at one point, adding in her rich brogue, "*and it was a wet one!*"

While directing *Night Watch*, he also co-produced *Promenade, All!*, a light-hearted look at four generations of an American business family starring Hume Cronyn, Anne Jackson, and Eli Wallach. Written by David Robison and directed by Arthur Storch, it reunited Coe with his former partner Arthur Cantor. "Once he split with Joyce, I think he was a little happier," Cantor says. "He came to me and said, 'Let's work together again.' And we worked together very harmoniously. The play didn't make it, but it was a good show."

That wasn't how the critics felt when it opened on April 16, 1972. The play's reviews ranged from snide to dismissive, and it closed after only forty-eight performances. In Coe's Broadway career, he did better financially as well as artistically on long shots. He was now supporting himself and two families, however, and had to take sure shots. *Promenade, All*, a likeable show with marquee names, was a sure shot that missed.

• • •

Coe brought his renewed professional vigor to television as well. TV in the early 1970s, however, was a far cry from the world of *Philco-Goodyear*. Many industry founders had retired, replaced by men who had climbed the corporate ladder in sales. "Programs come into being to attract an audience," *Variety* television editor Les Brown wrote during this period. "Not to feed their minds or to elevate them morally or spiritually, but to deliver them to an advertiser." Many of those who make TV shows abandoned any pretense of cultural aspiration and now began referring to their work as "the product."

Even during this period, though, Coe was responsible for several quality dramas. In 1972, he made his only two shows for ABC, the network he blamed for the death of live television. On *If You Give a Dance, You Gotta Pay the Band*, Coe worked with two other live TV stalwarts: Herbert Brodkin, the show's executive producer, and his old patron and nemesis David Susskind, here the producer. Coe directed the show, which aired on December 19. The story by Stanley L. Gray, an ex-con and former drug addict, focused on two black inner-city kids struggling against their surroundings.

The script, Gray's first for television, was too long, and he recalls Coe sensitively helping him make the needed cuts. Gray found Susskind arrogant, and thought Coe (who probably got the job through Susskind) seemed almost subservient to him. Yet Coe's discomfiture with that subservience struck Gray as a measure of his dignity.

Critical reaction to the show was enthusiastic. Ron Powers of the Chicago *Sun-Times* called it "one of the finest and most courageous [plays] ever to appear on TV" and Bernie Harrison of the Washington *Star-News* called it "a lovely play," adding "Coe's direction is uncannily good." In another sign of Coe's remarkable talent-scouting abilities, it also praised the two lead actors, one of whom was eleven-year-old Larry (now Laurence) Fishburne, in his debut performance.

Two days before *Dance/Band* aired, another Coe show appeared on ABC. Given free rein to develop a dramatic program as he saw fit, he came up with the idea of short stories of different lengths on a common theme. *Of Men and Women*, a dramatic anthology-within-an-anthology, showed he had not lost his capacity for innovative TV drama.

The hour-long show featured four stories by as many writers, all dealing with relations between men and women. Directed by Jerry Thorpe, Charles S. Dubin, and Peter Medak, the stories ranged in length from six to eighteen minutes. A. E. Hotchner's "The Brave and Happy Life" starred George Maharis as a man who believes his wife has been killed in a plane crash. He runs to the consoling arms of his lover, only to learn his wife never boarded the plane. Don Petersen's "Hot Machine, Cold Machine" featured Jackie Cooper as a befuddled widower who learns his way around a laundromat from Cloris Leachman.

Terence Rattigan's "All on Her Own" was a one-woman piece starring Lee Remick as a woman coming to terms with her husband's death. And Harvey Jacobs's "Why He Was Late for Work" starred Bill Bixby as a good Samaritan who tries to help a blind man on the street (Burgess Meredith). The blind man, deranged, turns on him, accusing him of having slept with his wife. A mob then gathers and pounces on Bixby.

The latter episode's dark humor may have prevented ABC from picking the show up as a series. "One of the ABC executives said my piece was the one that ruined the show," Jacobs recalls. Kay Gardella of New York's *Daily News* wrote that Coe had been inspired to do *Of Men and Women* by the success of *Love, American Style*, ABC's light, frothy comedy anthology. ABC felt its audience could handle sweetness and light better than bittersweet irony, but key segments of the audience didn't agree: *Of Men and Women* won its time period in New York and Los Angeles. Like Coe's dramatic anthologies of the 1950s, though, it did better in the big cities than the hinterland.

Coe's next effort for television would flabbergast anyone familiar with his quality dramas. It was a 1973 pilot for a situation comedy starring Michele Lee as a spirited single woman on her own. *The Michele Lee Show* opens with a jiggle shot of Miss Lee in a tight pullover running toward the camera while a vapid song drones on about seeing what the day will bring. When her typically eccentric next-door neighbor wanders in through her unlocked apartment door, he says, "Believe me, a young lady living alone should have locks." Perkily and charmingly, she retorts, "And bagels!" Don't even ask about the plot.

Even allowing for the modest standards of mid-1970s sitcoms, this is undistinguished work. There's no point in assailing Coe for doing this tripe: he had to get shows on the air if he was going to put money in the bank. And if quality shows like *Of Men and Women* and *Dance/Band* couldn't get him steady work in TV, he would go where the money was— or where he thought it was.

• • •

In the spring of 1973, when Coe was just starting to revive his career, he learned that Joyce was depressed. He asked Bob Costello, his unit production manager on *Mr. Peepers* and now a successful television producer, if he could find work for her. On two later occasions Costello did, getting Joyce jobs as an assistant casting director on PBS's *The Adams Chronicles* and as a production secretary on the ABC soap opera *Ryan's Hope*. Coe also called Adeline Garner Shell, one of Joyce's roommates at the Osborne, the elegant old Manhattan apartment house where she lived before her marriage to Coe. "You should keep in touch with her," he said, "because she really is a wonderful person."

• • •

Not long after he separated from Joyce, a new love came into Coe's life. Eleanor Cogbill was a tall, blonde woman in her early thirties, a freelance artist from Pittsburgh with a pleasant disposition and a gentle nature. "She acceded to him," says Arthur Cantor. "That's what he needed. She never gave him a rough time."

In 1974, Cantor asked Coe to direct *In Praise of Love*, which he was going to produce on Broadway. In effect, Coe would now be working for a man he had trained. Written by Terence Rattigan, the play starred Rex Harrison as a British writer and Julie Harris as his terminally ill wife. Each thinks the other is unaware of the situation and tries to shield the other from the news.

The egotistical Harrison was extremely difficult to work with. Twenty years earlier, Coe might have managed, but time and liquor had worn him down. As Rattigan wrote the play's early scenes, Harrison's character appears as a boor, indifferent to his wife's fate. But as soon as the curtain rose, Harrison was looking at his wife's medical charts in order to build sympathy for his character. Normally, Rattigan would have helped Coe oppose this tampering with the script, but the British playwright had pneumonia and could not attend New York rehearsals.

Then there was a pitched battle over the script two days before the show's December 10, 1974, opening, with Harrison threatening to abandon the play unless Julie Harris's role was cut in order to accentuate his own. Frequently, Harrison simply ignored Coe. "Rex Harrison gave him a terrible time," Arthur Cantor adds. "He didn't know how to cope with it, so he drank. And the more he drank, the less he could cope." Coe was off the wagon for good.

He still managed to stage a good show, although it got mixed reviews. Martin Gottfried had savaged Coe's last two shows, but wrote in the *New York Post*, "Aspiring to be no more than a touching diversion, well done, it is just that. . . . Fred Coe has given it just the production it requires." John Beaufort of the *Christian Science Monitor* also called it touching and praised the "meticulousness of Coe's direction." But Jack Kroll of *Newsweek* called it "flimsy and sentimental" while T. E. Kalem of *Time* said, "This is a soap bubble of a play. It floats about weightlessly. . . . Expiring at last, it drops to earth in the form of a sentimental teary splat."

Still, the play was critic-proof, and ran through May, when it closed after 199 performances. The manner of its closing was another Harrison affront: at a time when Coe needed—and had—a hit show to help him financially, Harrison stopped doing the still-popular show because he didn't feel like working in New York's summer heat. Audiences came mainly to see him, and the show died when he left.

• • •

The Adams Chronicles was one of the most ambitious dramatic series ever undertaken by National Educational Television, the immediate predecessor of PBS. But when series producer Virginia Kassel asked Fred Coe to produce an episode, he declined: a multi-generational saga about the Massachusetts family that gave this country its second and sixth presidents struck him as a starchy historical pageant. "I don't trust anything where someone writes with a feather," he told Eleanor Cogbill.

Kassel, who conceived of the series as part of America's Bicentennial celebration, persisted, however, and Coe signed on in February of 1975, agreeing to produce and direct four of its thirteen episodes. As a condition of his working on the series, he asked Kassel to hire Bob Costello, his unit production manager on *Mr. Peepers*, as coordinating producer.

"[Fred] was beginning to feel the effects of a very rigorous life," Kassel says. "He said he was tireder than he'd ever been." He didn't want to undertake anything of many months' duration, and thought he needed backup. Now a successful television producer in his own right, Costello was a known quantity.

Coe produced and directed Episode 9, featuring John Quincy Adams's term as president and Episode 10, about his subsequent and more successful work as a congressman. We don't know whether Coe identified with the man Tad Mosel, who wrote both episodes, called "old Johnny Q." But well he might have: John Quincy Adams was an intense man described as "more a natural force . . . than a mere human being," one who devoted too much to work and too little to family. Coe also produced and directed Episodes 12 and 13, focusing on John Quincy Adams's grandchildren. Those episodes were written by two more of Coe's Golden Age protégés: Sam Hall and Roger O. Hirson.

Premiering on January 20, 1976, *The Adams Chronicles* featured 300 principal actors, 800 extras, 250 sets, and two soundstages in a studio at 460 West 54th Street. Location shooting was done in Rhode Island, New York State, Philadelphia, and Washington, D.C. Five other directors worked on the series: Paul Bogart, James Cellan Jones, Barry Davis, Bill Glenn, and Anthony Page. The series was budgeted at $5.2 million, but added between $1.4 and $2 million in cost overruns.

One reason for the cost overruns was a Writers' Guild Strike against the show. When resolved, it led to a highly compressed shooting schedule and generous quantities of overtime pay. All thirteen episodes were taped in a fifteen-week period starting around Memorial Day of 1975 and ending some two weeks after Labor Day. The series was produced in a stressful atmosphere of barely contained chaos, much like the working conditions of live TV.

"These strikes were quite crippling and Fred kept going and kept people's spirits up," Virginia Kassel says. "He was a hard taskmaster on his actors and cameramen. But he imposed discipline at a time when we didn't know from day to day whether we would be able to proceed. He never wavered, never felt uneasy and never gave anyone a sense of panic. It was quite extraordinary." He would pay a price for the months of grueling work, however.

He smoked constantly, often stacking three or four packs of cigarettes on the control room console. Coe was set to direct the sequence on *John Quincy Adams—President* where John Adams dies, but felt so poorly he turned to Bob Costello, asked him to direct it, and went home. Another time, when the two went to lunch near the studio, Coe had to take a cab—it was too much of a physical strain for him to walk a block and a half to the restaurant and back.

Mentally, though, he was as sharp as ever. During a rehearsal of Episode 12, he and Sam Hall watched the actors rehearse. As Coe read the script a few lines ahead of the actors, he would point to a line coming up and whisper to Hall that the actor was going to have trouble. To Hall's astonishment, in every case, the actor would stumble or stop and give the line a puzzled look.

Tad Mosel calls Coe's work on *The Adams Chronicles* among the best direction his scripts ever received. The critics, though, were of two minds about the 1976 series: *The New Republic* called *John Quincy Adams—President* a well-shaped hour, but the *Saturday Review* said Coe's episodes had a heavy-handed civics-text quality, something it felt was true of the series as a whole. Despite such mixed reviews, *The Adams Chronicles* was popular: its first three episodes drew 12 to 14 percent of the audience in the New York City area, up from the 5 percent PBS shows usually got.

Coe received three Emmy nominations for his work on *The Adams Chronicles*: two as a producer of a limited series (i.e., miniseries) and one as director of *John Quincy Adams—President*. When Roger O. Hirson arrived for the Emmy Awards telecast May 17, 1976, in Los Angeles, the empty seat in front of him bore Coe's name. The recently remarried Hirson was eager to see him and introduce him to his new wife. But at ceremony's end, the seat was still vacant.

Coe's health and fortunes were waning, and Bob Costello saw a parallel. The Adams family flourished early in U.S. history, but went into decline when the industrialists took over. Coe was a man of his times, Costello thought. He was wonderful during the Golden Age of Television, and did some very successful work later on. But he hadn't risen on the crest of the wave.

• • •

When *The Adams Chronicles* finished taping in September of 1975, Coe was having sharp back pains. He went to see his doctor, and learned that his aorta had been weakened by years of smoking and drinking. He was in the hospital for a month, getting strong enough to undergo an operation for an aneurysm, a condition in which the aorta in his chest area had ballooned, becoming dangerously thin and weak. Because he smoked so much, his lungs had to be drained of fluid before an operation could even be attempted.

During Coe's month in the hospital, he had several regular visitors: Eleanor Cogbill, his son John, and Joyce. Despite the ongoing emotional trench warfare between Fred and Joyce Coe, there was still an underlying mutual fondness: Tad Mosel felt they were closer during their years of separation than when they had been together.

The operation, conducted in October, was successful, with a large aneurysm on the aorta in Coe's chest repaired. "Successful" is a relative term, however: Coe's aorta was enlarged all the way down through his abdomen. The operation saved his life, but revealed that much of this important artery was weakened.

In the short run, though, Coe had prevailed. Paddy Chayefsky, Arthur Penn, and Herb Gardner came to see him in the hospital one day. "The mood was very buoyant because Fred had come through," Arthur Penn recalls. "He was sitting there swearing he was never going to smoke or drink again, which we knew was a lot of bullshit." When Coe laughed, his throat would catch, the result of his smoking. But, Herb Gardner thought, the laugh in his hospital bed was the same as in the back of the theater on *A Thousand Clowns*. You wouldn't know there had been bad days.

When Coe returned to the apartment he now shared with Eleanor Cogbill on 65th Street, he still wasn't well. He remained in bed for three months in late 1975, where he edited his episodes of *The Adams Chronicles* on videotape playback equipment. Eleanor took his temperature, kept a temperature chart, helped him to the bathroom, got up every four hours at night to give him pills, bathed and sponged him, and prepared three meals a day for him. When Alice Coe met Eleanor in the fall of 1975, she didn't think Eleanor was her ex-husband's lover, but his nurse.

Eleanor also let out Coe's shirts because he gained a lot of weight after the operation. Harry Muheim, one of his writers, was amazed when he met him again. "He sounded the same and his attitude was pretty much the same," Muheim recalls, "but all of his ideas were now coming out of a fat man."

After the operation, Coe spent the Christmas of 1975 at Alice's home in Fort Lauderdale. His visits with her always had a soothing effect upon him, but in New York, he was a different person. "If he was working, he didn't drink," Eleanor Cogbill says. "But at night he'd go out, get drunk, insult people and forget he'd done it." He lost many friends: he didn't remember what he said, or why people didn't want to associate with him.

A. E. Hotchner often ran into Coe at Dick Edwards's. "Fred began a flow of disintegration," Hotchner recalls. "He was drinking too much, his complexion turned bad, and he lost his enthusiasm for production. You could almost see him dying a little bit at a time." Fred Coe was married to one woman, living with a second, and abidingly fond of a third. He wanted to be a good father to Sue and Sam, but was often at odds with their mother. He was trying to restart his career, yet his drinking made that unlikely. "It was like a soap opera," Eleanor Cogbill muses. "And you know, he never did like soap operas."

• • •

On November 7, 1977, Coe and Joyce sold the house on Baiting Hollow Road to author Gail Sheehy. After Coe lost the house, he still went out to the Hamptons, staying with Bob and Sybil Costello in Amagansett. "It was kind of sad," Costello says. "He'd just stretch out and think, and you didn't know where he was." Even here, Coe sought the shadows. In the living room, he could have stretched out on the daybed near the picture window with sunlight pouring in and a view of the waves breaking on Amagansett Beach. Instead, he chose another daybed, in a darker corner of the living room.

By early 1978, Coe hadn't worked in almost three years and was depleting his savings. He cut back his assistant, Tom Greene, from full-time status to half-time, with his agent, Priscilla Morgan, hiring Greene on a half-time basis. He apparently fell behind in his payments to Joyce, who filed several court actions for nonpayment of alimony and child support against him that spring.

Meanwhile, in Fort Lauderdale, Alice was regretfully giving up her share of the real estate office she ran with another woman. The year before, Coe had asked her to forgo weekly $200 support payments he still sent her. In agreeing to this, she neglected to mention that it would cost her the ability to maintain her share of the business. In June of 1978, Alice returned to Nashville. A woman starting over in her early sixties, she was worried about her prospects, briefly moving in with a friend who helped her find work.

• • •

On March 30, 1978, the Writers' Guild East gave Coe its first annual Evelyn Burkey Memorial Award, which goes to the person most helpful to writers. (It would later go to Walter Cronkite, Art Buchwald, South African playwright Athol Fugard, and Horton Foote, among others.) The award was presented at the Writers' Guild East's annual dinner, held at the Essex House Hotel. Coe attended with Eleanor Cogbill. There to honor their "Pappy" were Paddy Chayefsky, Horton Foote, Tad Mosel, JP Miller, Sumner Locke Elliott, Robert Alan Aurthur, Herb Gardner, N. Richard Nash, and director Delbert Mann.

The mood was festive, with the table where Coe and most of the writers sat dominated by the hyperkinetic gregariousness of Paddy Chayefsky. The buoyant spirits and horseplay almost made it seem like a class reunion. But to JP Miller, neither Robert Alan Aurthur nor Coe, both of whom continued to smoke, looked well. Eight months later, Aurthur was dead of lung cancer.

The ceremony featured Chayefsky's glowing tribute to Coe and Coe's brief and hesitant remarks of acceptance. He then invited his party to the Russian Tea Room. As Tad Mosel surveyed the group of writers Coe first assembled in Studio 8G, he wondered if anyone but Coe could have done it. "If you took all of his writers and put us together without Fred, I'm not sure we would have gotten along so well," Mosel says. "But Fred had that way of making people get along with each other, do you know?"

By 1978, many of Coe's writers had gone on to success in Hollywood. But he was firmly mired in yesteryear, ignoring Mosel's dictum, "It's okay to look back at the past, but you shouldn't stare." He wanted to restage several of the best episodes of *Philco-Goodyear Playhouse* under the rubric *Camera 50*. While in Hollywood working on an unsuccessful TV pilot, he met a young limousine driver who reminded him of Wally Cox. His resulting idea: a *Mr. Peepers Jr.* series. Almost as sad as the mess he had made of his life and the increasingly broken state of his health is that Fred Coe, once a paragon of innovation, had now become so relentlessly derivative in a futile effort to revive his glory days.

Remarkably, he still managed to convey optimism to his troops. Sometime in the mid-1970s, he got together with Harry Mark Petrakis, the author of *A Dream of Kings*. It was about midnight and Petrakis was exhausted. The effervescent Coe wanted to go to Elaine's, saying they'd probably meet some writers (his favorite class of people) there. But Petrakis was tired and begged off.

And on a warm May afternoon in 1978, writer David Karp ran into Coe on the street near Lincoln Center. Coe grinned and enthusiastically told Karp about his latest project. "We're going to make it this time, Pappy," he said with the boundless optimism of a Mississippi Delta planter convinced cotton prices will rise. "I got a real hunch about this one!"

At the same time, his self-destructiveness was spiraling out of control. Increasingly, he came to resemble Harvey Weems, protagonist of Horton Foote's drama *The Midnight Caller*, which had aired on *Philco-Goodyear Playhouse*. Years before, Weems's marriage to Helen, his true love, was forbidden by his parents. She salvages her life; he doesn't. Every night, he shows up drunkly bellowing at her rooming house. "I tried to save him," Helen laments. "I wanted to save him like I never wanted to do anything in my life. But . . . [h]ow could I have won? How can you save someone that doesn't want to be saved? Because he doesn't want to be saved. Not from drink, not from loneliness, not from death."

• • •

By the spring of 1979, Coe had not worked in four years, with one project after another failing to get off the ground. He was rescued from idleness by executive producer Ray Katz, who decided to remake *The Miracle Worker* for television. Melissa Gilbert played the Helen Keller role originally performed by Patty Duke. Duke, now grown up, assumed the Annie Sullivan role originated by Anne Bancroft.

Katz invited Coe and writer William Gibson to participate in the film. In late February and early March, there were rehearsals in Los Angeles, then a two-week practice run at the Poinciana Playhouse in Palm Beach, Florida, followed by filming back in Los Angeles.

Paul Aaron, the film's young director, had made two previous movies and worked on Broadway, successfully directing a revival of Paddy Chayefsky's *The Tenth Man*, starring Richard Dreyfuss. Aaron had ideas of his own about the film, and when he first met Coe, said he would do things differently than Coe and Arthur Penn had done seventeen years earlier. They were working in color, not black and white, the film was for home rather than theater audiences, and the temper of the times had changed.

"When I come to things I will do differently from Arthur Penn, will you be okay with that?" Aaron asked. "Absolutely," Coe replied. He may have thought it would be okay, but it wasn't.

Coe was highly critical of Aaron's work (as was Patty Duke). "He had a movie in his mind and I had a movie in mine," Aaron says. "I said, 'Why do this again? Why don't you just show the Arthur Penn movie? If you want me to do it, then I'm gonna do it.' He paid lip service to that, but when push came to shove, Fred was not always a happy camper. We had some real fights."

In Palm Beach, Aaron threatened to walk off the film; Ray Katz talked him out of it. During filming back in Los Angeles, Coe planned to discuss the *Mr. Peepers Jr.* project with writer Harry Muheim. But enmeshed in battle, Coe had little time for him. "He was agitated [about that], because he was unfailingly considerate," Muheim says. He listened to Coe, in an adjoining room, engage in a shouting match by phone with Aaron. When Coe emerged, he looked haggard and drawn.

Delbert Mann, in Los Angeles for pre-production on Hallmark Hall of Fame's *All Quiet on the Western Front*, had lunch with Coe at the MGM commissary. Coe had not looked healthy to Mann at the Burkey award dinner, but at least he was energetic. Now, Mann was shocked: his mentor had deteriorated desperately. He walked heavily, on the soles of his feet, shuffled like a sick old man, and had lost much of his energy and feistiness.

In the end, Coe would have little artistic input on this version of *The Miracle Worker*, and perhaps it's just as well. The remake did well critically, and received five Emmy nominations, winning one for outstanding drama special, and another for Patty Duke-Astin as best actress. But the film is still a low-budget knockoff of the original, oddly unmoving and bathed in inappropriately bright California sunshine. Ultimately, director Paul Aaron was right: the best course is to rent a video of the Arthur Penn film.

* * *

With a week of filming left on *The Miracle Worker*, Coe woke on Saturday, April 28, and felt ill. He called Alice in Nashville and asked her to assemble the remaining members of the gang so he could see them on his way back to New York. Then he stayed in bed the rest of the day. On Saturday night, he felt worse, and late that evening, Eleanor Cogbill called an ambulance for him.

In his abdomen, his weakened aorta had enlarged, forming another aneurysm. And like a balloon under pressure, it had burst. As the ambulance sped him and Eleanor to UCLA Medical Center, his blood pressure was dropping rapidly. At the hospital, an angiogram was done and Coe was taken immediately into surgery. Ever the trouper, he handed Eleanor production notes and instructions for *Miracle Worker* executive producer Ray Katz.

The last time Eleanor saw him, they were sticking needles in him and he was in a lot of pain. He said, "I'm sorry about this." She said there was nothing to be sorry about. He said he loved her, and they wheeled him away.

Coe survived the surgery, but had lost too much blood. Just after 10:30 P.M. on Sunday, he went into cardiac arrest, and died at 11:20 P.M. It was Sunday, April 29, 1979, the sixty-fifth anniversary of his father's admission to St. Joseph's Hospital in Memphis. Just like the father he never met, he died by failing to survive a hospital stay aggravated by chronically neglecting his health.

Coe was known for having a big heart, but since childhood, his had been weakened. He pounded it with heavy drinking, heavy smoking, a poor diet, constant work, a stressful personal life, no exercise, and a hair-trigger temper. Neither his father nor his grandfathers made it out of their forties. The closest male ancestor on his father's side to outlive him was his great-great-grandfather Anson Coe (1784–1856). In retrospect, what's remarkable about his death at sixty-four is not that it was tragically premature, although it was, but that he lived as long as he did.

Following his death, Ray Katz stepped in as producer of *The Miracle Worker*. Even here, there's an analogy between Coe and D. W. Griffith: In 1935, after his career had gone into decline, Griffith was invited to England to remake *Broken Blossoms*. But he fought with the producer and left the film, which went on without him.

What would Coe have thought of his last project? "He may have looked at the film and thought, 'I hate it.' We'll never know," says Paul Aaron. "He had other visions. But so clearly, his visions belonged to other times, to work already done." And at the time of Coe's death, his brand of television drama did seem passé. But critic Andrew Sarris's tribute to Griffith applies equally well to Coe: "The cinema of Griffith . . . is no more outmoded than the drama of Aeschylus."

Delbert Mann, in Czechoslovakia working on *All Quiet on the Western Front*, received the news from his wife, Ann. When he and Coe had met at the MGM Commissary, he felt he wouldn't see him again, and was grateful for that last opportunity.

Several days later, Bo Goldman was in a health club on the roof of One Lincoln Center in Manhattan, talking with his agent in Los Angeles.

"I can't reach Ray Katz," his agent complained. "He's all screwed up because Fred Coe died."

"What?!"

"Yeah, well, Fred Coe died," the agent said. "Didn't you know that, honey?"

Goldman felt like he'd been hit in the stomach, yet wasn't really surprised.

"No, I didn't," he said angrily. "Why didn't you tell me?"

"Why would I tell you that?"

"You knew how close I was to Fred."

"Oh well," his agent said. "Death isn't a biggie with me."

•   •   •

The funeral service was held on May 4 at Madison Avenue Presbyterian Church, where the paths of Fred and Alice Coe had accidentally crossed that of Joyce Beeler thirty years earlier. It was well attended by many from the entertainment industry who had worked with Coe. Alice, John, and Laurie were there, as were Joyce, Sue and Sam, and Eleanor Cogbill.

Organized by Joyce, the service featured an impressive group of eulogists: Paddy Chayefsky, Horton Foote, Tad Mosel, Sumner Locke Elliott, Lillian Gish, Arthur Penn, Arthur Cantor, and Bo Goldman. Goldman catalogued Coe's rich lode of idiosyncracies in a eulogy laden with affectionate humor. Arthur Penn addressed his remarks to Coe's children, telling them what an extraordinary man he thought their father had been. Speaking with his customarily succinct eloquence, Tad Mosel called Coe the golden light of the Golden Age.

But his eloquence was too succinct for Lillian Gish, seated among the mourners. "She said, 'Well, Tad was too brief!'" Mosel recalls. "And unfortunately, she had a voice that carried." Gish would have another dramatic moment: when she finished her own eulogy, she paused at Coe's coffin on the way back to her seat. "She put her hand on the coffin and said, 'Oh dear Fred, we will never forget you,'" recalls Ann Levack, Coe's assistant in the early 1970s. "It was just so touching."

Coe was buried that afternoon at Green River Cemetery in the Hamptons, the final resting place of painter Jackson Pollock and writer A. J. Liebling. Because Coe didn't like ties, he was buried without one.

A West Coast memorial service was organized, also on May 4, by David Karp and David Shaw, and was held in the board room of the Writers' Guild in Los Angeles. On June 17, a memorial service was held by Coe's boyhood friends in Nashville at Singing Hills Presbyterian Church, the new location of Hillsboro Presbyterian, where he began his dramatic career as the teenaged impresario of the Hillsboro Players. In its obituary, the *New York Times* called him "a man for all media." The *Los Angeles Times* said he was a pioneer of television drama, and added "some industry notables say he virtually created the art."

While Coe left a glorious professional legacy, his inability to manage his personal life found one last expression from beyond the grave. Shortly after his death, his will was read, marking what John Coe's friend Bill Weylock calls "a grotesque episode." Despite what Coe may have told Eleanor Cogbill, she was not in his will. Neither was Alice. Or John or Laurie. Or Laurie's children, Corinne Marie and Sam. Neither, for that matter, were Joyce's children, Sue and Sam. Joyce Coe was Fred Coe's sole heir. "The only thing that bothered me was that the children didn't get anything," Alice says. "I know Fred loved John and Laurie, but he was not good at details of any kind whatsoever."

• • •

Assessing Coe's accomplishments on *Philco-Goodyear Television Playhouse*, Max Wilk writes in *The Golden Age of Television*, "In years to come, when courses are given in the history of television, *Philco-Goodyear* will be in the curriculum . . . if not all of it." Fred Coe's *Philco-Goodyear Playhouse* is not the best-known dramatic show in American television history. But in terms of the programs it aired and the talents it spawned, it is the most important.

His Broadway legacy alone is astonishing: *The Trip to Bountiful*, *Two For the Seesaw*, *All the Way Home*, and *A Thousand Clowns*, all part of the

American canon, would not have been staged were it not for him. He was not at the finish line for *Fiddler on the Roof*, but got it started when no other producer would. He also produced *The Miracle Worker*, *Wait Until Dark*, and *Gideon*, directed *In Praise of Love* and, off-Broadway, *Journey to the Day*.

These shows were important, and many of them successful. They encompass many moods and genres: inspirational psychodrama, harrowing thriller, bittersweet comedy, a gentle meditation on man's place in the universe. Horton Foote once said that in his television drama, Coe was equally at home in Tad Mosel's Midwest, Paddy Chayefsky's Bronx, Thornton Wilder's New England, and Tennessee Williams's Mississippi. The same is true in the theater: the thematic and tonal range of his stage plays is almost as broad as the sum of human experience. And while his film resume is brief, he still produced two superb films: *The Miracle Worker*, and *A Thousand Clowns*, which he also directed.

On September 8, 1980, Delbert Mann organized a tribute to Coe at the Tennessee Performing Arts Center in Nashville. It was a black-tie evening featuring readings of poetry and prose by a member of the Royal Shakespeare Company and by a Coe discovery—Princess Grace of Monaco. In connection with the event, Mann and his wife Ann put together a fifteen-page illustrated booklet, *A Remembrance of "Pappy,"* featuring articles by Ann Mann and tributes from Paddy Chayefsky, Horton Foote, Tad Mosel, JP Miller, David Swift, and David Shaw.

Miller recalled how he once stumbled into Coe's office, green and untested, only to leave with several assignments and the start of a career. He thanked Coe, adding, "Thanks again, Pappy. If you need writers wherever you are, I hope you'll save a spot for me."

On December 20, 1982, NBC aired a live national broadcast of Carson McCullers's *The Member of the Wedding* from the Tennessee Performing Arts Center. Produced by David Rintels, it starred Pearl Bailey, Dana Hill, and Howard E. Rollins Jr., and was directed by Delbert Mann. After the broadcast, Mann organized a benefit for the newly created Fred Coe Memorial Fund for Artists-in-Theatre at Vanderbilt University. And in 1986, Coe was voted into the Academy of Television Arts and Sciences Hall of Fame, along with Steve Allen, Walt Disney, Jackie Gleason, Mary Tyler Moore, former CBS president Frank Stanton, and *Kukla, Fran and Ollie* creator Burr Tillstrom.

Despite this signal honor, it is the concluding irony of Coe's life that his greatest influence came not in television, but in the Hollywood feature film. Countless screenwriters, directors, and actors trained by Coe at *Philco-Goodyear Playhouse* made the transition to the west coast and celluloid that their mentor never could. Today, television drama has its moments, but the electronic theater created by Coe and his contemporaries in the 1950s is nowhere in evidence.

"Car chases are the polyester suits of television," says JP Miller. "But that's what they think of as action. There's no such thing as internal action, what Fred Coe used to get. You create a magnificent human drama and push the camera right up close to Kim Stanley and she doesn't do anything but respond inside and maybe there's a slight twitch of her eyelid or something. And it breaks your heart. That's all gone. You have to be hit over the head with a brick now."

Not that the other media Coe worked in are doing much better. Feature films increasingly display the blockbuster mentality (high concept, low thoughtfulness). Each season, Broadway becomes less a showcase for serious original drama and more an amusement park, with growing emphasis on special effects and impressive scenery. It's disquieting to realize that if Coe were alive and healthy today, there might be room for him on the margins of American culture—a good off-off-Broadway theater, an independent filmmaker or a specialty cable channel—but not at the center, a place he once occupied with such distinction.

Coe spoke with Cecil Smith of the *Los Angeles Times* on the Simi Valley location of *The Miracle Worker* shortly before his death, and the talk turned to television. As a warm breeze ruffled the tall grass, Coe said some of the dramatic series on TV weren't so bad, but that the medium had become more administrative than creative. "I don't recognize it much anymore," he said.

Of course he didn't. From a diverse, vibrant, and experimental medium—one with its share of failures, to be sure—television drama has devolved into a swarm of formulaic action series, disease of the week movies, tabloid horrors ripped from yesterday's headlines, or series dramas with a diverse but heartwarming crew of (choose one, depending upon this season's fashion) doctors, lawyers, policemen, cowboys, or spacemen who took a wrong turn at the Crab Nebula. It was Fred Coe's miserable fate to be the consummate dramatic artist in a medium largely devoid of artistic integrity.

Today, Fred Coe is forgotten. He lives on through the Fred Coe Visiting Artist Program at Vanderbilt. He's a member of the Academy of Television Arts and Sciences Hall of Fame, and a bust of him stands in the Academy's courtyard in North Hollywood, next to the bust of Paddy Chayefsky. He lives on through his sons, John and Sam, and his daughters, Laurie and Sue.

But where he doesn't live, and where he should, is in America's cultural memory out of gratitude for his enduring contributions to, and influence on, American television, theater, and film in the second half of the twentieth century. "A lot of producers want their names out in front of everything," says Porter Van Zandt. "But Fred was just not that way. It wasn't all about him, it was about the play. I think that's one of the reasons why it's been so easy to forget him," he adds. "But the people who worked with him don't forget."

APPENDIX 1

The Television Work of Fred Coe

NBC Television Theater (NBC, 1945–1948): Floor Manager, Director, then
   Producer/Director
Philco Television Playhouse (NBC, 1948–1951): Producer
   Philco-Goodyear Television Playhouse (NBC, 1951–1954): Producer
Mr. Peepers (NBC, 1952–1955): Producer
Bonino (NBC, 1953): Producer
First Person Playhouse (NBC, 1953): Producer
Producers Showcase (NBC, 1954–1955): Producer
Playwrights '56 (NBC, 1955–1956): Producer
The Red Mill (DuPont Show of the Month) (CBS, 1958): Producer
Playhouse 90 (CBS, 1958–1960): One of three rotating producers
Three Roads to Rome (ITV, England, 1961): Producer
Theatre '62 (CBS, 1961–1962): Producer
Fourteenth Annual Emmy Awards (NBC, 1962): Producer
The Final War of Olly Winter (CBS Playhouse, 1967): Producer
All the Way Home (Hallmark Hall of Fame) (NBC, 1971): Director
Of Men and Women (ABC, 1972): Producer
If You Give a Dance, You Gotta Pay the Band (ABC Theater, 1972): Director
The Adams Chronicles (PBS, 1976): Producer/Director of four of thirteen
   episodes
The Miracle Worker (NBC Movie of the Week, 1979): Producer

Awards and Nominations

1952: **Peabody Award** (for Mr. Peepers)
1952: Emmy nomination (as producer of Philco-Goodyear Television Playhouse)
1953: **Peabody Award** (for Philco-Goodyear Television Playhouse)
1953: **Sylvania Award** (for Marty)
1953: **Look Magazine Award** (as best television producer)

1953: Emmy nomination (as producer of *Philco-Goodyear Television Playhouse*)

1954: **Look Magazine Award** (as best television producer)

1954: **Sylvania Award** (as producer of *Philco-Goodyear Television Playhouse*; shares award with Gordon Duff)

1954: **Variety Showmanship Award**

1954: Emmy nomination (as producer of *Philco-Goodyear Television Playhouse*)

1955: **Christopher Award**

1955: **Emmy Award** (as producer of *Producers Showcase*)

1958: **Look Magazine Television Award** (for *The Plot to Kill Stalin*)

1967: Emmy nomination (as producer of *The Final War of Olly Winter*)

1971: **Peabody Award** (for *All the Way Home*)

1976: Emmy nomination (as producer of a limited series: *The Adams Chronicles*)

1976: **Peabody Award** (for *The Adams Chronicles*)

1976: Emmy nomination (as director in a drama series; "John Quincy Adams: President" episode of *The Adams Chronicles*)

1977: Emmy nomination (as outstanding producer of a limited series: *The Adams Chronicles*)

1978: **Evelyn F. Burkey Memorial Award** (presented by the Writers' Guild East to the individual who has done the most to help writers)

1980: **Emmy Award** (as producer of an outstanding drama special for *The Miracle Worker*)

1986: **Inducted into the Hall of Fame of the Academy of Television Arts and Sciences**

APPENDIX 2

The Stage Plays of Fred Coe

Broadway

The Day Will Come (National Theatre, 1944): Actor, Stage Manager
The Trip to Bountiful (Henry Miller's Theatre, 1953): Producer
Two for the Seesaw (Booth Theatre, 1958): Producer
The Miracle Worker (The Playhouse, 1959): Producer
All the Way Home (Belasco Theatre, 1960): Producer
Gideon (Plymouth Theater, 1961): Producer
A Thousand Clowns (Eugene O'Neill Theatre, 1962): Producer/Director
Fiddler on the Roof (1964): Original Producer
Xmas in Las Vegas (Ethel Barrymore Theater, 1965): Producer/Director
Wait Until Dark (Ethel Barrymore Theater, 1966): Producer
Georgy (Winter Garden, 1970): Producer
Night Watch (Morosco Theater, 1972): Director
Promenade All (Alvin Theater, 1972): Producer
In Praise of Love (Morosco Theater, 1974): Director

Off-Broadway, Regional, and Tours

Bonanza (Nixon Theater, Pittsburgh) (1944): Stage Manager
Journey to the Day (Westport, Connecticut) (ca. 1961): Producer
A Matter of Position (Walnut Street Theater, Philadelphia) (1962): Producer/Director
Journey to the Day (Theater de Lys, Greenwich Village) (1963): Producer/Director
A Thousand Clowns: tour (ca. 1964)
Wait Until Dark: tour (1967)
The Enemy Is Dead (Berkshire Theater Festival, Stockbridge, Mass.) (1972): Producer

The Early Years

ca. 1931–1937: Producer/director, The Hillsboro Players, Nashville, Tennessee

1935–1938: Actor/stagehand/technician, Nashville Community Playhouse

1938–1939: Director, Summer Workshop, Nashville Community Playhouse

1940: Director, *It's Morning* (Yale University Theatre)

1940–1944: Producer/director, Town Theatre, Columbia, South Carolina

Awards and Nominations

1960: **Tony Award** (as producer of *The Miracle Worker*)

1961: Tony nomination (as producer of *All the Way Home*; nomination shared with Arthur Cantor)

1962: Tony nomination (as best dramatic producer; nomination shared with Arthur Cantor)

1962: Tony nomination (as producer of *Gideon*; nomination shared with Arthur Cantor)

1962: **Distinguished Career Award** (presented by Southeastern Theater Conference)

1963: Tony nomination (as producer of *A Thousand Clowns*)

APPENDIX 3

The Films of Fred Coe

The Left-Handed Gun (Warner Bros., 1958): Producer
The Miracle Worker (United Artists, 1962): Producer
A Thousand Clowns (United Artists, 1965): Producer/Director
This Property Is Condemned (Paramount/Seven Arts, 1966): Original Pro-
   ducer; received screenplay credit with Francis Ford Coppola and Edith
   Sommer
Me, Natalie (National General Pictures, 1969): Director

Awards and Nominations

1960: **Grand Prix**, Union de la Critique du Cinema (Belgium) (for *The
   Left-Handed Gun*)
1965: Academy Award nomination (as producer of *A Thousand Clowns*)

NOTES

Key to Abbreviations and Sources

Frequently cited periodicals are referred to by initials:

NYCR	New York Theatre Critics' Reviews
NYHT	New York Herald Tribune
NYT	New York Times
TVG	TV Guide

Unless otherwise noted, all interviews were conducted by the author. Individuals who appear frequently are identified by their initials:

ACA	Arthur Cantor	JPM	JP Miller
AC	Alice Coe	TM	Tad Mosel
EC	Eleanor Cogbill	BN	Bill Nichols
BC	Bob Costello	AP	Arthur Penn
BG	Bo Goldman	DS	David Shaw
EG	Everett Greenbaum	DSW	David Swift
DM	Delbert Mann	PW	Pat Weaver

Several interviews with John and Laurie Coe on 3/19/94 are marked 3/19/94a to indicate that they were interviewed individually during the day and 3/19/94b for a joint interview that evening at the Old Spaghetti Factory in downtown Atlanta. Two interviews with Bob Costello are labelled 6/18/93a (afternoon interview with him at his house in Amagansett) and 6/18/93b (evening interview with him and his wife, Sybil, at Estia Restaurant in East Hampton.) Quotes from 1950s live television dramas usually come from kinescopes housed at one of two locations:

SHSW	State Historical Society of Wisconsin
UCLA	University of California at Los Angeles Film and Television Archive

1   A Death in the Family

A complete chronology of the Coe family can be found in J. Gardner Bartlett's *Robert Coe, Puritan: His Ancestors and Descendants, 1340–1910* (Boston: Self-published, 1911). A copy is on file in the history and genealogy department of the Los Angeles Public Library.

4   "It was a land of smokehouses": Ben Robertson, *Red Hills and Cotton: An Upcountry Memory* (Columbia, S.C.: University of South Carolina Press, 1973), 5–6.

4   he was light-hearted and full of fun: Interview with Vera (Coe) Dawes, 6/9/94. Interview conducted by Christine Jones.

4   Hayden Lumpkin Coe was fair but strict: Interview with Vera (Coe) Dawes, 6/27/94. Interview conducted by Christine Jones.

4   three more children arrived: Bartlett, *Robert Coe, Puritan*, 403.

4   the patriarch . . . who died of kidney failure: "City News," Asheville *Gazette-News*, 3/12/04, 8.

5   widow Sarah Hughs . . . back to Richland: *Robert Coe, Puritan*, 403.

5   Coe was running alongside a moving engine: Interview with Vera (Coe) Dawes, 6/27/94. Interview conducted by Christine Jones.

5   When Frederick Coe was well enough . . . his seven-year-old sister Vera came upstairs: Ibid.

5   "I have it bad and am proud of it": Frederick Coe letter to Annette Harrell, 7/14/09.

5   were secretly married: Information about date and place of the wedding is from flyleaf of Annette Coe's Bible. Copy in the possession of Kate Wells.

6   "If we do grow old as the years pass": Frederick Coe letter to Annette Harrell Coe, 1/3/10.

6   He had chronic appendicitis: Interview with AC, 11/19/91.

6   On July 23 . . . he died of septicemia: Death certificate of Frederick Hayden Hughs Coe.

6   "It was as if she came from nowhere": Interview with Laurie Coe, 3/19/94a.

6   Local lore says the Mississippi Delta: James C. Cobb, *The Most Southern Place on Earth: The Mississippi Delta and the Roots of Regional Identity* (New York: Oxford University Press, 1992), vii.

6   President Theodore Roosevelt's big-game hunting: Ibid., 125–126.

7   "one of those milky white winter mornings": Tennessee Williams, *27 Wagons Full of Cotton and Other Plays* (New York: New Directions, 1953), 197.

7   His full name. . . . "South Carolina, U.S.A.": Delayed birth certificate of Frederick Hayden Hughs Coe, filled out by Coe and his mother in 1943. Copy in possession of the author.

7   "It makes them extremely capable": Interview with Leslie Stevens, 4/13/94.

7   Kate Wells . . . guesses this was because: Interview with Kate Wells, 8/31/93.

7   Young Fred Coe . . . sometimes wondered if he were illegitimate: Interview with AC, 4/17/92.

7   "He probably never had a chance": Interview with Kate Wells, 12/4/93.

8   as a result of childhood rheumatic fever: Interview with AC, 4/17/92.

8   "Duck—Mo! Mo! Mo!": Interview with Kate Wells, 4/22/92.

8   with a bookshelf including: Annette Coe's books are now in the possession of Kate Wells.

8   When she left Alligator: Interview with AC, 11/19/91.

8   "beyond schools, beyond roads and rivers": G. Gordon Mahy, Jr., *Murdoch of Buckhorn* (Nashville: The Parthenon Press, 1946), 59.

8   Roads across the mountains were impassable: Eunice Tolbert Johnson, *History of Perry County* (Hazard, Ky.: Hazard Chapter of the D.A.R, 1953), 71.

8   it was a two-and-a-half-hour ride: Mahy, *Murdoch of Buckhorn*, 85.

8   Brainard Memorial Hospital . . . was a one-doctor, one-nurse: *Buckhorn: The Story of a Christian Enterprise on Squabble Creek in the Mountains of Kentucky*, 19. Copy on file in Perry County Library, Hazard, Ky.

9   Annette Coe and a Dr. Turner: The name of the physician Annette Coe worked with comes from the "Buckhorn News" column of the 3/30/23 *Hazard Herald*. Copy on microfilm in Perry County Library, Hazard, Ky.

9   When she was gone, her son waited: Interviews with John Coe, 3/19/94a, and BG, 3/3/93 and 3/8/93.

2   A Romantic Conversation

Much of the information in this chapter on Nashville in the 1920s and 1930s is taken from Don H. Doyle's *Nashville Since the 1920's* (Knoxville: The University of Tennessee Press, 1985).

11   the "Fugitives": Leading members of the Fugitives were John Crowe Ransom, Allen Tate, Robert Penn Warren, Laura Riding, and Donald Davidson. They produced a distinguished body of poetry, and, in Warren's case, novels. Although their magazine, *The Fugitive*, only lasted from 1922 through 1925, it received national acclaim, and, according to H. L. Mencken, constituted the entire literature of the state of Tennessee.

11   her active interest in culture: Interview with Martha Geistman (Mrs. Colin Campbell), 4/22/93.

11   puppet shows: Interview with Frank "Spiller" Campbell, 9/1/93.

11   the seventh grade's class poet: *The Volunteer* (1928), 61. Copy on file in the Special Collections Department in Heard Library at Vanderbilt University.

11   the Depression came to Nashville: Doyle, *Nashville Since the 1920's*, 85.

11   large numbers of poor and homeless: Ibid., 86.

12   Morrell Fisher liked to clown around: Donald Phillips letter to JK, received 5/26/93.

12   Donald Phillips felt: Interview with Donald Phillips, 8/30/93.

12   "His ferocity came from": Interview with JPM, 2/2/94.

12   W. F. Christopher . . . suggested . . . start an amateur theatrical group: Interview with Jane Geistman (Mrs. Goodall Bailey), 4/20/93.

12   The stage . . . no more than fifteen to twenty feet wide: Interview with Martha Geistman (Mrs. Colin Campbell), 4/22/93.

12   with spotlights in tin cans: Interview with AC, 5/4/92.

12   One side of the stage was a wall: Interview with Max Souby, 6/8/93.

12   "Stand up, Becky!": Interview with Jeanne (Stephenson) Bodfish, 3/2/93.

13   accidentally jumped from: Interview with Jeanne (Stephenson) Bodfish, 9/2/93.

13   "She's upstairs, lying prostitute": Interview with Jane Geistman (Mrs. Goodall Bailey), 8/30/93.

13   "This is amateur night in Dixie!": Interview with Phyllis Adams, 4/6/92.

13   On Sunday evenings . . . would pay court: Interviews with Jeanne (Stephenson) Bodfish, 2/25/93, 3/2/93, and 9/2/93.

13   "I can't remember very much": Nancy Anderson, "New TV Role for Ivan Dixon," *Burbank Daily Review*, 1/12/67, 16.

13   He picked DiMaggio: Fred Coe, "Ten a Year—Or Bust!," *NYHT*, 5/11/59, 15.

13   "See that boy in the blue sweater?": Interview with AC, 11/19/91.

14   Alice was a seven-month baby: Interview with AC, 8/29/93.

14   she was a fighter: Ibid.

14   One Sunday night in the fall of 1934: This account of "the romantic conversation" is pieced together based on JK interviews with Jeanne (Stephenson) Bodfish, 2/25/93, 4/14/93, 6/1/93 and 8/30/93, and her letter of 4/28/94.

14   "His work life was his life": Interview with AC, 5/9/94.

14   "I've decided to go with": Ibid., 8/30/93.

15   they went to Hettie Rae's: Ibid., 4/13/92, 5/6/93, and 8/30/93.

15   the New Deal: Doyle, *Nashville Since the 1920's*, 94.

15   many members of Fred Coe's gang: AC letter to JK, received 8/16/93.

15   the Hillsboro Players performed: Interview with DM, 4/30/93.

15   a tall, shy student: Interview with DM, 10/6/93.

15   Delbert Mann had met Coe: Ann and Delbert Mann, *A Remembrance of "Pappy,"* 4.

15   Mann escorted Alice: Interview with DM, 10/6/93.

16   she accompanied him to Nashville's Union Station: Interview with AC, 9/4/93.

16   New Haven was where Captain John Coe: Bartlett, *Robert Coe, Puritan*, 87.

3   The Battle of Sumter Street

17   People believing an invasion from Mars: Erik Barnouw, *The Golden Web: A History of Broadcasting in the United States 1933–1953* (New York: Oxford University Press, 1968), 87–88.

17   Alice asked him to forgo his letters: Interview with AC, 4/17/92.

17   "There was not a day that passed": Interview with Melville Bernstein, 10/23/93.

18   Coe and Alice . . . thought television might amount: Interview with AC, 2/19/93.

18   Coe directed with skill: Interview with Sarah (Click) Ferry, 8/1/93.

18   "Fred seemed to make a deep impression": Ibid.

18   Coe is one of only two: Otto Preminger, *Preminger: An Autobiography* (Garden City, N.Y.: Doubleday, 1977), 63.

18   major producers . . . who trained at Yale: Worthington Miner of *Studio One*, while not a student at the Yale School of Drama, also attended Yale as an undergraduate.

19   The *Tennessean* questioned: "Playhouse Gives Artistic 'Caesar,'" Nashville *Tennessean*, 8/16/39, 7.

19   "a credit to its young director": Mortimer Trull, "'Twelfth Night' Wins Praise at Playhouse," Nashville *Banner*, 8/15/40, 3.

19   *Twelfth Night* was less daringly experimental: John Thompson, "'Twelfth Night' By Workshop Well Received," Nashville *Tennessean*, 8/15/40, 7.

19   The post . . . paid $1,500: C. Robert Jones, "The Town Theatre of Columbia, South Carolina 1919–1974," unpublished master's thesis, University of Georgia (1973), 113.

19   "You mean 'the War Between the States'": Interview with Allen Whitehead, 11/3/93.

19   Fred Coe would later affectionately parody: The action of *This Time, Next Year* takes place in a Southern state capital which is probably modeled on Columbia.

19   Building it up . . . helped to end the Depression: John Hammond Moore, *Columbia and Richland County* (Columbia, S.C.: University of South Carolina Press, 1993), 393.

20   the past is not dead, it's not even past: William Faulkner, *Requiem for a Nun* (New York: Random House, 1950), 92.

20   slim and sandy-haired: "Town Theater Director Plunges Into New Duties," *The State* (Columbia, S.C.), 9/4/40, 2.

20   he thought Coe was a student: Miriam Glovier Rabb, "Community Theater Should Not Be Carbon Copy of Broadway, Director Coe Says," *The Record* (Columbia, S.C.), 2/3/44, 5.

20   he began talking excitedly without waiting: "Town Theater Director Plunges Into New Duties," *The State*, 9/4/40, 2.

20   "If we have hard production problems": "Columbia Stage Society Soon Opens New Season," *The State*, 9/15/40, 1-D.

20   "They were in debt": Interview with AC, 8/31/93.

20   To attract larger crowds: Jones, "The Town Theatre of Columbia," 115.

20   theater membership either doubled or tripled: In "The Town Theatre of Columbia," C. Robert Jones writes on p. 113 that the theater's membership doubled, from about 650 to 1,249, between 1940–1941 and 1943–1944. But "'Man Who Came to Dinner' Opens Town Theater Season," an article in *The State* (9/21/41) says theater membership was 410 at the end of the 1940–1941 season, meaning that if the 1,249 figure is valid for 1943–1944, then membership actually tripled.

20   Coe bounced a check: Interview with AC, 3/27/92.

20   She was the stabilizer: Interview with Martha Geistman (Mrs. Colin Campbell), 4/22/93.

20   it sometimes seemed she was more Coe's mother: Interview with AC, 4/13/92.

21   Coe was quick to party: Interviews with Charles Wickenberg, 11/12/93, and Jo (Zula) Brown, 3/23/94.

21   "We never drank in Columbia": Interview with AC, 4/17/92.

21   Fred Coe provided the Theatre with a boost: Jones, "The Town Theatre of Columbia," 113.

21   "We've had some good directors since then": Interview with Jo (Zula) Brown, 10/27/93.

21   "Fred just thought that was great": Interview with Charles Wickenberg, 11/12/93.

21   His lighting . . . drew praise: Margaret Vale, "Town Theater Cast Pleases In "Liliom" Presentation," *The State*, 4/4/41, 6-B.

21   he designed the stage set for *H.M.S. Pinafore*: Margaret Vale, "'H.M.S. Pinafore' at the Town Theater for Bundles for Britain," *The State*, 2/23/41, 3-A.

21   Coe said many outstanding plays had been written: Program for Town Theatre's production of *H.M.S. Pinafore*, February/March 1941. Copies on file at Town Theatre and in possession of author.

21   Coe and Alice were listening: Interview with AC, 4/28/94.

22   Columbia . . . responded with wartime salvage drives: Moore, *Columbia and Richland County*, 396.

22   women with husbands . . . at Fort Jackson: Interview with Jo (Zula) Brown, 3/23/94.

22   Classified 4F: Interview with AC, 4/17/92.

22   He had a file of 175 enlisted men: "Khaki Returns to the Theater in Columbia," *The State*, 9/21/41, 10-A.

22   "It was for anyone who didn't mind rehearsing": Interview with Jo (Zula) Brown, 10/27/93.

22   Coe found women who perfectly fit: Interview with Jo (Zula) Brown, 10/27/93.

22   he directed . . . *Rebecca* . . . a year and a half before it reached Broadway: The Town Theatre's production of *Rebecca* premiered in June 1943; the Broadway production premiered in January 1945.

22   winning a Hollywood contract: Jones, "The Town Theatre of Columbia," 114.

22   "so simple, so plain": Interview with Allen Whitehead, 11/3/93.

22   The ideal community theater . . . does not attempt: Rabb, "Community Theater Should Not Be Carbon Copy," *The Record*, 2/3/44, 5.

23   "I was beginning to lose it": Ibid.

23   "Not to be maudlin about it": Interview with Jo (Zula) Brown, 10/27/93.

23   "A couple of nights after we opened": Ibid.

23   Shurr . . . told Coe he belonged on Broadway: Interview with AC, 11/19/91.

23   "The theater was a little oasis": Interview with AP, 10/26/93.

23   "Fred was always very generous": Ibid., 12/13/91.

23   Shurr and Penn . . . brought food: Interview with AC, 2/19/93.

23   a secretarial job for Alice: Ibid., 11/19/91.

24   "His resignation, and that of his gifted young wife": Margaret Vale, "Director Coe's Finale, 'Bundling Play,' Promises To Be Town Theater Hit," *The State*, 6/11/44, 6-B.

24   In later years, he usually said: See, for example, Schiff, "Fred Coe: Grand 'Old' Man of Television," *New York Post*, 8/31/59, 35, and "Hanging Out: Robert Alan Aurthur," *Esquire*, May 1973, 48.

24 Paddy Chayefsky was wounded: John Clum, *Paddy Chayefsky* (Boston: Twayne, 1976), 19.

24 David Shaw . . . fought against . . . Afrika Korps: Michael Shnayerson, *Irwin Shaw: A Biography* (New York: G. P. Putnam's Sons, 1989), 123.

24 Donald Phillips . . . survived a direct hit: Donald Phillips letter to JK received 5/26/93.

24 "She helped him get started": Interview with Ira Skutch, 2/24/93.

4   The Birth of a Medium

27 When Coe arrived in New York that June: Interviews with AC, 3/27/92, 4/13/92, and 4/9/93.

27 He and Alice lived on her secretarial salary: Ibid., 3/27/92.

27 In an era soon to witness: Morris, *Manhattan '45*, 73, 81.

28 Alice only had one blouse: Interview with Jeanne (Stephenson) Bodfish, 9/2/93.

28 During their first Christmas: Interview with AC, 4/9/93.

28 "confused . . . a mixture of would-be realism": Lewis Nichols, "The Wandering Jew," *NYT*, 9/8/44, 17.

28 A lead actor quit the show: "Casting Woes Ignored!: Nixon's 'Bonanza' Broadway-Bound," *Pittsburgh Press*, 12/31/44, 14.

28 To bring in some money: Interview with AC, 3/25/93.

28 Alice told Jack Davies they were preparing: Ibid., 4/17/92.

28 he was not a popular man at NBC: Ira Skutch, *I Remember Television* (Metuchen, N.J.: The Directors Guild of America and The Scarecrow Press, 1989), 38.

28 a lone voice of showmanship: "John Royal Dies in N.Y. at 91," *Variety*, 2/15/78, 38.

29 a flashy man . . . who wore a flower: Interview with Don Pike, 3/5/93.

29 After watching Mae West: "John Royal Dies in N.Y. at 91," *Variety*, 2/15/78, 38.

29 Royal hired him as a floor manager: Interview with AC, 11/19/91.

29 "I always felt John Royal was *his* father": Interview with BG, 3/8/93.

29 When Coe was hired: "Television Signs Off to Change Channels," *NYT*, 2/28/46, 18, and Skutch, *I Remember Television*, 41.

29 it began to air Sunday night dramas: Harry Castleman and Walter J. Podrazik, *Watching TV: Four Decades of American Television* (New York: McGraw-Hill, 1982), 18.

29 Temperatures rose to 100 degrees: Skutch, *I Remember Television*, 40.

29 "We used to call the lighting director": Interview with Don Pike, 3/5/93.

30 Berlin and Tokyo: Oliver E. Allen, *New York, New York* (New York: Atheneum, 1990), 283.

30 "It was the town of all towns": Morris, *Manhattan '45*, 6–7 and 12.

30 One of his first shows: William Hawes, *American Television Drama: The Experimental Years* (University, Ala.: University of Alabama Press, 1986), 105.

30 he had stagehands construct sets: Interview with Ira Skutch, 2/16/93.

30   They had more experience: Edward Sobol, "A Director's Headaches," *NYT*, 6/13/48, 11.

31   "Fred was aware of the restrictions": Interview with Don Pike, 3/15/93. One of the best accounts of what a live television director went through during the pressurized countdown to airtime is Coe's chapter, "Problems in the Studio," in John Royal's *Television Production Problems* (New York: McGraw-Hill, 1948), 113–123.

31   When Adna Karns . . . visited him: Interview with Adna Karns, 2/22/93.

31   The Waldorf-Astoria had already wired: Morris, *Manhattan '45*, 250.

31   "This new form of entertainment": John Royal, "The Royal Hotfoot for Video's Haloed Heads," *Variety*, 1/9/46, 119.

31   In 1946, there were seven commercial television stations: Frank Sturcken, *Live Television: The Golden Age of 1946–1958 in New York* (Jefferson, N.C.: McFarland & Company, 1990), 13.

31   In 1949, there would be: *Les Brown's Encyclopedia of Television* (New York: Zoetrope, 1982), 491.

31   The NBC television network: Castleman and Podrazik, *Watching TV*, 15.

31   in 1947, the cable was extended: Jack Gould, "NBC to Launch Television Service on Friday between Washington and New York," *NYT*, 6/24/47, 46.

31   Boston and Richmond were added: Interview with Stephen A. Flynn, 5/7/92.

31   By July 1948, NBC had eight more: "NBC Television Network: A Working Reality," NBC ad in *Variety*, 7/28/48, 52–53.

31   But by year's end, the coaxial cable: Tim Brooks and Earle Marsh, *The Complete Directory to Prime Time Network TV Shows, 1946–Present* (New York: Ballantine Books, 1992), xiii.

31   It had the then-impressive audience: Castleman and Podrazik, *Watching TV*, 20.

31   the 1947 World Series . . . had an audience of 3.9 million: Ibid., 30.

32   "as if television had been re-invented": Ibid., 36.

32   "the performers": Ibid., 21.

32   "These full-length plays": "Petticoat Fever" review, *Variety*, 11/28/45, 40.

32   there was a television blackout: "Television Signs Off to Change Channels," *NYT*, 2/28/46, 18.

32   NBC proposed the construction of Television City: Jack Gould, "The News of Radio: Industry Considering 'Television City' Here as Means of Reducing Costs," *NYT*, 11/20/47, 58.

32   the failure of . . . Television City: Skutch, *I Remember Television*, 65.

33   Although *Watching TV* authors: Castleman and Podrazik, *Watching TV*, 21.

33   "It's usually considered in bad taste": *Lights Out* review, *Variety*, 7/3/46, 31.

33   She narrated travel films: Skutch, *I Remember Television*, 43.

33   The show was cancelled: Castleman and Podrazik, *Watching TV*, 28.

33   "But the guy's dead!": "It Happens in Tele, Too," *Variety*, 9/11/46, 40.

34   In Nashville, you lived in a house: Interview with AC, 4/2/93.

34   "A friend of mine just moved out": Ibid., 3/27/92.

34   he later called it "rotten": "Hanging Out: Robert Alan Aurthur," *Esquire*, May 1973, 48.

34   with some trimming: *This Time Next Year* review, *Variety*, 10/1/47, 33.

34   "Theatre Guild Makes Auspicious": Bob Stahl, "Theatre Guild Makes Auspicious Tele Bow, Despite Decrepit Script," *Variety*, 11/12/47, 34.

34   "The Theatre Guild, venerable doyen": Jack Gould, "Theatre Guild Makes Video Bow on NBC With Production of 'John Ferguson'," *NYT*, 11/16/47, Sec. 2, 11.

35   On April 22, 1948, NBC added: Sarah Rouse and Katharine Loughney, *3 Decades of Television: A Catalog of Television Programs Acquired by the Library of Congress 1949–1979* (Washington, D.C.: Library of Congress, 1979), iv.

35   Studio 8G had been: Interview with Don Pike, 3/17/93.

36   "I want that red convertible": Interview with AC, 4/13/92.

36   Coe threw him in water over his head: Interviews with John Coe, 3/19/94a and with AC, 4/28/94.

36   "I made it without a father": Interview with John Coe, 3/19/94a.

36   "He was disgusted with what he was doing": Interviews with Adna Karns, 2/22/93 and 3/2/93.

5   His Loyalties Tear Him Apart

37   In the fall of 1948, Mrs. Ruth Wellborn: "The Rise of Television," *Newsweek*, 12/20/48, 50.

37   In 1947, there had been 16,000: *Les Brown's Encyclopedia*, 492.

37   Now there were 190,000: Ibid., 492.

37   there would be nearly twelve million: "11,748,400 TV Sets in U.S.," *Variety*, 3/28/51, 26.

37   The television industry lost fifteen million dollars: "TV B'casters Took $15,000,000 Lacing in '48," *Variety*, 12/28/49, 22.

38   "one of Kraft's fine dairy-related": Douglas Copland, "The Irony Board," *The New Republic*, 11/2/92, 12.

38   Three weeks after being advertised: Gerard Jones, *Honey, I'm Home!* (New York: Grove Weidenfeld, 1992), 31.

38   In 1945, James Petrillo: Castleman and Podrazik, *Watching TV*, 17.

38   imposing "the freeze": ibid., 37.

39   at $17,39 a week: "Philco's 17G Nut For 'Playhouse' A New High in TV," *Variety*, 9/22/48, 25.

39   "The Equity-Philco presentation": Jack Gould, "Television in Review," *NYT*, 10/10/48, Section 2, 11.

39   "perhaps the most brilliant": "The Rise of Television," *Newsweek*, 12/20/48, 51.

39   "the cast, under the capable direction": "Tele Follow-up Comment," *Variety*, 10/13/48, 32.

39   He had to know where cameras and boom mikes were: Information in this paragraph and the next two comes from interview with DM, 4/30/93.

40   "I seldom slept": Franklin J. Schaffner, *Worthington Miner* (Metuchen, N.J.: The Directors Guild of America and the Scarecrow Press, 1985), 11.

40   "It's like nothing before it": "Is There a Doctor in the House?", *Variety*, 11/1/50, 29.

40   "He almost killed himself": Interview with Adrienne Luraschi, 4/9/92.

40   "A success on all counts": "Tele Follow-up Comment," *Variety*, 1/12/49, 30.

41   But because the stage manager was distracted: Interview with Hildy Parks, 4/16/94.

41   "Cue the nun!": Ibid.

41   But because a sound man: Interview with DM, 4/29/92.

41   two weeks after the broadcast: "'Philco Playhouse' Status in Doubt; 126G Over Budget," *Variety*, 1/26/49, 31.

41   "so many grains of sand": Wilk, *The Golden Age of Television*, 127.

41   "We don't know, and it is a blessing": Fred Coe, "Televising Shakespeare," *Theatre Arts*, April 1951, 56.

41   "should have been left within": "Tele Follow-up Comment," *Variety*, 3/30/49, 30.

41   "Philco tangled with farce": "Tele Follow-up Comment," *Variety*, 2/1/50, 32.

41   "an unbelievable story": "Tele Follow-up Comment," *Variety*, 2/8/50, 56.

42   "The networks admit": "Video's '50 Accent on Writing," *Variety*, 12/21/49, 27.

42   The show's cancellation was announced in March: "Radio and Television," *NYT*, 3/30/49, 50.

42   But by June, Talent Associates agreed: "Bestsellers as Philco Format," *Variety*, 6/15/49, 25.

42   "By the end of that first year, I was a basket case": Wilk, *The Golden Age of Television*, 127.

42   The show had only one rehearsal: Skutch, *I Remember Television*, 89.

42   "Even on the printed page": Jack Gould, "Programs in Review," *NYT*, 9/25/49, Sec. 2, 11.

42   Pierson Mapes . . . went to Philadelphia: Interview with Ira Skutch, 10/22/91.

42   "In [my] grand design": Wilk, *The Golden Age of Television*, 241.

43   Weaver was in the habit: Kenneth Bilby, *The General: David Sarnoff and the Rise of the Communications Industry* (New York: Harper and Row, 1986), 256.

43   "I called him into the office and gave him a fight talk": Interview with PW, 10/21/91.

43   "I told him he should not go": Ibid., 3/3/93.

43   he changed *Philco's* lead-in: Ibid., 10/21/91.

43   "Fred was always a director": Interview with DM, 3/20/92.

43   the script girl was an important figure: Information in this paragraph comes from 3/20/92 interview with DM.

44   a campus celebrity for her beauty: See Lillian McLaughlin, "'I'm a Career Girl,' Says Relays Queen," Des Moines *Tribune*, 4/26/46, 1.

44 she had come to New York . . . with the goal of singing at the Metropolitan Opera: Ibid.

44 Alice . . . recalls recommending her to Coe: Interview with AC, 4/13/92. Memories of those who worked for *Philco* and even one of Joyce's roommates bolster Alice's recollection: 5/3/94 interview with Rhoda (Rosenthal) Herrick of the *Philco Television Playhouse* staff ("She met Fred's wife first, singing in the choir at church") and 9/20/94 interview with Adeline (Garner) Shell, one of Joyce's two roommates during this period.

44 he crossed the line from admiration to infatuation: 7/26/94 interview with TM. "His first marriage broke up because he had an affair with Joyce. Everybody knew that."

44 He started coming home late, sometimes not even calling: Alice G. Coe vs. Frederick H. Coe, Circuit Court of the Fifteenth Judicial Circuit of Florida, Broward County (1952), No. 16853, Bill of Complaint, 2.

44 "Oh," Coe said . . . "Maybe you're not": Interview with AC, 4/13/92.

44 "When this child is born": Ibid.

44 much like that of a leprechaun: Skutch, *I Remember Television*, 87.

45 "Fred went right through the ceiling": Interview with DM, 4/30/93.

45 "Let's cut it": Ibid.

46 "What's he like?": Interview with DS, 3/26/92.

46 "He had this marvelous talent": Ibid., 5/5/93.

46 "Pappy". . . who had never known his own father: Thanks to Ann Mann for this insight.

46 "I worked with many good producers": Interview with TM, 10/18/91.

46 "It was pretty common knowledge": Interview with Larry Elikann, 3/28/92.

46 "Joyce was sexy-looking": Interview with Adrienne Luraschi, 4/9/92.

47 Coe had begun staying out: Coe vs. Coe, Bill of Complaint, 2.

47 she would infuriate him: Interview with AC, 4/17/92.

47 Carol Saroyan . . . gave a small party: Interview with Carol (Saroyan) Matthau, 6/3/93.

47 "'I am in love'": Interview with Phyllis Adams, 4/6/92.

47 In March, Alice . . . took John: Coe vs. Coe, Bill of Complaint, 2.

48 "Where does a man go": *The Symbol, Philco Television Playhouse*, 1/7/51 (UCLA).

48 Impressed by her performance: Interview with AC, 4/13/92.

48 "Where's the goddamn pencil": Interview with Adrienne Luraschi, 5/3/93.

48 "It was black tie": Schaffner, *Worthington Miner*, 219.

49 "There's nothing duller": Vernon Scott, "Coe on Loss of 'Live' TV Drama," N.Y. *Morning Telegraph*, 9/25/58, 2.

49 another five in 1949: Live dramatic anthologies premiering that year were *Colgate Theater* (NBC), *Silver Theater* (CBS), *Theatre Hour* (CBS), *NBC Dramatic Theater* and *Program Playhouse* (DuMont).

49   and another eleven in . . . 1950: Live dramatic anthologies premiering that year were *Robert Montgomery Presents Your Lucky Strike Theater* (NBC), *Armstrong Circle Theater* (NBC), *Starlight Theater* (CBS), *Stage 13* (CBS), *Cameo Theater* (NBC), *Masterpiece Playhouse* (NBC), *Nash Airflyte Theatre* (CBS), *Lux Video Theatre* (CBS), *Pulitzer Prize Playhouse* (ABC), *Prudential Family Theater* (CBS), and *Somerset Maugham Theatre* (NBC).

49   "The shortage of material": Fred Coe, "TV Drama's Declaration of Independence," *Theatre Arts*, June 1954, 31.

49   "The Van Gogh program cut the umbilical cord": Ibid.

49   Weekly casting lists prepared by staff members: Copies of those casting lists, saved by Delbert Mann, are in his possession and that of the author.

49   "H.R. Hays's adult and perceptive": "Tele Follow-up Comment," *Variety*, 3/8/50, 34.

49   Unable to find much original: "Plagiarism Charge vs. Philco, NBC-TV Filed On Semmelweiss Tale," *Variety*, 3/14/51, 25.

50   "the books they could get rights to" Interview with DS, 5/5/93.

50   the best play for a given medium: Edward Sobol, "A Director's Headaches," *NYT*, 6/13/48, 11.

50   "[The] shortage of television story properties": "Script Shortage Still No. 1 Problem While Networks See No Easy Solution," *Variety*, 4/5/50, 35.

50   In July 1950 Charles Underhill: Charles Underhill, "New Opportunities for Television Writers," *Variety*, 7/26/50, 51.

50   NBC's *Colgate Theater* was already making: "TV Writer is Today's Kingpin," *Variety*, 4/26/50, 31.

50   "The originals we usually get": Val Adams, "Video Birthday: Kraft Theatre Observes Fourth Anniversary," *NYT*, 5/6/51, Sec. 2, 9.

50   "a tepid satire of politics": Tom Stempel, *Storytellers to the Nation: A History of American Television Writing* (New York: Continuum, 1992), 34.

50   writers were banned from *Kraft* rehearsals: Ibid., 35.

51   was praised . . . as one of *Philco*'s best shows: "Tele Follow-up Comment," *Variety*, 4/11/51, 34.

51   "On camera day, the star and his agent": Interview with DSW, 3/27/92.

52   "Philco Playhouse took an unfair": "Griffith & TV Intolerance," *Variety*, 4/25/51, 34.

52   Gish told Coe: *The Birth of the Movies*, *Philco Television Playhouse*, 4/22/51, David Susskind Papers (SHSW).

52   "He didn't do everything the first time": Kevin Brownlow and David Gill, *D. W. Griffith: Father of Film*, PBS *American Masters* documentary airing 3/24/93 on KCET-TV, Los Angeles.

52   "He shut out the world": Ibid.

52   In February 1951 it was No. 6 in the Trendex: "Trendex Top 10," *Variety*, 2/14/51, 23.

52   and No. 4 in the Hooperatings: "Sugar Ray Tops Berle," *Variety*, 2/28/51, 27.

52   the Nielsen ratings: "Nielsen's October TV Ratings," *Variety*, 11/29/50, 28.

53   the 1995 *Complete Directory*: Tim Brooks and Earle Marsh, *The Complete Directory to Prime Time Network TV Shows, 1946–Present* (New York: Ballantine Books, 1995), 1277.

53   "He was really the model": Interview with Bud Yorkin, 2/19/94.

53   "You could write his memos": Interview with Rhoda (Rosenthal) Herrick, 5/3/94.

53   "That show used to drive me wild": Interview with Dick Smith, 5/28/93.

54   the first television broadcast seen simultaneously: "TV Spans U.S. as Truman Talks at Parley," by Jack Gould, *NYT*, 9/5/51, 1.

54   Samuel Goldwyn . . . advocated forming a posse: Irving Settel and William Laas, *A Pictorial History of American Television* (New York: Grosset & Dunlap, 1969), 71.

54   "I don't know what the hell": Interview with BC, 4/14/92.

55   "the gathering of energy and experience": Sturcken, *Live Television*, 37.

6   A Certain Time and Place

56   Through the closed door: Interview with DM, ca. 10/15/91.

57   "He would be hollering": Interview with Adrienne Luraschi, 4/9/92.

57   Toward the end of one show: Interview with O. Tamburri, 4/14/92.

57   The normally placid Delbert Mann: Ann and Delbert Mann, *A Remembrance of "Pappy,"* 7.

57   "Incredible . . . It was incredible": Interview with AP, 5/11/92.

58   "Ah want to see their eyes!": Delbert Mann, "An Appreciation of Fred Coe," *Variety*, 5/23/56, 31.

58   he didn't believe in closeups for their own sake: "Coe is TV Discovery," *Cue* (N.Y.), 12/11/48, 24.

58   "The 75-millimeter is tougher": Interview with Jack Coffey, 6/1/93.

58   Young & Rubicam . . . would insist on: Interviews with Delbert Mann, 3/20/92, Arthur Penn, 11/13/91, and Bill Nichols, 4/4/92 and 4/8/92. See also Skutch, *I Remember Television*, 98.

58   when $600 to $750 was a standard: "The 'Freelance' Production Chart," *Variety*, 6/3/53, 27.

58   unable to face her: Interview with AC, 4/13/92.

59   "I don't want you to get": Interview with AC, 4/13/92.

59   "It would seem from your letter": AC letter to JK, received 5/30/94.

59   "I heard Joyce felt": Interview with Adrienne Luraschi, 4/9/92.

60   "Joyce and I are going to be married": Interview with AC, 4/17/92.

60   "Reading scripts, hiring directors": Ceplair, "Fred Coe: Forgotten Genius," *Emmy*, July/August 1982, 43.

60   Sutton . . . in full General Grant uniform: Ann and Delbert Mann, *A Remembrance of "Pappy,"* 8.

60   "I'd see him on the street": Interview with E. G. Marshall, 5/6/92.

60   One of his writers said: David Karp, "A Memory of Fred Coe, 1914–1979," *The Writers' Guild of America Newsletter*, June 1979, 19.

60   In his early days at NBC: "He Searches for Excitement," TVG, 3/1/58, 24.

60   "He dressed like Banana Republic": Interview with Laurie Coe, 3/8/94.

60   "As a razor-backed producer": Fred Coe, untitled memo of 9/11/52 to DM, Vincent Donehue, et al., in the David Susskind Papers, State Historical Society of Wisconsin, Shelf List, Box 9: "Fred Coe, Correspondence, January 1950—November 1954."

61   "He was terribly supportive": Interview with Horton Foote, 10/29/91.

61   "People were just overcome": Ibid., 4/21/92.

62   "allusive, delicate and elegiac": Gore Vidal, "Television Drama, Circa 1956," *Theatre Arts*, December 1956, 85.

62   "a Chekhov of the Texas small town": Fred Coe, "TV Drama's Declaration of Independence," *Theatre Arts*, June 1954, 88.

62   "Miss Martha gives a peal": Horton Foote, *Harrison, Texas* (New York: Harcourt, Brace and Company, 1956), 3.

62   Foote eliminated the scene: Barbara Moore and David G. Yellin, *Horton Foote's Three Trips to Bountiful* (Dallas: Southern Methodist University Press, 1993), 15–16.

62   Foote pared away the more obviously dramatic: Ibid., 15.

62   Influenced by Arthur Miller's *Death of a Salesman*: Shaun Considine, 5/10/95 letter to JK.

62   Coe encouraged him to write: Ibid.

62   "Chayefsky's works are as authentically Bronx": Bernard Kalb, "The Author," *Saturday Review*, 4/16/55, 13.

62   It was loosely based on a *Reader's Digest* article: Max Wilk, *The Golden Age of Television: Notes from the Survivors* (New York: Delacorte Press, 1976), 129.

63   "This is a nice story, Pappy": Interview with Herb Gardner, 5/11/94.

63   "You get a sense that Coe helped create": Interview with Ron Simon, 11/15/94.

63   "How's it going with that script?": Interview with DM, ca. 1/14/91.

64   "Dramas that undertake": Jack Gould, "N.B.C. Playhouse Offers Valid and Moving Hour With Production of Paddy Chayefsky's 'Marty'," *NYT*, 5/27/53, 43.

64   "Hi, Marty, what do you feel": Interview with Rod Steiger, 10/23/93.

65   "You don't write in pictures": Interview with N. Richard Nash, 10/30/93.

65   "Give it to me in a sentence": Ibid.

66   "We didn't sit in reverence": Interview with BC, 4/21/92.

66   "I've never been": Interview with Eva Marie Saint, 5/6/92.

66   "In a strange way": Interview with JPM, 10/22/91.

66   To direct most of the shows: Several episodes of *First Person Playhouse* were directed by Bob Costello, later unit production manager on *Mr. Peepers*.

66   "I got a call one day": Interview with AP, 11/13/91.

67   "I remember talking with Fred": Ibid., 5/11/92.

67 "Fred Coe, one of TV's bright young veterans": "'First Person': Program of the Week," *TVG*, 8/21/53, 13.

67 "How's the little Tad?": Interview with TM, 10/22/93.

67 still working as a ticket clerk: Interview with TM, 10/18/91, and his essay in Ann and Delbert Mann, *A Remembrance of "Pappy,"* 15.

68 "Can you imagine being asked": Interview with TM, 10/18/91.

68 "You can sit at your typewriter": Quoted in Ceplair, "Fred Coe: Forgotten Genius," *Emmy*, July/August 1982, 42.

68 Coe . . . intended to open *Philco-Goodyear*'s fall 1953 season: Interview with TM, 7/20/93.

68 "his writings have a naked lyrical quality": Henry Hewes, "Six Authors in Search of a Sponsor," *Saturday Review*, 8/14/54, 22.

69 "With the best will in the world": Review of *The Morning Shirt*, London *Times*, 9/4/61, 5A.

69 JP Miller was a hulking, 6'3 Texan: Interview with JPM, 10/22/91 and as quoted in Michael Winship, *Television* (New York: Random House, 1988), 26.

69 "I sold a script": Interview with JPM, 10/22/91.

69 "Fred understood that you don't get milk": Ibid.

70 "The protagonist . . . is the force for good": Reginald Rose, *Six Television Plays* (New York: Simon and Schuster, 1956), 204.

70 "I'm not per se a social writer": Moore and Yellin, *Horton Foote's Three Trips*, 27.

70 maverick producers such as Fred Coe: Other leading producers of live television drama include Felix Jackson, George Schaefer, Robert Montgomery, and Martin Manulis.

70 "It was a hysterical period": Interview with Eli Wallach, 4/13/92.

71 Phil Loeb. . . . checked into New York's Taft Hotel: "Phil Loeb Dies; Actor, Unionist," *Variety*, 9/7/55, 65.

71 "Young and R. put a lot of pressure": Interview with BN, 4/4/92.

71 Pierson Mapes . . . kept a copy of *Red Channels*: Skutch, *I Remember Television*, 98.

71 "If we had a particularly good script": Interview with BN, 4/4/92.

71 Several times, Coe had to talk: Ann and Delbert Mann, *A Remembrance of "Pappy,"* 7.

71 Young & Rubicam refused to approve her: Interview with DM, 4/29/92.

71 the executive . . . gushed expansively: Ibid.

71 "Use her": Ibid. DM was present both at the luncheon and later in Coe's office.

72 "It would probably be annulled": *The Huntress*, airdate 2/14/54 (UCLA).

72 "He was an interplanetary": Ibid.

72 "Fred's attitude was": Interviews with AP, 11/13/91 and 5/11/92.

72 "I think that, like a lot": Interview with Walter Bernstein, 11/15/95.

72 "If anyone came from the sponsor": Quoted in Wilk, *The Golden Age of Television*, 135.

72   "Fred screamed at him so loud": Interview with JPM, 10/22/91.

73   "The sponsor *pays* for this show": Interview with Harry Muheim, 6/6/93.

73   acquiescence to such a move would be a blow: "A Case for TV Dramas," *Variety*, 3/17/54, 23.

73   called the show the "Phil-Coe" Hour: "Special Citation for Philco-Goodyear Television Playhouse," *Variety*, 4/21/54, 29.

73   "Fred drove all the writers mad": Interview with Mary Phipps, 2/2/94.

73   "We are confident that the next five years": Fred Coe, "TV Drama's Declaration of Independence," *Theatre Arts*, June 1954, 88.

73   the advertising agency . . . was displeased: "Radio & Television: The Week in Review," *Time*, 8/30/54, 55.

74   "One week there'd be a story about a blind old lady": Ibid.

74   "I'm sure Fred was still": Interview with PW, 4/10/92.

74   "One of the reasons it was fun": Robert Alan Aurthur, "An Appreciation of Fred Coe," *Variety*, 5/23/56, 31.

74   leaving *Philco* was not a demotion: Interview with PW, 5/4/92.

74   "I think he was glad to be rid": Interview with DM, 3/20/92.

74   "a complete motion picture studio": Settel and Laas, *A Pictorial History of Television*, 108.

75   Coe was making $270 a month: Interview with AC, 3/27/92.

7   Mr. Peepers

76   Six years after the end of World War II: Interviews with DSW, 3/27/92 and 4/30/92.

77   "An ant lion is poised": Everett Greenbaum, *The Goldenberg Who Couldn't Dance* (New York: Harcourt Brace Jovanovich, 1980), 104.

77   "Aw, look, Pappy": *Mr. Peepers* pilot, airdate 5/15/52 (UCLA).

77   "Ah think we better hear": Quoted in Max Wilk, *The Golden Age of Television*, 75.

78   "We had a weather balloon": Interviews with BC, 4/14/92, 4/20/92, and 2/25/93.

78   was originally set for an eight-show run: Wilk, *The Golden Age of Television*, 75.

78   "In a dull season": "Mr. Peepers," *Time*, 7/28/52, 42.

78   "a lead-pipe cinch": "On the Air," *The Hollywood Reporter*, 7/7/52, 10.

78   "is dreamy-eyed, moves in vague motions": Val Adams, "The Amiable 'Mr. Peepers' in the Flesh," *NYT*, 7/27/52, Sec. 2, 9.

78   He was born in Detroit: Harry Gilroy, "A Peep at Mr. Peepers—and Wally Cox," *NYT Magazine*, 1/11/53, 14.

78   Cox became the roommate of Marlon Brando: "Back to School with Mr. Peepers," *TVG*, 9/4/53, 5.

79   "He took me and Fred": Interview with DSW, 3/27/92.

79   "probably the most non-aggressive man": "Back to School with Mr. Peepers," *TVG*, 9/4/53, 6

79   he earned $1,500 a week: Harry Gilroy, "A Peep at Mr. Peepers," *NYT Magazine*, 1/11/53, 14.

79　that rose to $2,500 a week: Fritz Goodwin, "Taking Another Peep at Mr. Peepers," *TVG*, 11/18/67, 32.

79　"one scene where he got caught": Interview with BC, 8/1/93.

79　"She couldn't remember her lines": Interview with BN, 4/4/92.

80　"When she was first on": Interview with DSW, 3/27/92.

80　"David wanted to make a more": Interview with BN, 4/4/92.

80　"Roscoe, it's good to see you": *Mr. Peepers*, airdate 9/18/52 (UCLA).

80　"I shouldn't have done this": Interview with DSW, 3/27/92.

81　NBC logged 15,000 calls and letters: Harry Gilroy, "A Peep at Mr. Peepers," *NYT Magazine*, 1/11/53, 14.

81　"For me, being on the show": Quoted in Wilk, *The Golden Age of Television*, 75.

81　"In those days, the network": Interview with DSW, 3/27/92.

82　"Fred had a tendency": Ibid.

82　His budget was so small: Interview with EG, 5/4/92.

82　"Have fun with Freddie the Frog": Ibid., 7/9/93.

82　"Up yours, too": Ibid.

82　a producer at NBC learned of his job: Greenbaum, *Goldenberg*, 96–97.

83　"We've been looking for you": Ibid., 98.

83　"Because that's how they get your name": Ibid., 120.

83　"It's good that we weren't": Interview with EG, 7/9/93.

83　"At first, I was very afraid": Ibid.

83　When they drew a blank: Greenbaum, *Goldenberg*, 114–115.

84　"'Why don't you change the guy's attitude *here?*'": Wilk, *The Golden Age of Television*, 80.

84　"I became very nervous": Interview with EG, 5/4/92.

84　"I suppose we brought Mom in": Interview with DSW, 8/4/93.

84　"Of course . . . I knew I knew you": *Mr. Peepers*, airdate 2/13/55 (UCLA).

85　*TV Guide* ran an article: "Peepers' Gadgets . . . And How They Work," *TVG*, 4/24/53, 10.

85　"Mr. Peepers should be more": Jack Gould, "Radio and Television," *NYT*, 8/13/52, 29.

85　"What's she like?": *Mr. Peepers*, airdate 10/18/53 (UCLA).

85　"too high-brow, too low-brow": "The Rise and Fall of Mr. Peepers," *TVG*, 7/30/55, 20.

85　"Appeal of 'Mr. Peepers'": "Tele Follow-up Comment, *Variety*, 12/24/52, 26.

85　"a lot of people have been bitten": *Mr. Peepers*, airdate 2/13/55 (UCLA).

85　"Don't touch Wally": Interview with Georgann Johnson (who changed her name from "Georgiann" to "Georgann" subsequent to appearing on *Mr. Peepers*), 7/20/93.

86　"I felt like I was the most straight": Interview with Georgann Johnson, 7/29/93.

86　"Coe was marvelous": Quoted in Wilk, *The Golden Age of Television*, 80.

86　"Sometimes during rehearsal": Interview with EG, 7/9/93.

86   "What time do they throw?": Mr. *Peepers*, airdate 4/26/53 (UCLA).

86   "Ezio Pinza was not a sitcom actor": Interview with DS, 4/17/92.

86   Swift thought Bonino: Interview with DSW, 3/27/92.

86   "interesting but not earth-shaking": Television reviews, *Variety*, 9/16/53, 31.

86   Gerard Jones's study: Gerard Jones, *Honey, I'm Home!*, 45–46.

87   Coe instructed Fritzell and Greenbaum: "The Rise and Fall of Mr. Peepers," *TVG*, 7/30/55, 21.

87   "When I see something I like": "Mr. Peepers' Plunge," *Life*, 5/31/54, 68.

87   "Do you like large families?": Mr. *Peepers*, airdate 10/18/53 (UCLA).

87   "The advantage of live TV": "Mr. & Mrs. Frederic Remington Announce the Marriage of their Daughter . . . ," *TVG*, 5/21/54, 17.

87   "Jim, who always had terrible luck": Interview with EG, 7/9/93.

87   "She's all I've got": Mr. *Peepers*, airdate 5/23/54 (UCLA).

88   With 40 million viewers: Greenbaum, *Goldenberg*, 123.

88   "Mr. *Peepers* comes close": Mr. *Peepers* review, *TVG*, 5/28/54, 22.

88   Everett Greenbaum had opposed: Interview with EG, 7/30/93.

88   Mahlon Fox . . . had to make: Interview with Mahlon Fox, 8/2/93.

88   The audience was salted with unemployed actors: Interview with EG, 7/30/93.

88   "It's possible that *Peepers*'s quiet humor": "The Rise and Fall of Mr. Peepers," *TVG*, 7/30/55, 21.

89   Jack Gould . . . felt that constituted a snub: Jack Gould, "Peabody Awards," *NYT*, 4/26/53, Sec. 2, 11.

89   "Practically all of the characters": Television Reviews, *Variety*, 9/22/54, 29.

89   like a barometer: "The Rise and Fall of Mr. Peepers," *TVG*, 7/30/55, 20.

89   "Much of the style and mood": Jack Gould, "TV: 'Hit Parade' Miss," *NYT*, 5/18/55, 63.

90   "with a new time spot": "The Rise and Fall of Mr. Peepers," *TVG*, 7/30/55, 20.

90   Coe offered to sustain Fritzell and Greenbaum: Interview with EG, 8/11/93.

8   A Silent Telephone

91   "Television's vicious programming cycle": "Rise & Fall of Hour Dramas," *Variety*, 7/20/55, 27.

91   "We are reaching out": Robert Lewis Shayon, "Unusual Plays Wanted—But Don't Offend Anyone," *Saturday Review*, 2/13/54, 32.

92   "I'm a college graduate": Reginald Rose, *Six Television Plays*, 205.

92   "From all accounts . . . dealers holding": "Dixie Pressure on TV Talent," *Variety*, 6/20/56, 17.

92   as late as December of 1954: Greenfield, *Television*, 132.

93   "everyone was having second thoughts": Sturcken, *Live Television*, 68.

93   "It was very luxurious": Interview with Dominick Dunne, 4/17/92.

94   "You look like a nice girl": Interview with Jane (Wetherell) Aurthur, 6/23/93.

94   "The color technicians went wild": Philip Hamburger, "Television," *The New Yorker*, 10/30/54, 96.

94   the show's . . . segments fared increasingly worse: "Ginger 19.6, 'Lucy' 40.8," *Variety*, 10/20/54, 23.

94   NBC would probably write off: "Specs Just '1-Season Wonder'?" *Variety*, 10/20/54, 23.

95   Lindsay and Crouse didn't like: Interview with AP, 7/20/93.

95   "Fred came into the control room": Ibid.

95   "a fine production": Jack Gould, "Television: 'State of the Union'," *NYT*, 11/17/54, 45.

95   "a stunning TV production": "Lindsay-Crouse Upgrade State of the Specs," *Variety*, 11/17/54, 35.

95   In October, a new ratings service: Castleman and Podrazik, *Watching TV*, 90.

95   "It's no longer considered": "Specs No Longer a Bad Word," *Variety*, 12/1/54, 25.

96   "a little dated": Jack Gould, "Television in Review," *NYT*, 1/12/55, 36.

96   "A reticent, abstract play": Brooks Atkinson, *Broadway* (New York: Limelight Editions, 1990), 273.

96   Miller . . . had done a cut-and-paste job: Interview with JPM, 7/21/93.

96   Coe called a script conference: Ann and Delbert Mann, *A Remembrance of "Pappy,"* 7; Interview with DM, 11/22/93.

96   "What's your image?": Interview with JPM, 7/21/93.

96   "Fred quietly tore": Interview with DM, 10/15/91.

96   "I had never done an adaptation": Interview with JPM, 7/21/93.

96   "expertly wrought adaptation": *Yellow Jack* review, *Variety*, 1/12/55. 35.

96   Jack Gould called it excellent: Jack Gould, "Television in Review, *NYT*, 1/12/55, 36.

96   "Otis Riggs, the set designer": Interview with BN, 6/22/93.

96   "That would be total nonsense": Interview with Mike Dann, 10/4/93.

97   "When we were blocking": Interview with AP, 7/20/93.

97   "I just want to thank you": Fred Coe letter to DM, 1/19/55. Copy in Delbert Mann's papers at Heard Library, Vanderbilt University. Box 3, *Yellow Jack* file. Copyright National Broadcasting Company, Inc. All Rights Reserved.

97   "Nothing ever suited her": Interview with BN, 10/20/93.

97   "I had been so preoccupied": Shelley Winters, *Shelley II: The Middle of My Century* (New York: Simon and Schuster, 1989), 312.

97   "Before camp, he was camp": Interview with Dominick Dunne, 4/19/92.

97   "Sumner could do an imitation": Ibid., 11/6/93.

97   it lacked the substance: Jack Gould, "TV: Double Feature," *NYT*, 2/9/55, 37.

97   none of the stars brought their characters to life: *The Women* review, *Variety*, 2/9/55, 37.

98   "Fred kind of sloughed it off": Interview with Larry Elikann, 3/28/92.

98   between 65 and 75 million viewers: Castleman and Podrazik, *Watching TV*, 91.

98   only three subsequent shows have been watched by a higher percentage: According to the 1993 Nielsen Television Index of Top 100 Network Programs, the last

episode of M*A*S*H had a 60.2 rating, the "Who Shot J.R.?" episode of *Dallas*, 53.3, and the eighth episode of *Roots*, 51.1. According to Nielsen NTI Pocket Piece of 3/7/55, *Peter Pan* had a 51.0. This rating does not appear in television reference books because in 1960, Nielsen changed its formula for computing ratings, and, as a result, *Peter Pan*'s rating by contemporary standards may be slightly lower—or slightly higher.

98   *Peter Pan* parties were held: "Robbing Peter to Pay Pan," *Variety*, 3/9/55, 27.

98   Traffic thinned on the nation's roads: Kenneth Bilby, *The General: David Sarnoff and the Rise of the Communications Industry* (New York: Harper & Row, 1986), 255.

98   it knocked it out of the Top 10: ". . . But No 'Lucy'," *Variety*, 3/16/55, 27.

98   "Surely there must be": Jack Gould, "Television: Neverland," *NYT*, 3/8/55, 33.

98   "Television's role was to": Jack Gould, "Delightful 'Peter Pan,'" *NYT*, 3/13/55, Sec. 2, 15.

98   "Spec[tacular]s Just": "Specs Just '1-Season Wonder'?" *Variety*, 10/20/54, 23.

98   "Fred was really the genius": Interview with PW, 3/3/93.

99   "Seldom has so much coin": *Reunion in Vienna* review, *Variety*, 4/6/55, 29.

99   "The cavernous stone corridors": *Darkness at Noon* review, *Variety*, 5/4/55, 29.

99   Riggs designed: Explanation of how *Darkness at Noon* set worked synthesized from interview with DM, 10/19/93.

99   "television viewing is not often": Jack Gould, "TV: 'Darkness at Noon'," *NYT*, 5/4/55, 40.

100   "'Forest' Petrifies": "'Forest' Petrifies CBS Competition," *Variety*, 6/1/55, 25.

100   Coe was not only leaving the show: "Fred Coe Exiting NBC to Produce Own TV Films? Lawyers With Dual Production-Client Status Accented," *Variety*, 9/7/55, 23.

100   "Fred Coe was looked up to": Interview with Mike Dann, 11/3/93.

101   "They're going to have to devise": J. P. Shanley, "Faces on TV This Week," *NYT*, 9/18/55.

101   "He came to rehearsal so few times": Interview with DM, 10/6/93.

101   "I think Fred almost lost his mind": Interview with Dominick Dunne, 11/6/93.

101   Mann . . . refused to speak to him: Interview with DM, 10/6/93.

101   Coe would have fired: Interview with DS, 5/5/93.

101   they . . . worked all night to relight: Interview with DM, 10/6/93.

102   "Babylon had two million people": *Our Town*, airdate 9/19/55 (UCLA).

102   "Eva Marie Saint was responsible": J. P. Shanley, "TV: 'Our Town' Still is Entertaining," *NYT*, 9/20/55, 62.

102   "stunning": *Our Town* review, *Variety*, 9/21/55, 34.

102   "Given the dubious decision": Wendell Brogen, "Television," *The New Republic*, 10/3/55, 23.

102   "Mr. 'Philco Playhouse' himself": "Reunion on Tuesday," *Variety*, 9/14/55, 26.

102   "None that I know of": Interviews with Jane (Wetherell) Aurthur, 6/23/93, and Everett Chambers, 8/3/93.

102   Gore Vidal affirms: Gore Vidal 11/5/93 letter to JK.

103   "Fred was calling the shots": Interview with DS, 5/5/93.

103   "Fred never relinquished": Interview with AP, 10/26/93.

103   There, he was befriended: Robert Alan Aurthur, "52 Plays a Year, All Original, All Live," *TVG*, 3/17/73, 7.

103   "Write it without describing": Ibid.

103   "Not only is this unfair": Sidney Poitier, *This Life* (New York: Alfred A. Knopf, 1980), 179.

103   including paying him $2,000: Robert Alan Aurthur, "52 Plays a Year," 10.

103   Two Southern newspapers: Ibid.

104   "I'm talking to the guy who wrote it": Ibid.

104   "*Philco-Goodyear* writers were different": Interview with TM, 10/18/91.

104   At one of them, Alice met: Interviews with AC, 3/5/93 and 12/18/93.

104   Coe held out for *Playwrights '56*: Sturcken, *Live Television*, 119.

105   In April of 1954 the U.S. Supreme Court ruled: Castleman and Podrazik, *Watching TV*, 99.

105   "It's going to die": Interview with Jane (Wetherell) Aurthur, 6/23/93.

105   "It didn't have the glamor": Interview with Dominick Dunne, 11/6/93.

105   "the Coe-terie of tip-top": *The Keyhole* review, *Variety*, 5/30/56, 23.

105   "In doing 'The Answer'": Jack Gould, "TV: Fantasy of Bombs and Angels," *NYT*, 10/5/55, 71.

106   "Can you do a Hemingway?": Interview with A. E. Hotchner, 10/29/93.

106   "They came in and asked to speak": Ibid.

107   Jack Gould gave the Faulkner: Jack Gould, "TV: Faulkner's 'Sound and Fury,'" *NYT*, 12/7/55, 79.

107   "In the shadow of that giant": "In a Tough Spot," *Newsweek*, 1/2/56, 41.

107   "For about the first 10 minutes": *The Waiting Place* review, *Variety*, 12/28/55, 31.

107   "Everybody's interested in gimmicks": Sid Shalit, "Who's Afraid of the Big Bad Wolf? Not Fred Coe!" *New York Daily News*, 1/17/56, 47.

108   "We're doing the run-through": Interview with Bill Klages, 10/19/93.

108   In March, Pontiac announced: "Pontiac's Detour on 'Playwrights,'" *Variety*, 3/7/56, 22.

108   "How are things going?": Interview with Jane (Wetherell) Aurthur, 6/23/93.

108   "Fred would take chairs": Interview with Larry Elikann, 3/28/92.

108   *Playwrights* had higher ratings: Val Adams, "TV Drama Series Will Bow July 3," *NYT*, 4/25/56, 71.

109   "Fred was just caught": Interview with Mike Dann, 10/4/93.

109   Miner quit after an adaptation: Castleman and Podrazik, *Watching TV*, 113.

109   the show's leading directors: Ibid., 114.

109   First on *Dotto*, and then *Twenty-One*: Ibid., 125.

109   Abel Green . . . said *Philco-Goodyear*: "An Appreciation of Fred Coe," *Variety*, 5/23/56, 32.

110   "Fred was very unhappy": Interview with BN, 4/8/92.

110   "A composite of that guy": Sturcken, *Live Television*, 82.

110   he rented a farmhouse in nearby Watermill: "Alice Coe Itinerary, 1951–1979," 3. In possession of the author.

110   the resignation of Pat Weaver: "'Bob & Pat' Now 'Bob & Co.',", *Variety*, 9/12/56, 23.

110   NBC's new top programming executive: Castleman and Podrazik, *Watching TV*, 111.

110   "the slide-rule boys": "Road to Success: Research," *Variety*, 6/6/56, 23.

110   "The best of it was really": Tom Stempel, *Storytellers to the Nation*, 56.

110   "I have not deluded myself": Gore Vidal, "Television Drama, Circa 1956," *Theatre Arts*, December 1956, 86.

111   "Television has, for all its limitations": Gore Vidal, *Visit to a Small Planet and Other Television Plays* (Boston: Little, Brown and Company, 1956), xviii.

111   "Television drama through the first decade": Jeff Greenfield, *Television: The First 50 Years* (New York: Harry N. Abrams, 1977), 129.

111   "In its golden years": Settel and Laas, *A Pictorial History of Television*, 99.

111   In May of 1956 . . . Coe had signed: Val Adams, "Fred Coe and N.B.C. Agree on New Pact," *NYT*, 4/30/56, 47.

111   Except for trouble-shooting: "'That Old (TV) Gang of Mine'," *Variety*, 11/27/57, 39

111   "Nearly all of my people": Interview with PW, 12/2/91.

111   "I have a clear memory of Fred": Interview with Harry Muheim, 6/6/93.

112   "I would like to produce shows": "Coe Will Leave N.B.C.-TV Dec. 16," *NYT*, 11/27/57, 55.

112   "I kept going back to the office": Interview with Everett Chambers, 8/3/93.

112   On December 4, *Variety* reported: "TV 'Playhouse 90' in Dual-Producer Setup; Dicker Coe," *Variety*, 12/4/57, 29.

112   And on December 16: "Producer Gets C.B.S. Pact," *NYT*, 12/16/57, 51.

112   Coe's agent, Priscilla Morgan, had held: Interview with Priscilla Morgan, 6/22/93.

112   In 1957, sailings of passenger liners: Morris, *Manhattan '45*, 268.

9   Live TV's Last Stand

113   television . . . in New York and four other cities: Castleman and Podrazik, *Watching TV*, 20. The four others were Philadelphia, Chicago, Schenectady, New York, and Los Angeles.

113   496 TV stations . . . and $1.3 billion: Sturcken, *Live Television*, 101.

113   "there was a tremendous vacuum": John Crosby, "A Plea for Experiment," *NYHT*, 3/24/58, Sec. 2, 1.

113   "Television can't afford": John P. Shanley, "Fred Coe—Pioneer's Viewpoint," *NYT*, 9/14/58, Sec. 2, 15.

114   "As the TV season proceeds": Quoted in William Boddy, *Fifties Television: The Industry and Its Critics* (Urbana and Chicago: University of Illinois Press, 1993), 189.

114   "These plays . . . held consistently high ratings": Barnouw, *The Image Empire*, 32–33.

114   not as "well liked . . . as other shows": Boddy, *Fifties Television*, 201.

114   Rod Serling acknowledged: Rod Serling, "TV in the Can vs. TV in the Flesh," *NYT Magazine*, 11/24/57, 56–57.

114   "I think the most deplorable thing": Matt Messina, "Coe Sets 'Stalin' TVer," New York *Daily News*, 8/20/58, 63.

115   "You can't blame a city": Vernon Scott, "Coe on Loss of 'Live' TV Drama," New York *Morning Telegraph*, 9/25/58, 2.

115   Of the ten highest-rated shows: Gordon F. Sander, *Serling: The Rise and Twilight of Television's Last Angry Man* (New York: Dutton, 1992), 139.

115   "The best acting was by the Rocky Mountains": Castleman and Podrazik, *Watching TV*, 127.

115   " 'Live' TV: It Went Thataway": *Variety*, 5/4/60, 23.

115   "horse-ass opera": Quoted in Sturcken, *Live Television*, 126.

115   Stevens found Coe a capable: Interview with Leslie Stevens, 3/5/94.

115   Vidal says . . . brought in his own people: Gore Vidal, 11/5/93 and 3/29/94 letters to JK.

115   Arthur Penn . . . Vidal was simply unavailable: Interview with AP, 2/2/94.

115   "very lively viewing": Ruth Waterbury, " 'Left-Hand Gun' Hits Mark," *Los Angeles Examiner*, 5/8/58, Sec. 3, 6.

116   "[an] example of sniffling celluloid": *The Left-Handed Gun* review, *Cue*, 5/24/58, 9.

116   "What do you think?": Interview with Leslie Stevens, 3/5/94.

116   "She took it to all the big fancy producers": Interview with AP, 10/26/93.

116   Gibson says . . . first suggested Fonda: William Gibson, *The Seesaw Log* (New York: Alfred A. Knopf, 1959), 11.

117   Penn says it was Coe's idea: Interview with AP, 10/26/93.

117   "I've got a girl": Howard Teichmann, *Fonda: My Life* (New York: New American Library, 1981), 255.

117   "Start it rolling": Ibid., 259.

117   Coe was able to get the Booth Theater: Ibid., 260.

117   finance the show, and book out-of-town theaters: Gibson, *The Seesaw Log*, 25–26.

117   "Well, if *that* doesn't show": Ibid., 44.

117   "His manner was . . . firm": Ibid., 57.

118   "Fred was the best producer": Interview with William Gibson, 1/28/94.

118   "Fonda was extremely nervous": Interview with AP, 2/2/94.

118   "*Don't* call the director *boy!*" : Interview with Joe Harris, 2/3/94.

118   "Bill did write a book": Interview with Porter Van Zandt, 2/10/94.

118   "I had watched men more harrowed": Gibson, *The Seesaw Log*, 106.

118   "a tender style of writing": Brooks Atkinson, "The Theatre: 'Two for the Seesaw',"
      NYT, 1/17/58, 15.

118   *Mirror* said to "rush": Robert Coleman, "'Two for the Seesaw' a Hit," New York
      Daily Mirror, 1/17/58, 18.

118   gave Coe "credit": John Chapman, "'Two for Seesaw' Captivating," New York
      Daily News, 1/17/58, 43.

118   "Henry Fonda is naturally": Richard Watts Jr., "Two on the Aisle," *New York Post*,
      1/17/58, 40.

119   "I don't mean Fonda's role": Gibson, *The Seesaw Log*, 96.

119   "In 1957 . . . Mr. Gibson looked haggard": Maurice Zolotow, "Stage Team Re-
      visited," *NYT*, 10/18/59, Sec. 2, 1.

119   "We told her to go home": Judith Crist, "Fred Coe Back on Broadway," *NYHT*,
      8/23/59, Sec. 4, 2.

119   In Philadelphia, there wasn't a strong advance sale: Interview with AP, 2/2/94.

120   "Sooner or later, Miss Bancroft": Brooks Atkinson, "Miracle Worker," *NYT*,
      11/1/59, Sec. 2, 1.

120   Bancroft was out of commission: Nan Robertson, "Broadway Slugging Match,"
      NYT, 12/20/59, Sec. 2, 5.

120   "The child was all tensed up": Ibid.

120   "Patty and Annie took such spills": Ibid.

120   "an emotional play on a painfully touching subject": Richard Watts Jr., "Two on
      the Aisle," *New York Post*, 10/20/59, 48.

120   "the loose narrative technique": Brooks Atkinson, "Theatre: Giver of Light,"
      NYT, 10/20/59, 44.

120   "We doubt that 'The Miracle Worker'": Robert Coleman, "'Miracle' Magnificent
      Drama," *Daily Mirror*, 10/20/59, 39.

120   "Robert Alan Aurthur's adaptation": *The Red Mill* review, *Variety*, 4/23/58, 27.

121   "It was a mess": Interview with BG, 3/8/93.

121   "We taped in long segments": Interview with DM, 1/31/94.

121   Perhaps no other American producer has accomplished: Thanks to Bill Nichols
      for this insight.

121   It was conceived by . . . Hubbell Robinson: Joel Engel, *Rod Serling: The Dreams and
      Nightmares of Life in the Twilight Zone* (New York: Contemporary Books, 1989),
      127.

122   "This is not the great temple": John P. Shanley, "Fred Coe—Pioneer's Viewpoint,"
      NYT, 9/14/58, Sec. 2, 15.

122   "Fred would buy expensive clothes": Interview with BG, 3/8/93.

122   "The point I wanted to make": Interview with DM, 1/31/94.

123   *The New Republic* praised: Frank R. Pierson, "The Dying TV Drama," *The New
      Republic*, 2/2/59, 22.

123   a "johnny one-note plateau": "Playhouse 90—The Plot to Kill Stalin," *Variety*,
      10/1/58, 29.

123   Jack Gould . . . questioned the wisdom: Jack Gould, "TV: A Real-Life Drama," *NYT*, 9/26/58, 53.

123   "That was a filthy slander": "Menshikov Calls TV Play 'Slander'," *NYT*, 10/7/58, 69.

123   Two days later, the Soviet government announced: "Moscow Closes CBS News Bureau," *NYT*, 10/9/58, 15.

123   A *New York Times* editorial harshly criticized: "Soviet Censorship," *NYT*, 10/9/58, 36.

123   "One stupid mistake": Jack Gould, "A Plot Backfires," *NYT*, 10/12/58, Sec. 2, 13.

123   The Overseas Press Club sent a note: "Protest Sent Soviet," *NYT*, 10/26/58, 3.

123   A CBS engineer . . . unable to get a visa: E. W. Kenworthy, "Soviet Excludes Official of C.B.S.," *NYT*, 10/23/58, 62.

123   "Fred always seemed to carry": David Karp, "A Memory of Fred Coe, 1914–1979," *The Writers' Guild of America Newsletter*, June 1979, 19.

123   "Fred was . . . a kind of gentle and sweet semi-literate": Ibid.

123   "even though a graduate of": Greenbaum, *Goldenberg*, 112. Despite Greenbaum's assertion, Coe did not get a degree from Yale Drama.

124   "Southerners were sort of frowned on": Interview with BN, 6/22/93.

124   "He is known to be hot-headed": Donald Davidson, "The Artist as Southerner," *The Saturday Review of Literature*, 5/15/26, 1.

124   "One felt in him the swamp ferment": Greenbaum, *Goldenberg*, 112.

124   "He was deceptively brilliant": Interview with Roger O. Hirson, 2/14/94.

124   "He had probably the best bullshit detector": Interview with BG, 3/8/93.

124   Frankenheimer says Coe exuded the feeling: Quoted in Michael Winship, *Television* (New York: Random House, 1988), 28.

124   "He gave us a climate in which we could function": Interview with John Frankenheimer, 2/21/94.

125   he was going to quit writing, move to Riverhead: Interview with JPM, 7/21/93.

125   "Pappy, I like it": Ibid., 10/22/91.

125   "Now, Piper Laurie is a great actress": Ibid.

125   "original and effective": Frank R. Pierson, "The Dying TV Drama," *The New Republic*, 2/2/59, 22.

125   "Under John Frankenheimer's direction": "Tele Follow-up Comment," *Variety*, 10/8/58, 35.

126   "*The Days of Wine and Roses* makes a strong": Fred Coe 2/24/60 letter to Guy della Cioppa. Copies in Fred Coe's papers at the SHSW and in the possession of the author. Copyright CBS Entertainment, a division of CBS Inc.

126   Procter & Gamble's decision to spend: "CBS-TV's Pay-As-You-Go Staff," *Variety*, 10/15/58, 23.

126   the first on-location taping: "Tele Follow-up Comment: Playhouse 90 review," *Variety*, 10/22/58, 34.

126   "We were up on Mulholland Drive": Interview with Adri Butler, 2/11/94.

126   "In the first scene, Sterling Hayden poses": Interview with Roger O. Hirson, 2/14/94.

126   "Fred Coe, who ordinarily infuses": "Tele Follow-up Comment," *Variety*, 11/5/58, 52.

126   "He would never do anything like that": Interview with BG, 5/28/93.

127   "We built the Mississippi River": Interview with Charles Cappleman, 4/15/93.

127   "Everybody said that show couldn't be done": Interview with John Frankenheimer, 2/21/94.

127   "The gifted Fred Coe-John Frankenheimer combo": "Tele Follow-up Comment," *Variety*, 11/26/58, 33.

128   "By tomorrow, the world's weariest group": John P. Shanley, "Hard Work As 'The Bell Tolls'," *NYT*, 3/8/59, Sec. 2, 11.

128   "In this play, all of the characters": Ibid.

128   "So he gets costumed": Interview with A. E. Hotchner, 2/2/94.

128   the taping retakes Frankenheimer's perfectionism required: "Hemingway's Answer to TV 'Bell' Version: 'Wonderful Theatre'," *Variety*, 4/1/59, 21.

128   "He started to drink, and disappeared": Interview with John Frankenheimer, 2/21/94.

128   "CBS didn't turn any wrath on me": Interview with A. E. Hotchner, 3/4/94.

128   "brilliantly fulfilled": Jack Gould, "TV: 'For Whom the Bell Tolls,' Part I," *NYT*, 3/13/59, 59.

129   *Variety* found the 1943 movie version: *For Whom the Bell Tolls* review, *Variety*, 3/18/59, 55.

129   a criticism it voiced of Part Two as well: "Tele Follow-up Comment: Playhouse 90 (Part II)," *Variety*, 3/25/59, 42.

129   "Abercrombie and Fitch out of": "Hemingway's Answer to TV 'Bell' Version," *Variety*, 4/1/59, 21.

129   "I thought she was terrific": Interview with Roger O. Hirson, 2/14/94.

129   "And you don't care, do you?": Interview with Mab Ashforth, 7/26/94.

129   they went rowing in a backwater lagoon: Interview with William Gibson, 1/28/94.

129   "Fred said Joyce wanted to have children": Interview with AC, 9/2/93. Also: Interview with Mab Ashforth, 7/26/94.

129   perhaps he never should have married: Interview with AC, 2/19/93.

130   CBS executives tried to talk him out of it: Interview with BG, 5/28/93.

130   "The crew went nuts": Ibid.

130   " 'Well, I've created another monster' ": Ibid.

130   "I hope we will continue": Fred Coe letter to DM, 12/4/59. Copies in Delbert Mann's papers at Vanderbilt University and in possession of the author. Copyright CBS Entertainment, a division of CBS Inc.

131   "When I worked for Fred, I didn't know": Interview with Roger O. Hirson, 2/14/94.

131   a brave but futile attempt: Greenfield, *Television*, 132.

131   Coe . . . proposed that the networks join forces: "He Searches for Excitement," *TVG*, 3/1/58, 24.

131 "Fred was a genius": Interview with Ethel Winant, 10/12/93.

131 "[Saudek's] words must have fallen oddly": Frank R. Pierson, "The Dying TV Drama," *The New Republic*, 2/2/59, 22.

132 Lucille Ball and Desi Arnaz made their final: Castleman and Podrazik, *Watching TV*, 133.

132 "To have a solid place in the community": Atkinson, *Broadway*, 495.

132 "Television no longer deserves daily criticism": Quoted in Sturcken, *Live Television*, 3.

10   Fiddler off the Roof

135 Normally, Tad Mosel looked forward: Interview with TM, 2/2/94.

135 "Pappy, how would you like": Ibid.

136 "a *Philco-Goodyear* package": Interview with TM, 10/18/91.

136 Coe would later deride CBS: "Hanging Out: Robert Alan Aurthur," *Esquire*, May 1973, 50.

136 he bordered on genius: Interview with ACA, 6/20/93.

136 *All the Way Home* went into rehearsal still short: Ibid., 5/3/94.

136 "He was very good with scripts": Ibid., 11/29/91.

136 "That was a tragedy to Fred and me": Interview with TM, 2/2/94.

136 "a parade of people": Ibid.

137 "If I were Mary": Interview with TM, 7/20/93.

137 "You've never had anything": Tad Mosel, *All the Way Home* (New York: Ivan Obolensky, 1961), 127.

137 "My mother always said": Interview with TM, 2/2/94.

137 "In New Haven, we were one-third": Herbert Mitgang, "Two From the Books: Drama is Based on The Agee Prize Novel," *NYT*, 11/27/60, Sec. 2, 1.

137 "Tad Mosel has . . . had the taste and wisdom": Howard Taubman, "Theatre: Version of Agee's 'Death in the Family'," *NYT*, 12/1/60, 42.

137 "a fine, sensitive new playwright": Robert Coleman, "'All Way Home' Misses Mark," *New York Mirror*, 12/1/60. See NYCR, 166 (1960).

137 By Thursday, only $3,500 worth of tickets: Louis Calta, "'All Way Home' Plans to Close," *NYT*, 12/2/60, 35.

137 "Most people believe the Warner Bros. movies": Interview with ACA, 6/20/93.

138 The show's advertising was cancelled: 'The Miracle,' subheading in Robert Alden article "Advertising: Michigan Bank Opens a Drive Against Competitors," *NYT* 12/9/60, 46.

138 "Oh, for Chrissakes": Interview with ACA, 6/20/93.

138 "Do you think that review": Ibid.

138 "My God, you can't close": Ibid.

138 On Thursday night, ticket sales were only: Arthur Gelb, "Agee-Mosel Play Gains a Reprieve," *NYT*, 12/5/60, 42.

138 a spokesman . . . said it would continue: Calta, "'All Way Home' Plans to Close," *NYT*, 12/2/60, 35.

138   Friday night's ticket sales: Gelb, "Agee-Mosel Play Gains a Reprieve," *NYT*, 12/5/60, 42.

138   On Sunday morning, he called Ingram Ash: 'The Miracle,' subheading in Alden article "Advertising: Michigan Bank Opens a Drive . . . ," *NYT*, 12/9/60, 46.

139   "It's a Broadway miracle": Gelb, "Agee-Mosel Play Gains a Reprieve," *NYT*, 12/5/60, 42.

139   "Fred and I decided that a closeup": Interview with AP, 12/13/91.

139   "How many voters made their choice": Settel and Laas, *A Pictorial History of Television*, 147–148. Coe later became an unpaid television adviser to President Kennedy, who invited him and Joyce to an intimate luncheon at the White House on May 24, 1961. Among the guests was one of Coe's discoveries, Princess Grace of Monaco.

140   "the modesty and sweetness of legend": Howard Taubman, "Theatre: Biblical Drama," *NYT*, 11/10/61, 38.

140   a play of enormous power: John McClain, New York *Journal-American*, 11/10/61. See *NYCR* 175 (1961).

140   "What is missing this morning": Walter Kerr, "First Night Report: 'Gideon'," *NYHT*, 11/10/61, 12.

140   Gideon's aggrieved line: Norman Nadel, "'Gideon' Opens at Plymouth," New York *World-Telegram and Sun*, 11/10/61. See *NYCR*, 177 (1961).

140   "'Hello, Pappy?'": Interview with Herb Gardner, 5/11/94.

140   But when Coe felt the director wasn't: Interview with Porter Van Zandt, 2/10/94.

141   *Clowns* was probably Coe's favorite: Interview with ACA, 11/23/91.

141   "You know why it works so well?": Interview with Herb Gardner, 5/11/94.

141   Finding Jason Robards: Interviews with Phyllis Adams, 5/24/93, and George Jenkins, 5/24/93.

141   "Pappy, don't you think": Interview with Herb Gardner, 5/11/94.

141   "You had to pack a dinner basket": Interview with ACA, 6/20/93.

141   "Isn't Mr. Robards as guilty of guff": Walter Kerr, "First Night Report: 'A Thousand Clowns,'" *NYHT*, 4/6/62, 16.

141   By the fall of 1962, *Clowns* already had twenty-six road companies: Interview with Jeanne (Stephenson) Bodfish, 9/2/93, reporting a conversation with Coe.

141   More than thirty summers later: Interview with Herb Gardner, 5/11/94.

142   After the show, Coe rushed to the hospital: Max Souby 8/9/93 letter to JK.

142   he and Joyce sat at the piano: Interview with Laurie Coe, 3/18/94.

142   Joyce's artificial elegance: Ibid.

142   "I'm sure Fred got a little tyrannical": Interview with JPM, 7/21/93.

142   "Fred would get drinking": Interview with AP, 7/20/93.

142   "You cannot improvise": Henry T. Murdock, "'A Matter of Position' Bows in World Premiere," *Philadelphia Inquirer*, 10/1/62, 21.

142   "For a while there": Ernest Schier, Philadelphia *Evening Bulletin*, 10/1/62, 31.

142   Coe and Arthur Cantor cut it: Interview with ACA, 11/29/91.

143 "Coe's been doing these small-screen kitchen dramas": Quoted in Harry Muheim's unpublished article, "A Night at Groucho's." In possession of Harry Muheim and the author.

143 Coe took an option to produce: Interview with JPM, 7/21/93.

143 "He would say, 'We're gonna do it'": Ibid., 10/22/93.

143 "You son of a bitch . . . we were gonna make": Ibid.

143 "We were a family": Robert Alan Aurthur, "An Appreciation of Fred Coe," *Variety*, 5/23/56, 31.

144 "I got on the phone and *begged*": Interview with John Coe, 3/19/94a.

144 "His sense of justice was keen": Interview with BG, 3/8/93.

144 "My father held court": Interview with John Coe, 3/20/94.

144 "He was a giant to me": Ibid., 3/19/94a.

145 "I hate this film business": Interview with David Hays, 5/9/94.

145 Gibson knew that if he sold: Interview with William Gibson, 1/28/94.

145 The film earned $2 million: "Big Rental Pictures of 1962," *Variety*, 1/9/63, 13.

145 Gibson, slyly noting Hollywood's Byzantine: Interview with William Gibson, 1/28/94.

145 "He was a drinker": Francis Ford Coppola, 2/23/95 letter to JK.

146 "Fred behaved very badly": Interview with Horton Foote, 7/19/93.

146 "He always kept his word": Interview with Herb Gardner, 5/11/94.

146 "'The worst thing that can happen'": Interview with David Karp, 2/1/94.

146 Principal photography . . . was shot between mid-May and mid-August: "'Clowns' Rolls Monday," *Hollywood Reporter*, 5/14/64, 2, and "'Thousand Clowns' Winds," *Hollywood Reporter*, 8/14/64. Latter clip is in *Thousand Clowns* file at the Library of the Academy of Motion Picture Arts and Sciences.

146 "Herb revealed his dissatisfaction": Ralph Rosenblum and Robert Karen, *When the Shooting Stops . . . the Cutting Begins* (New York: The Viking Press, 1979), 172.

147 "Most of the film you see": Interview with Herb Gardner, 5/11/94.

147 Rosenblum . . . talks about top New York directors: Rosenblum and Karen, *When the Shooting Stops*, 233–234.

147 "At the very end, he asked": Interview with Herb Gardner, 5/11/94.

147 It also earned over $2 million: "Big Rental Pictures of 1966," *Variety*, 1/4/67, 8.

147 "Fred rose so high": Interview with DM, 4/29/92.

147 Coe proposed a series: Interview with AP, 2/23/94.

147 he made *Three Roads to Rome*: Interview with TM, 7/20/93.

147 "Fred gave me two of them": Interview with BG, 3/8/93.

147 "He kept asking me, 'Where's Fred?'": Ibid.

147 Reviewing *Notorious*, *Variety* said: Theatre '62 review (*The Spiral Staircase*), *Variety*, 10/11/61, 36.

147 "How wise is it": *Spellbound* review, *Variety*, 2/14/62, 36.

148 "Goldman did an okay job": Theatre '62 review, *Variety*, 3/14/62.

148 "I'm not claiming pretensions": "The Paradine Case," *Show*, March 1962, 19.

148   "The lowest I ever stooped": "Hanging Out: Robert Alan Aurthur," *Esquire*, May 1973, 54.

148   "They want to do a series": Interview with David Karp, 2/1/94.

148   Coe was torn by two instincts: Ibid.

148   "The sponsor, if he buys": Marie Torre, "Coe Defends TV Controls By Sponsors," *NYHT*, 6/28/61, 22.

148   Coe had agreed with the American Gas Association: John P. Shanley, "Producer Backs Sponsor Control," *NYT*, 6/28/61, 71.

148   "It's supposed to be only in Hollywood": Hal Humphrey, "Whatever Happened to Fred Coe of Alligator, Miss.," Los Angeles *Mirror*, 7/5/61, 14.

149   "He was asking me stuff": Interview with DS, 5/5/93.

149   "The next few years should see": "The Paradine Case," *Show* magazine, March 1962, 19.

149   Prince was hesitant: Interview with Joseph Stein, 4/16/94.

149   "It's not my cup of tea": Interview with Sheldon Harnick, 4/28/94.

149   "The boys were surprised": "Hanging Out: Robert Alan Aurthur," 54. Despite his status as a gentile from the rural South, Coe may have had access to the folk material of *Fiddler* from a direct source: Meyer Kline, a dry-goods merchant in Alligator, Mississippi, who left Czarist Russia as a sixteen-year-old in 1897. Information on Kline comes from 1920 U.S. Census report for Alligator.

149   "Fred was really important": Interview with Joseph Stein, 4/16/94.

149   Mostel played hard-to-get: Jared Brown, *Zero Mostel: A Biography* (New York: Atheneum, 1989), 210.

149   "Don't be so fast in refusing": Ibid.

149   fourteen musicals were scheduled: Stuart W. Little, "Musical Postponed in Theater Shortage," *NYHT*, 11/6/63, 17.

150   Coe . . . wrote to William Paley: "Hanging Out: Robert Alan Aurthur," 58.

150   "Paley never ceased to be": David Halberstam, *The Powers That Be* (New York: Alfred A. Knopf, 1979), 32.

150   "Suddenly, no one was interested": "Hanging Out: Robert Alan Aurthur," 58.

150   "He said, 'I can cope'": Interview with ACA, 11/29/91.

150   "I don't know what's happening" Richard Altman with Mervyn Kaufman, *The Making of a Musical: Fiddler on the Roof* (New York: Crown, 1971), 22.

150   By the fall of 1963, Prince was Coe's co-producer: The earliest mention I find of Prince's involvement in the show comes in Stuart W. Little, "Musical Postponed," *NYHT*, 11/6/63, 17.

150   Coe later recalled he and Prince agreed: "Hanging Out: Robert Alan Aurthur," 58.

151   "Harold Prince said": Interview with BG, 3/8/93.

151   "Fred would rarely show up": Interview with Sheldon Harnick, 4/28/94.

151   Prince was exasperated . . . became the show's sole producer: The report of Coe's dropping out as co-producer comes in a three-inch column item headlined "Roundup," part of Louis Calta's article "News Along the Rialto: Strauss Operetta

Due in September" in the 7/12/64 *NYT*, Sec. 2, 1. Prince's call would have come between then and 6/11/64, when an article on page 12 of the NYHT, "Robbins Casts Middle-Aged Dancers," lists Prince and Coe as co-producers.

151   In 1973, it became the longest-running show: Atkinson, *Broadway*, 290.

151   By the early 1970s, it had grossed: Ibid., 461.

151   by 1989, *Fiddler's* worldwide box-office grosses: Carol Ilson, *Harold Prince: From "Pajama Game" to "Phantom of the Opera"* (Ann Arbor: UMI Research Press, 1989), 106.

151   Coe used to tell his son John: Interview with John Coe, 3/19/94b.

151   For the next dozen years . . . backers supported: Ilson, *Harold Prince*, 107.

151   "I'm sorry I had to do that": "Hanging Out: Robert Alan Aurthur," 58.

151   Hirson had lavished great skill: Lewis Funke, "Roger O. Hirson's 'Journey to the Day' Probes Mental Histories," *NYT*, 11/12/63, 49.

152   "I said to my kids, 'You gotta come in'": Interview with Roger O. Hirson, 2/14/94.

152   "Mr. Richardson has symbols strewn": Whitney Bolton, "'Xmas in Las Vegas' Is Another Loser," *Morning Telegraph*, 11/6/65, 3.

152   "It seems incredible": John McClain, "Xmas in Las Vegas: Cast Tries in Vain," *Journal-American*, 11/5/65. See NYCR, 286 (1965).

11   *"The Terrible Goddamn Thing Is . . ."*

153   as far as she knew, Coe and Joyce Beeler: Interview with Adrienne Luraschi, 4/9/92.

153   "They were the perfect couple": Interviews with Jane Aurthur, 6/20/93 and 10/20/93.

154   "I think she envisioned": Interview with Rhoda (Rosenthal) Herrick, 5/3/94.

154   "Fred Coe was a great drinking partner": Interview with TM, 6/9/93.

154   "He looked like an aging choir boy": Sumner Locke Elliott, *Some Doves and Pythons* (New York: Harper & Row, 1966), 170.

154   "to pass from daylight sweetness": Ibid., 177.

154   "the tone, the look of indecision": Ibid., 175.

154   Coe could begin the evening: Interview with JPM, 10/22/91.

154   From Penn's viewpoint, things were going well: Interview with AP, 7/30/94.

154   "He called in tears almost": Interview with Kate Wells, 4/22/92.

155   "I found the father": Ibid., 12/8/93.

155   John Houseman has described: Greenfield, *Television*, 162.

155   "They're calling our bluff": Kay Gardella, "Mosel Returns to TV with 'Secrets'," New York *Daily News*, 5/12/68, 32.

156   "It was a very tough show": Interview with Ronald Ribman, 7/28/94.

156   CBS President Thomas Dawson worried: Interview with Barbara Schultz, 8/1/94.

156   CBS had to offer slots at discount rates: Richard K. Doan, "Viewers, Critics Cheer CBS Play," *TVG*, 2/11/67, A-1, and interview with Barbara Schultz, 8/1/94.

156   Kellogg's Cornflakes was the only advertiser: Interview with Ronald Ribman, 7/28/94.

156   CBS ran promotional spots for its own programs: Interview with Laurie Coe, 3/18/94.

156   and took a $300,000 loss: Doan, "Viewers, Critics Cheer CBS Play."

156   "Thanks to Fred": Interview with Ronald Ribman, 7/28/94.

156   Neither Bogart nor Ribman recalls: Interviews with Paul Bogart, 8/5/94, and Ronald Ribman, 7/28/94.

156   "The Golden Age" . . . "the palmiest season": "In All Ways An Occasion" (CBS advertisement), *NYT*, 2/1/67, 78.

157   some erratic behavior: Interview with Harry Mark Petrakis, 8/3/94.

157   were sleeping apart: Interview with John Coe (3/19/94a,) who noticed that Coe and Joyce took separate rooms at their hotel suite in Rome.

157   she apparently sought help: Interview with Barbara Bolton, 8/10/94. Joyce consulted Bolton about possible therapists.

157   "He never understood what her needs were": Interview with Mab Ashforth, 7/26/94.

157   Joyce felt Coe was abusing her: Interview with Barbara Schultz, 8/1/94.

157   "I did hear one time": Interview with JPM, 7/30/94.

157   Joyce locked herself into: Interview with John Coe, 3/20/94.

157   "I never felt it was totally Fred's fault": Interview with Barbara Bolton, 8/10/94.

158   Some days he came downstairs: Interview with Jan (Monkhouse) Jessel, 8/14/93.

158   "his familiar duck-footed amble": "Hanging Out: Robert Alan Aurthur," 48.

158   an expert at showing raw nerves: *Me, Natalie* review, *Cue*, 7/19/69, 72.

159   she took a full bottle of sleeping pills: Patty Duke and Kenneth Turan, *Call Me Anna: The Biography of Patty Duke* (New York: Bantam Books, 1987), 196.

159   Coe went to the hospital: Ibid.

159   "We went through crisis here": Interview with John Coe, 3/19/94a.

159   "Fred saved the picture": Interview with George Jenkins, 5/24/93.

159   "Fred, you were a son of a bitch": Interview with Dick Smith, 5/28/93.

159   "At least you're trying": Interview with Laurie Coe, 3/18/94.

159   "I thought she was cold": Interview with Jan (Monkhouse) Jessel, 8/14/93.

160   "What [Patty Duke] ultimately does": *Me, Natalie* review, *Cue*, 7/19/69, 72.

160   "'Me, Natalie' has just the unaffected": Winfred Blevins, "'Me, Natalie' a Charmer," Los Angeles *Herald-Examiner*, 9/10/69, B-9.

160   "When raw nerves are exposed": *Me, Natalie* review, *Cue*, 7/19/69, 72.

160   But the *Los Angeles Times* called: Charles Champlin, "'Me, Natalie': Transition of Girl to Woman," *Los Angeles Times*, 9/9/69, Sec. 4, 1.

160   "It was a nice movie": Interview with BG, 3/8/93.

160   "Something about the movie obviously moved him": Interview with Peter Hunt, 7/30/94.

161   Myers walked right past him: Interview with Milt Myers, 5/21/95.

161   "He was a very sweet man": Interview with Peter Hunt, 7/30/94.

161   "It was very painful": Ibid.

161   Coe . . . stormed into the lobby: Ibid.

161   Hunt's phone rang: Ibid.

161   One of these blasts: Ibid.

162   "Oh, isn't it wonderful": Interview with William Gibson, 1/28/94.

162   "Fred never resented it": Interview with Dominick Dunne, 4/19/92.

162   "The terrible goddamn thing": Interview with Harry Muheim, 6/6/93.

162   John recalls that Joyce: Interview with John Coe, 3/20/94.

162   He sat in the living room and complained: Interview with Ann Levack, 9/29/93.

163   "That day he had called": Interview with TM, 6/9/93.

163   "We went out afterwards": Ibid., 10/22/93.

163   "There was never anything but closeness": Interview with AC, 9/2/93.

163   "He seemed to be all right": Interview with Yvette Schumer, 2/7/94.

163   "Fred didn't talk a lot": Interview with BC, 6/18/93.

163   "He raised us all": Interview with Laurie Coe, 3/19/94a.

164   "Fred was in a very benign period": Interview with TM, 7/26/94.

165   "The whole time I worked for him": Interview with Ann Levack, 9/29/93.

12   *Rendezvous at the Russian Tea Room*

166   Aurthur praised Coe's still-youthful: "Hanging Out: Robert Alan Aurthur," 48.

166   "a few more pounds": Ibid.

167   "In the 1970's a veneer": Atkinson, *Broadway*, 469.

167   "The call for a good": Richard Watts, "Theatre: Very Suspicious Characters," *New York Post*, 2/29/72. See NYCR, 370 (1972).

167   "superb": Betty Rollin, "Night Watch" review, WNBC-TV, 2/28/72. See NYCR, 372 (1972).

167   "the twists and turns": Douglas Watt, "Joan Hackett Is Fascinating in the Thriller 'Night Watch,'" *New York Daily News*, 2/29/72. See NYCR, 370 (1972).

167   a shameless imitation of *Sleuth*: Martin Gottfried, "Theatre: Night Watch," *Women's Wear Daily*, 3/1/72. See NYCR, 371 (1972).

167   "Ah, he gave me a kiss!": Interview with Margaret (Sheffield) Mannoni, 1/19/95.

167   "Once he split with Joyce": Interview with Arthur Cantor, 6/20/93.

167   it closed after only forty-eight performances: *Promenade, All!* closing notice, *Variety*, 5/31/72, 56.

168   "Programs come into being": Les Brown, *Televi$ion: The Business Behind the Box* (New York, Harcourt Brace Jovanovich, 1971), 173.

168   he recalls Coe sensitively helping him: Interview with Stanley Gray, 2/8/95.

168   Coe . . . seemed almost subservient: Ibid.

168   "one of the finest and most courageous": Ron Powers, "Radio and TV Deck Halls for Holidays," *Chicago Sun-Times*, 12/22/72, Sec. 2, 6.

168   "a lovely play . . . uncannily good": Bernie Harrison, "Three Cheers for 'A Dance,'" *Washington Star-News*, 12/19/72, C-7.

168   Given free rein: Cecil Smith, "Coe Producing 2 TV Anthologies," *Los Angeles Times*, 7/4/72, Sec. 4, 16.

169   "One of the ABC executives said my piece": Interview with Harvey Jacobs, 11/8/94.

169   Coe had been inspired to do: Kay Gardella, "Fred Coe Test Anthology in 'Of Men and Women'," *New York Daily News*, 12/19/72.

169   *Of Men and Women* won its time period: Ibid.

169   *The Michele Lee Show* opens: A kinescope of the pilot is on file at the Wisconsin Center for Film and Theater Research, Madison.

169   He asked Bob Costello: Interviews with BC, 4/14/92 and 6/18/93b.

170   "You should keep in touch'": Interview with Adeline (Garner) Shell, 9/20/94.

170   "She acceded to him": Interview with ACA, 11/29/91.

170   As Rattigan wrote the play's early scenes: Roy Moseley with Philip and Martin Masheter, *Rex Harrison: A Biography* (New York: St. Martin's Press, 1987), 291.

170   Normally, Rattigan would have helped: Ibid.

170   Harrison threatening to abandon the play: Ibid., 289.

170   "Rex Harrison gave him": Interview with ACA, 11/29/91.

170   "Aspiring to be no more": Martin Gottfried, "Theater: Love Comes to the Morosco," *New York Post*, 12/11/74. See NYCR, 150 (1974).

170   John Beaufort . . . called it touching: John Beaufort, "Gallantry Is Back on the Broadway Stage," *Christian Science Monitor*, 12/13/74. See NYCR, 153 (1974).

170   "flimsy and sentimental": Jack Kroll, "Vivat Rex," NYCR, 151 (1974).

170   "This is a soap bubble": T. E. Kalem, "Quick, Rex, the Kleenex," *Time*, 12/23/74. See NYCR, 152 (1974).

171   Harrison stopped doing the still-popular show: Moseley, *Rex Harrison*, 294.

171   "I don't trust anything": Interview with EC, 12/14/91.

171   "[Fred] was beginning to feel the effects": Interview with Virginia Kassel, 11/17/94.

171   "old Johnny Q": Bruce Cook, "Public Television's Big Splash," *American Film*, December 1975, 8.

171   "more a natural force": Jack Shepherd, *The Adams Chronicles: Four Generations of Greatness* (Boston: Little, Brown), 1975, 216.

171   *The Adams Chronicles* featured 300 actors, 800 extras: C. Gerald Fraser, "Adams Saga . . . Ending Taping Here," NYT, 9/15/75, 38.

171   The series was budgeted at $5.2 million: Richard F. Shepard, "TV Makes History With Adams Saga," NYT, 6/5/75, 48.

171   between $1.4 and $2 million in cost overruns: The $1.4 million figure is from Les Brown, "WNET Drops 2 Shows as 'Adams' Costs Mount," NYT, 10/1/75, 89; $2 million is cited in the review of "John Adams: Lawyer" in *Variety*, 1/28/76, 44.

172   "These strikes were quite crippling": Interview with Virginia Kassel, 11/17/94.

172   Coe . . . felt so poorly: Interview with BC, 6/18/93a.

172   Coe had to take a cab: Ibid.

172   Coe . . . would point to a line: Interview with Sam Hall, 10/21/93.

172   Tad Mosel calls Coe's work on *The Adams Chronicles*: Interview with TM, 7/20/93.

172   a well-shaped hour: Reed Whittemore, "Those Cultural Adamses," *The New Republic*, 4/3/76, 25.

172   a heavy-handed civics-text quality: Karl E. Meyer, "Television," *Saturday Review*, 5/1/76, 51.

172   its first three episodes drew 12 to 14 percent: "'Adams' Program Proves Popular," *NYT*, 2/7/76, 47.

172   When Roger O. Hirson arrived: Interview with Roger O. Hirson, 2/14/94.

172   Bob Costello saw a parallel: Interview with BC, 4/14/92.

173   Coe was having sharp back pains: Interview with Laurie Coe, 3/19/94a.

173   He was in the hospital for a month: Interview with EC, 4/29/93.

173   Tad Mosel felt they were closer: Interview with TM, 7/26/94.

173   "The mood was very buoyant": Interview with AP, 11/13/91.

173   the laugh . . . was the same: Interview with Herb Gardner, 5/11/94.

173   Eleanor took his temperature: "In the Matter of the Claim of Eleanor Cogbill against the Estate of Fred Coe, Decedent." Copy on file in Surrogate's Court, County of New York.

173   When Alice Coe met Eleanor: Interview with AC, 8/31/93.

173   Eleanor let out Coe's shirts: Interview with EC, 6/21/93.

173   "He sounded the same": Interview with Harry Muheim, 6/6/93.

173   "If he was working": Interview with EC, 5/5/94.

174   "Fred began a flow": Interview with A. E. Hotchner, 10/29/93.

174   "It was like a soap opera": Interview with EC, 6/21/93.

174   "It was kind of sad": Interview with BC, 2/25/93.

174   He cut back his assistant: Interview with EC, 12/14/91.

174   Joyce . . . filed several court actions: The index to the records of these actions is in New York State Supreme Court on Foley Square in lower Manhattan.

174   The year before, Coe had asked her: Interviews with AC, 9/2/93 and 11/8/94.

175   made it seem like a class reunion: Interview with EC, 6/21/93.

175   neither . . . Aurthur nor Coe . . . looked well: Interview with JPM, 7/21/93.

175   "If you took all of his writers": Interview with TM, 7/20/93.

175   "It's okay to look back at the past": Quoted by BC in 6/18/93a interview.

175   "We're going to make it this time": David Karp, "A Memory of Fred Coe," *The Writers' Guild of America Newsletter*, June 1979, 19.

176   "I tried to save him": Horton Foote, *Harrison, Texas* (New York: Harcourt, Brace, 1956), 174–175.

176   Katz invited Coe and writer William Gibson: Interview with William Gibson, 1/28/94.

176   Aaron had ideas of his own: Interview with Paul Aaron, 11/18/94.

176   "When I come to things": Ibid.

176   Aaron threatened to walk off: Ibid.

176   "He was agitated": Interview with Harry Muheim, 4/22/92.

176   Coe . . . in a shouting match: Ibid., 6/6/93.

177   his mentor had deteriorated: Interview with DM, 11/14/94.

177   He walked heavily: Ibid., 8/23/93.

177   had lost of much of his energy: Ibid., 10/15/91.

177   With a week of filming left: Most information in this paragraph is from 12/14/91 interview with EC. Second sentence is from 4/17/92 interview with AC.

177   At the hospital, an angiogram was done: Interview with EC, 12/14/91.

177   "I'm sorry about this": Interview with EC, 6/21/94.

177   Just after 10:30 . . . died at 11:20 P.M: Times are from Coe's death certificate, on file in the Office of Registrar-Recorder/County Clerk of Los Angeles.

177   The closest male ancestor . . . to outlive him: Bartlett, *Robert Coe, Puritan*, 276.

178   In 1935, after his career had gone into decline: See third episode of the documentary *D.W. Griffith: Father of Film* by Kevin Brownlow and David Gill, which aired on KCET-TV, Los Angeles, 3/24/93.

178   "He may have looked at the film and thought": Interview with Paul Aaron, 11/18/94.

178   "The cinema of Griffith . . . is no more outmoded": Quoted in Scott and Barbara Siegel, *The Encylopedia of Hollywood* (New York: Avon Books, 1990), 182.

178   Delbert Mann . . . received the news: Interviews with DM, 10/15/91 and 8/23/93.

178   "I can't reach Ray Katz": Interview with BG, 5/28/93.

178   Arthur Penn addressed his remarks: Interview with AP, 7/20/93.

179   "She said, 'Well, Tad'": Interview with TM, 7/20/93.

179   "She put her hand on the coffin": Interview with Ann Levack, 9/29/93.

179   Because Coe didn't like ties: Interview with EC, 6/21/93.

179   "a man for all media": Richard F. Shepard, "Fred Coe, Producer and Director In 'Golden Age' of TV, Dies at 65," *NYT*, 5/1/79, Sec. 4, 17.

179   "some industry notables say:" Tom Paegel, "Fred Coe, 64, Pioneer TV and Stage Director, Dies," *Los Angeles Times*, 5/2/79, Sec. 2, 6.

179   "a grotesque episode": Interview with Bill Weylock, 11/9/94.

179   "The only thing that bothered me": AC interview, 9/2/93.

179   "In years to come": Wilk, *The Golden Age of Television*, 138.

180   Coe was equally at home: Horton Foote, "An Appreciation of Fred Coe," *Variety*, 5/23/56, 32.

180   "Thanks again, Pappy": Quoted in Ann and Delbert Mann, *A Remembrance of Pappy*, 6.

180   his greatest influence came . . . in the Hollywood feature film: Thanks to Bo Goldman for this insight.

181   "Car chases are the polyester suits": Interview with JPM, 7/21/93.

181   "I don't recognize it much": Quoted in Cecil Smith, "Fred Coe: A Remembrance," *Los Angeles Times*, 5/3/79, Sec. 4, 36.

181   "A lot of producers want their names": Interview with Porter Van Zandt, 2/10/94.

SELECTED BIBLIOGRAPHY

Agee, James. *A Death in the Family*. New York: Bantam Books, 1969.

Allen, Oliver E. *New York, New York: A History of the World's Most Exhilarating and Challenging City*. New York: Atheneum, 1990.

Altman, Richard, with Meryvn Kaufman. *The Making of a Musical: Fiddler on the Roof*. New York: Crown, 1971.

Ambrose, Stephen E. *Eisenhower: The President*. New York: Simon and Schuster, 1984.

Atkinson, Brooks. *Broadway*. New York: Limelight Editions, 1990.

Barnouw, Erik. *The Image Empire*. New York: Oxford University Press, 1970.

Bartlett, J. Gardner. *Robert Coe, Puritan: His Ancestors and Descendants, 1340–1910*. Boston: self-published, 1911.

Brooks, Tim, and Earl Marsh. *The Complete Directory to Prime Time Network TV Shows, 1946–Present*. New York: Ballantine Books, 1995.

Bilby, Kenneth. *The General: David Sarnoff and the Rise of the Communications Industry*. New York: Harper & Row, 1986.

Boddy, William. *Fifties Television: The Industry and Its Critics*. Urbana and Chicago: University of Illinois Press, 1990.

Brown, Jared. *Zero Mostel: A Biography*. New York: Atheneum, 1989.

Brown, Les. *Les Brown's Encyclopedia of Television*. New York: Zoetrope, 1982.

———. *Les Brown's Encyclopedia of Television*. Detroit, Washington, D.C., and London: Visual Ink, 1992.

———. *Televi$ion: The Business Behind the Box*. New York: Harcourt, Brace, Jovanovich, Inc., 1971.

Carey, Gary. *Judy Holliday: An Intimate Life Story*. New York: Seaview Books, 1982.

Castleman, Harry, and Walter Podrazik. *Watching TV: Four Decades of American Television*. New York: McGraw-Hill Book Company, 1982.

Chayefsky, Paddy. *Television Plays*. New York: Simon and Schuster, 1955.

Cobb, James C. *The Most Southern Place on Earth: The Mississippi Delta and the Roots of Regional Identity*. New York: Oxford University Press, 1992.

Considine, Shaun. *Mad As Hell: The Life and Work of Paddy Chayefsky*. New York: Random House, 1994.

Doyle, Don H. *Nashville Since the 1920s*. Knoxville: University of Tennessee Press, 1985.

Duke, Patty, and Kenneth Turan. *Call Me Anna: The Biography of Patty Duke*. New York: Bantam Books, 1988.

Editors of Time-Life Books, *Shadow of the Atom: 1950–1960*. Alexandria, Virginia: Time-Life Books, 1970.

Elliott, Sumner Locke. *Some Doves and Pythons*. New York: Harper & Row, 1966.

Engel, Joel. *Rod Serling: The Dreams and Nightmares of Life in the Twilight Zone*. New York and Chicago: Contemporary Books, 1989.

Foote, Horton. *Harrison, Texas: Eight TV Plays*. New York: Harcourt, Brace, 1956.

Gianakos, Larry James. *Television Drama Series Programming: A Comprehensive Chronicle, 1947–1959*. Metuchen, N.J., and London: The Scarecrow Press, 1980.

Gibson, William. *The Seesaw Log*. New York: Alfred A. Knopf, 1959.

Gish, Lillian, and Ann Pinchot. *Lillian Gish: The Movies, Mr. Griffith, and Me*. Englewood Cliffs, N.J.: Prentice-Hall, Inc., 1969.

Goldstein, Norm. *The History of Television*. New York: Portland House, 1991.

Greenbaum, Everett. *The Goldenberg Who Couldn't Dance*. New York and London: Harcourt Brace Jovanovich, 1980.

Greenfield, Jeff. *Television: The First 50 Years*. New York: Harry N. Abrams, 1977.

Halberstam, David. *The Powers That Be*. New York: Alfred A. Knopf, 1979.

Hanson, Bruce K. *The Peter Pan Chronicles*. New York: Birch Lane Press, 1993.

Hawes, William. *A History of Anthology Television Drama Through 1958*. Ann Arbor, Michigan: UMI Dissertation Information Service, 1960.

———. *American Television Drama: The Experimental Years*. University, Ala.: University of Alabama Press, 1986.

Heldenfels, R. D. *Television's Greatest Year: 1954*. New York: Continuum, 1954.

Ilson, Carol. *Harold Prince: From "Pajama Game" to "Phantom of the Opera."* Ann Arbor, Michigan, and London: UMI Research Press, 1989.

Johnson, Eunice Tolbert. *History of Perry County*. Hazard, Ky.: Hazard Chapter of the D.A.R, 1953.

Jones, Gerard. *Honey, I'm Home!: Sitcoms, Selling the American Dream*. New York: Grove Weidenfeld, 1992.

Kisseloff, Jeff. *The Box: An Oral History of Television, 1920–1961*. New York: Viking, 1995.

McCullough, David. *Truman*. New York: Simon and Schuster, 1992.

McNeil, Alex. *Total Television: A Comprehensive Guide to Programming from 1948 to the Present*. New York: Penguin Books, 1984.

Mahy, Jr., G. Gordon. *Murdoch of Buckhorn*. Nashville: The Parthenon Press, 1946.

Mann, Ann, and Delbert Mann. *A Remembrance of "Pappy": Fred Coe, 1914–1979*. Privately circulated, 1980.

Moore, Barbara, and David G. Yellin. *Horton Foote's Three Trips to Bountiful*. Dallas: Southern Methodist University Press, 1993.

Moore, John Hammond. *Columbia & Richland County: A South Carolina Community, 1740–1990*. Columbia: University of South Carolina Press, 1993.

Morella, Joe, and Edward Z. Epstein. *Paul and Joanne: A Biography of Paul Newman and Joanne Woodward*. New York: Delacorte Press, 1988.

Morris, Jan. *Manhattan '45*. New York: Oxford University Press, 1987.

Mosel, Tad. *All the Way Home.* New York: Ivan Obolensky, 1961.

———. *Other People's Houses: Television Plays.* New York: Simon and Schuster, 1956.

Moseley, Roy, with Philip and Martin Masheter. *Rex Harrison: A Biography.* New York: St. Martin's Press, 1987.

Poitier, Sidney. *This Life.* New York: Alfred A. Knopf, 1980.

Preminger, Otto. *Preminger: An Autobiography.* Garden City, N.Y.: Doubleday & Company, 1977.

Ritchie, Michael. *Please Stand By: A Prehistory of Television.* Woodstock, N.Y.: The Overlook Press, 1994.

Robertson, Ben. *Red Hills and Cotton: An Upcountry Memory.* Columbia: University of South Carolina Press, 1991.

Rose, Reginald. *Six Television Plays.* New York: Simon and Schuster, 1956.

Rosenblum, Ralph, and Robert Karen. *When the Shooting Stops . . . The Cutting Begins.* New York: The Viking Press, 1979.

Royal, John. *Television Production Problems.* New York: McGraw-Hill, 1948.

Sander, Gordon F. *Serling: The Rise and Twilight of Television's Last Angry Man.* New York: Dutton, 1992.

Schaffner, Franklin. *Worthington Miner.* Metuchen, N.J., and London: Scarecrow Press, 1985.

Serling, Rod. *Patterns: Four Television Plays with the Author's Personal Commentaries.* New York: Simon and Schuster, 1955.

Settel, Irving, and William Laas. *A Pictorial History of Television.* New York: Grosset & Dunlap, 1969.

Shepherd, Jack. *The Adams Chronicles: Four Generations of Greatness.* Boston and Toronto: Little, Brown and Company, 1975.

Shulman, Arthur, and Roger Youman. *How Sweet It Was.* New York: Bonanza Books, 1966.

Siegel, Scott, and Barbara Siegel. *The Encylopedia of Hollywood.* New York: Avon Books, 1990.

Skutch, Ira. *I Remember Television.* Metuchen, N.J., and London: Scarecrow Press, 1989.

Stempel, Tom. *Storytellers to the Nation: A History of American Television Writing.* New York: Continuum, 1992.

Sturcken, Frank. *Live Television: The Golden Age of 1946–1958 in New York.* Jefferson, N.C., and London: McFarland and Company, 1990.

Udelson, Joseph H. *The Great Television Race: A History of the American Television Industry 1925–1941.* University, Alabama: The University of Alabama Press, 1982.

Vidal, Gore, ed. *Best Television Plays.* New York: Ballantine Books, 1956.

———. *Visit to a Small Planet and Other Television Plays.* Boston: Little, Brown, 1956.

Weaver, Pat, and Thomas M. Coffey. *The Best Seat in the House: The Golden Years of Radio and Television.* New York: Alfred A. Knopf, 1994.

Wheen, Francis. *Television: A History.* London: Century, 1985.

Wilk, Max. *The Golden Age of Television: Notes from the Survivors.* New York: Delacorte Press, 1976.

Winship, Michael. *Television.* New York: Random House, 1988.

INDEX

About the Author

Jon Krampner is an expatriate New Yorker who lives in Los Angeles. He is a contributing editor of *Emmy* magazine, and has written on television and entertainment subjects for the *Los Angeles Times*, *Playboy*, *Modern Maturity*, the *New York Times* Syndicate, and numerous other publications.